MW00411896

The
Korean War
1945-1953

Hugh Deane

 CHINA
BOOKS

& Periodicals, Inc.

San Francisco

ISBN 0-8351-2644-7

Library of Congress Number 99-62801

Printed in Canada
First Edition

Book and cover design by Linda Revel

China Books & Periodicals, Inc.
2929 Twenty-fourth Street
San Francisco, CA 94110
www.chinabooks.com

I did not think I was either a radical or a dreamer. I was a reporter who had found with shame and anguish that under our flag and often with our active encouragement there had come into being a police state so savage in its suppression of man's elemental liberties that it was difficult to find a parallel for it.

—MARK GAYN

Contents

*Thinking of the late
John S. Service*

Also by Hugh Deane:

**Good Deeds and Gunboats: Two Centuries of
American-Chinese Encounters**
China Books & Periodicals, San Francisco 1990

China and Korea: History That Shapes the Present

History That Shapes the Present

Sea water on three sides and forested mountain ranges on the fourth did not spare the Korean peninsula from invasions and less painful foreign influences over many centuries. But such intrusions also did not prevent the slow shaping of the people they encountered into a nation.

China, the neighboring giant, had the most profound and lasting influence. Invasions, migration, trade and much visitation and dialogue from China were the means, and Buddhism and Confucianism were the consequence and extended means.

Chinese commanderies or colonies occupied much of the peninsula in the late B.C. period and early A.D. centuries. Lolang, the largest and longest lasting of them, had a population of some 300,000 and a sinofied capital near what is now Pyongyang. The Chinese who brought their families and customs with them exploited the countryside as they had done at home and engaged in a thriving trade with the enormous and peaceful Han empire and Japan. Tomb artifacts, including splendid lacquerware, exemplify the Han cultural achievements at their finest. The Chinese language, schools and craft workshops were introduced. Chinese families became Sino-Korean families and Chinese craftsmen had Korean assistants. The role of the commanderies has been likened to that of the contemporary Roman colonies in Britain.[1]

A second enduring stream of influence flowed south from the nomadic peoples of the steppes, bringing alternative social structures, metal work and horses to local tribes and strengthening them so that they could stand up to and eventually subdue the Chinese presence. These tribes eventually federated and developed into states. Japan was an early recipient of Chinese and Korean influence and later was an invader. A principal reality was that Chinese and other foreign influences were Koreanized and absorbed into an innovative culture that is the sustenance of its nationalism.[2]

Visiting Pyongyang in October, 1997, three of us were taken through the Korean history museum and the folklore museum.[3] The exhibits make evident to informed observers a truth unacknowledged by the guides and the texts on the walls—that China contributed overwhelmingly to the shaping of Korean society. The commanderies are shrunk and minimized in the contemporary retellings and are even alleged to have been located outside the peninsula. Nationalism, freed from decades of Japanese restriction, is rewriting some established Korean history but correctly insists on recognition of the successful Koreanization of intruding cultural influences.[4]

In later centuries the peninsula was divided into Koreanized states but Chinese influence continued. Court records were kept in Chinese. Poets were likely to write in Chinese but their subjects often were Korean, many celebrating their pride in peaks, pines, wild hawks, crickets and rushing streams.

The written language exemplifies a Korean culture with Chinese connections. During the 15th century the court devised a remarkable phonetic alphabet that aided literacy, but Chinese characters were often used with it. Woodblock and moveable metal type printing made possible a wide variety of useful publications in both Chinese and Korean.

Korean inventiveness created devices to measure rainfall and the direction and velocity of wind, a triangulation means of measuring land elevations and distances, much improvement of military and naval weaponry, agricultural advances having to do with seedling transplanting and seed selection. Construction of an observatory made possible celestial study. Chinese Sung dynasty porcelain was studied and the superior celadon created. Korean artists—tomb painters, sculptors, poets, calligraphers, makers of jewelry, brocade and celadon—studied Chinese models but did not just copy them. They made their work distinctly Korean. Inadequate recognition of the splendor of their achievement has resulted in the enormous destruction of much of it in so many wars, including the latest, as well as inclinations to treat it as provincial.

Over many centuries Korea was a tribute-paying vassal of China. Korean kings received symbols of investiture from Chinese emperors. But most of that time Korean states handled internal affairs without interference. China was the formidable continental power, the Elder Brother and the source of great wisdom, and a succession of Korean dynasties perforce recognized this fact in sending gift-bearing delegations to Peking that also engaged in trading. But the resilient Korean culture that limited sinofication was a barrier to subjugation. Vassalage, largely ceremonial, was an historic compromise that lasted until near the end of the 19th century.

Invasions—Chinese, Mongol, Manchu and Japanese—were in general staunchly resisted. The Kokuryo kingdom, the northern of the three early kingdoms (the others were Silla in the southeast and Paekche in the southwest), conquered the declining Lolang colony in 313 A.D. and turned back massive Sui and Tang invasions intended to bring the peninsula into the Chinese empire. The unified Silla kingdom (668-935) allied itself with Tang in its quest for extended power but turned against it and forced its army to withdraw when Tang's objective of subjugation became evident. Intervals of relative peace made possible the strengthening of Koreanization.

The authors of *Korea Old and New* explain why Koguryo's victories were especially significant: "The conquest of Kokuryo was to be but one stage in the grand imperial design of both Sui and Tang to achieve hegemony over all of East Asia. Accordingly, had Kokuryo been beaten, Paekche and Silla as well likely would have fallen under Chinese dominion. But Kokuryo held firm, serving as a breakwater against which the repeated Chinese invasions foundered, and the peoples of the Korean peninsula thus were saved from the grave peril of foreign conquest."[5]

But hand in hand with the resistance to Chinese efforts to gain political control went a welcoming of Chinese ways. Silla, having forced out Chinese military forces, turned itself into a near replica of Tang China. And like Tang it was hospitable to a settlement of Arab traders. The Korea of the long-lasting Yi dynasty (1392-1910) was Confucianized by further waves of Chinese influence.

Late in the 16th century, in 1592, Hideyoshi Toyotomi, secure in power in Japan, invaded Korea in the belief that his armies could drive right through it and attack and defeat China. The invasion was initially a success. Seoul, looted and burned by Koreans hostile to the regime, fell in three weeks and Pyongyang a month later. Much of Korea was devastated, many of its architectural and artistic treasures destroyed, and hundreds of thousands of its people were killed or impoverished.

To verify their claims of mass executions, the samurai cut off the ears or noses of their victims and took them back to Japan for inspection and burial in huge mounds. The largest, called the Ear Mound, survives in Kyoto.[6]

But a seven-year struggle gave Korea victory. On the sea Admiral Yi Sun-sin's turtle ships, so-called because of their heavy protective plating, defeated Japanese fleets in a series of engagements, sinking supplies and reinforcements from Japan. On the land abused peasants were the backbone of guerrilla forces that burned crops and harassed Japanese camps. Chinese armies crossed the Yalu and joined the

Korean defense. Early in the second year of the war the Japanese force of nearly 200,000 had lost a third of its effectives. Toyotomi's death in September 1598 brought about the Japanese withdrawal.

In several respects the Hideyoshi performance foreshadowed 20th century events. In governing captured territory the Japanese tried to make Korea part of Japan. They introduced Japanese customs and language study. In defeat, the Japanese fell back to a Pusan enclave as the U.S.-South Korean forces were to do in 1950. Hideyoshi contributed to his own defeat by making the same mistake MacArthur was to make in North Korea—he divided his forces into armies that at critical moments failed to cooperate.

Class struggle shaped Korean events as well as nationalism. The peasants were routinely exploited and suffered with little relief from the recurrent famines caused by internal warfare and floods and other natural disasters. Periodically the exactions and hardships were so onerous that the villages turned to banditry and rebellion. Some 62 local rural uprisings took place in the 19th century. To be at all successful such uprisings had to be linked with dynastic contention, in which case basic policies were hardly changed by successes and relief was short-lived.

The Tonghak Rebellion

The history of China's revolution was preceded and influenced by the Taiping Rebellion of the mid-19th century. Korea's revolutionary strivings had a similar antecedent. They began, as the Taipings had, as a religious movement. In China, the leader Hong Xiuquan, when ill, had dreams and visions that encouraged him to try to convert a harassed and abused people to what might be called Christianity with Chinese characteristics. Choe Che-u, the son of a poor Korean scholar and a concubine, like Hong was frustrated by repeated failures to pass official examinations, and like Hong had religious visions when ill. His teachings blended parts of various religions into what he saw as a superior one. It made much more of magic than did that of the Taipings. Choe called it Eastern Learning (Tonghak) as opposed to the Western Learning (Sohak) of the Catholics.

Word of the Taiping successes in the 1850s shocked the court of the Yi dynasty, then in decline, and in all likelihood quickly reached Choe Che-u and inspired him to emulation. More important, the corruption and injustices that inflamed the Taiping adherents prevailed in Korea and turned great numbers of people into reformist zealots. Famine had claimed over two million victims in the early decades of the century and resulted in widespread begging, abandonment of babies, sales of daughters and banditry. Taxes were tripled. Debauchery and extravagance characterized the court and much of the elite. Offices were sold and the buyers compensated themselves by imposing illegal levies. The woes of the people were expressed in this popular couplet: "As the drips of the candle on the banquet table fall, so do the tears of the people; and as the music swells in merry-making, the outcry of the discontented masses becomes the more clamorous."[7]

The Taipings had a nationalist objective—to oust the alien Manchu dynasty. In the age of imperialism, a weakened Korea was prey to successive foreign interventions and the Tonghaks were soon inveighing against foreign threats, in particular the increasingly dominant Japanese. "Japanese and foreign rebels and thieves are now introduced into the bowels of our land and anarchy has now reached its zenith," one of their proclamations declared.

As Tonghak grew, it broadened its social concerns. Its membership soon included many more of the oppressed. It espoused the demands of the peasants, preached equality and promised bountiful times to come. It was increasingly drawn into armed revolt, its adherents armed for the most part with farm tools. It also had a persistent strain of ideological conservatism, respecting the monarchy and class structure and invoking Confucian principles. It was more reformist than revolutionary.

Tonghak growth was rapid. A court official in Cholla in the south said he heard of the Tonghak wherever he went and that there was not a shop woman or mountain boy who could not recite Tonghak scripture. Among those who joined in his youth was the eminent twentieth century nationalist leader Kim Ku, a rival of Syngman Rhee assassinated during the U.S. occupation, the killing probably ordered by Rhee.

Curious about Tonghak, as instructed "I did not eat any odorous foods and I bathed clean and wore new clothing to go to see them," Kim Ku wrote in his autobiography. Approaching, "I could hear people reading something aloud. It was different from the tone of chanting Buddhist sutras or other poems and sounded rather like singing songs in harmony." He was told that the principles "were that the wicked people of the last era of the world should renew themselves and lead new lives in order to become a new people. By doing so they would be able to serve the true king of the future in constructing a new nation..."[8]

The court at first temporized but then went after the Tonghak leadership. It seized and beheaded Choe Che-u and his associates in 1866. The movement was numbed as adherents fled into the mountains. But the social causes for Tonghak credibility were still there and the movement quietly revived.

The state of affairs moved a retired official to lament in a memorial that the nation had become like an aged tree, a rotten core inside a standing shell of bark. Corruption on high, foreign intrusions, class inequalities and worsening peasant grievances were skillfully exploited by a new Tonghak leadership headed by Choe Si-hyong and Chon Pong-jun. The movement spread in the early 1890s, recruiting in the north as well as in its strong southern base of Cholla, Kyongsang and Chungchong provinces. It compiled a bible of doctrine and magical incantations and an anthology of hymns, established a network of churches and parishes, and demonstrated and petitioned for the posthumous rehabilitation of its founder as well as for reduction of taxes and punishment of abusive officials.

On February 28, 1889, Hugh A. Dinsmore of the U.S. Legation informed the Secretary of State of the severe drought and famine in Cholla, where the Tonghaks were regaining strength. He wrote, "Rev. F. Ohlinger of the American Methodist Mission here but recently returned from the stricken district informs us that there is great suffering and a prospect of worse conditions. Though there is some rice offered for sale, it is at such a price that the poorer classes cannot buy, and these are driven to dire extremities."

The Tonghak peak was in 1893 and 1894. In the south especially Tonghak bands raided grain storehouses, assaulted government facilities, beat up and humiliated members of the elite and seized guns at arsenals. They were victorious in local armed clashes.

On May 16, 1893, Augustine Heard of the U.S. Legation informed Washington that the Tonghaks were "daily increasing" and drilling regularly though almost without arms. "They had erected a wall about their encampment, in the center of which was a large flag with the inscription 'Down with the Japanese and foreigners. May the right flourish.'"

Isabella Bird, a British geographer and popular career traveler, reported in her two-volume work on *Korea and Her Neighbors* that the Tonghaks had a considerable number of adherents in Seoul itself. She thus summed up one of the last Tonghak proclamations: "The Tonghaks asserted, and with undoubted truth, that officials in Korea, for their own purposes, closed the eyes and ears of the King to all news and reports of the wrongs inflicted on his people. That ministers of State, governors, and magistrates were all indifferent to the welfare of their country, and were bent only on enriching themselves... That examinations (the only avenues to official life) were nothing more than scenes of bribery, barter and sale, and were no longer tests of fitness for civil appointment. That officials cared not for the debt into which the country was fast sinking. That 'they were proud, vainglorious, adulterous, avaricious.' That many officials receiving appointments in the country lived in Seoul."

In 1894 clashes with the obdurate court developed into insurrection. Thousands of peasants, armed with a few rifles but mostly with bamboo spears and cudgels, crushed government troops sent against them, gaining control of much of the southwest and seizing Chonju, capital of Cholla. Government granaries were seized and their contents distributed.

Intervention by the imperialist powers was dominating in Korea as it was in China. Japan, Russia and China were the principal protagonists, each supported by a faction of leading Koreans. But a movement opposed to all foreign intervention developed in the 1880s. An Independence Club and a four-page Korean and English language semi-weekly newspaper named *The Independent*, both organized principally by Dr. Philip Jaisohn (So Chae-pol), initiated lively discussion and educated many who served the nationalist cause in later years. In February, 1897 the Independence Club declared in a memorial that "the great and glorious responsibility of defending the nation's rights has been forgotten. The consequence is that the powerful neighbors have been treating us as if we were nobody..."[9]

Imperialism, soon the most threatening by the Japanese, helped to end the Tonghak rebellion. Tonghak forces numbering tens of thousands marched on Seoul, but were decisively defeated by a force stiffened with a contingent of well-armed Japanese. Other defeats followed in Chonju and other locations. Captured Tonghak leaders were beheaded and Tonghak villages pillaged. In one area in 1895 government and Japanese troops reportedly killed 36,000 Tonghaks and suspects.[10]

The Tonghak rebellion raised the issue of national survival as well as economic injustice and political corruption, but leadership weaknesses helped to bring about its collapse. As one history commented, "...the Tonghak leaders lacked ideological conviction and revolutionary strategy; they rode the tiger of peasant antipathy but possessed no master plan to control and direct it."[11]

Japan's Aggression

The early Sino-Japanese war was declared on August 1, 1894. In less than a year Japanese forces, brought close to a peak of readiness, humbled opponents who fired cannonballs of painted mortar and wielded tin sabers the debilitated forces of an empire in decay. By the treaty of Shinonoseki in 1895 China was forced to cede Taiwan and accept Japanese domination of Korea.

Japan established a protectorate over Korea in 1905, able to do so as a byproduct of its victory over Russia in the war of 1904-05. The rival imperialisms accepted Japan's peninsular success, but a "righteous army" of guerrillas among whom were Tonghak survivors challenged the takeover. Japanese troops suppressed local uprisings by burning villages and killing some 12,000 people in the course of 12 months. They reported 1,450 engagements in 1908, 900 in 1909, and 147 in 1910, by which year the Japanese were strongly enough entrenched to formally annex Korea.

In 1945 Americans found that South Cholla, part of the principal Tonghak base, was the reddest area in South Korea, and that was partly because of the Tonghak heritage. Bruce Cumings noted that "the uprisings of 1946 resembled the Tonghak in some ways. Participants in the autumn uprisings borrowed their techniques from the Tonghak… They wielded the implements of their work, like scythes, hooks and hammers… They were able to summon huge crowds overnight by primitive communication methods: signal fires on hillsides, drums in the mountains, couriers, and word-of-mouth."[12]

On March 1, 1919, a Declaration of Independence, inspired by Woodrow Wilson's 14 points and signed by 33 prominent citizens, one of them the son of a Tonghak leader, was boldly announced in Seoul and read publicly in many places. "...May all the ancestors to the thousands and ten thousand generations aid us from within and all the force of the world aid us from without, and let the day we take hold be the day of our attainment."[13]

Over a million Koreans took part in supportive demonstrations. The Japanese police reported that disturbances had to be dealt with in all but seven of Korea's 218 counties. In the end, the foreign powers were indifferent to appeals for international support and the Japanese never hesitated to crack down harshly.

Baron Yoshimichi Hasegawa, in command of the early Japanese occupying forces, denounced the Korean resistance in a proclamation in these words: "...those who fail correctly to distinguish loyalty from treason have by wild and baseless rumors instigated peoples' minds and caused the rowdies in various places to rise in insurrection. These insurgents commit all sorts of horrible crimes, such as murdering peaceful people, both native and foreign, robbing their property, burning official and private buildings, and destroying means of communication. Their offenses are such as are not tolerated by heaven or earth." He said that villages to which offenders belong "shall be held collectively responsible and punished with rigor."[14]

Japanese deeds accompanied such rhetoric. In 1919 Japanese army planes even bombed Seoul. When Korean partisans attacked the town of Hunchi near the Yalu border and killed fourteen Japanese, six Japanese battalions burned local churches and schools and massacred some 400 Koreans.[15] In several years, by Korean count, the Japanese killed 7,500, wounded great numbers and took 45,000 prisoners.

But the idea of independence was fixed in the consciousness of many. Underground work began, an exiled nationalist regime was proclaimed in Shanghai and a guerrilla effort was born among Koreans in Manchuria.

A significant consequence of the March 1 declaration was the initiation of the Korean trade union movement. A year later, in 1920, the Labor Mutual Benefit Society was formed, succeeded three years later by the All Korean Workers and Peasants Society, legal but with limited powers.

In 1925 two underground organizations took up the struggle for social justice and independence the Korean Communist Party and the Communist-led National Federation of Trade Unions. On the 10th of June 1926 an impressive mass demonstration called for independence, the eight-hour day, distribution of land to peasants and civil liberties. In 1929, 10,000 strikers in Wonsan held out for three months, finally getting Japanese concessions. Orators have since called that "the birth of working class consciousness in Korea." During the next several years strikes took place in textile mills in Pusan, a rice mill in Inchon and factories and mines in the Pyongyang area. In Kwangju workers joined students clashing with Japanese students.

In the early 1930s Japan cracked down on union and related activities, breaking up strikes and adding many to the prison population. Union activity diminished and the leadership split into small sections. But an experienced leadership came to the fore in 1945 and quickly found that the U.S. XXIV Corps was as difficult to deal with as the Japanese had been.

Tokyo described its takeover of the peninsula as "the reunion of two brothers of the same family whom Nature had long separated," but the Korean brother continued to fare poorly. Helen Foster Snow (Nym Wales), who spent the summer of 1936 there, wrote that "the atmosphere was like being in a pneumatically sealed tube in which no sound could travel."[16]

Japan's forty year rule was characterized by police repression, economic and strategic developments that benefited the Japanese almost exclusively, and persistent but finally vain efforts to Japanize the language, personal names and culture. Its efforts were abetted by some 700,000 Japanese immigrants as well as by a small pampered Korean elite, elements of which served in the Japanese police and armed forces.

Like a castle built on a sandy beach, Japan's Korean construct quickly fell apart in the closing months of the lost war, challenged by a strong left nationalist movement that created the populist People's Republic in early September 1945.

U.S. Role

The early U.S. role in Korea was essentially imperialist, foretelling the future. In February of 1845, Zadoc Pratt representing New York's 11th district in the U.S. House of Representatives, introduced "a measure to extend commerce to Japan and Korea by dispatching a mission to them." Nothing came of this until the civil war had resolved the central domestic division, but then armed missions did follow.

In 1866 the *General Sherman*, an armed merchantman ship in British employ seeking trade, was refused permission to proceed up the Taedong River but did so anyway. It got as far as Pyongyang, firing its cannon as it went. After a number of hostile incidents it was attacked at night by Koreans, and all hands, ten Asians and five Westerners, were killed or drowned. American efforts to gain information and redress got nowhere.[17]

Kim Il Sung set down this account in his reminiscences: "...my great grandfather, together with some other villagers, collected ropes from all the houses and stretched them across the river between Konyu Islet and Mangyong Hill; then they rolled some stones into the river to block the way of the pirate ship.

"When he heard that the *General Sherman* had sailed up to Yanggak Islet and was killing people there with its cannons and guns, and that its crew were stealing the people's possessions and raping the women, he rushed to the walled city of Pyongyang at the head of the villagers. The people of the city, with the government army, loaded a lot of small boats with firewood, tied them together, set them on fire and floated then down to the aggressor ship, so that the American ship was set on fire and sank with all hands. I was told that my great grandfather played a major role in this attack."[18]

In Pyongyang today the place where the *General Sherman* anchored is pointed out to visitors and a cannon from the ship is a displayed trophy.

In 1867 the purchaser of Alaska and ardent advocate of westward expansion, Secretary of State William Henry Seward, with the help of a nephew, George F. Seward, consul in Shanghai, conceived of a joint expedition with the French that would avenge the killings and force a commercial treaty on the Korean regime, but unfavorable circumstances—among them the unsavory reputation of the General Sherman—forced him to back away. [19]

But in 1871 the U.S. made a further effort to do in Korea what Commodore Perry had achieved in Japan—to break open its closed door and inquire again into the fate of the *General Sherman*. Five warships with a complement of 1,230 men from the U.S. Asiatic Fleet undertook this task. But in what the *New York Herald* called the Little War with the Heathen, a fierce Korean defense discouraged American prospects. When their weapons emptied, the defenders threw sand into the faces of the attackers. The squadron sailed away without achieving its mission.[20]

The U.S. concluded a treaty with Korea in 1882, the first Western nation to do so. What became the most discussed and significant provision of this treaty—for Washington later something of an embarrassment—was this: "If other Powers deal unjustly or oppressively with either Government, the other willl exert their good offices, on being informed of the case, to bring about an amicable arrangement, thus showing their friendly feelings."

This clause led Korea to describe the United States as its "Elder Brother."[21]

The first U.S. minister, Lucius H. Foote, was warmly received by the Korean court. Responding to a request by King Kojong, the U.S. sent four military instructors to Seoul in 1889, one of whom was immediately appointed a vice defense minister. Evangelistic efforts by American Methodist and Presbyterian missionaries were an added U.S. presence and many remained steadfastly pro-Korean throughout the period of Japanese rule.

The U.S. had economic successes. Three American firms established Seoul amenities: the Seoul Electric Light Company, the Seoul Electric Car Company and the Seoul "Fresh Water" Water Company. About 100 Americans were living in the capital. Imports from the United States included kerosene from Standard Oil, Eagle Brand milk, Armour canned meats, Cross & Blackwell foods, clothing, cigarettes, California wine and mining machinery[22] The U.S. also had an interest in a large gold mine at Unsan in the north.

Washington soon turned out to be not a friend of Korea but a friend of Japan. As early as the fall of 1900 President Theodore Roosevelt thought that "Japan should have Korea in order that she might be a check on Russia."

W. W. Rockhill was chief adviser on Far Eastern matters to Secretary of State John Hay and Roosevelt, and this was his influential opinion: "The annexation of Korea to Japan seems absolutely indicated as the one great and final step westward of the extension of the Japanese Empire. I think when this comes along it will be better for the Korean people and also for the peace in the Far East."

A series of articles by an earlier George Kennan in the *Outlook*, a magazine close to Theodore Roosevelt, persuaded many that Roosevelt's pro-Japan policy in regard to Korea reflected realities. Korea was characterized by "filthiness, demoralization, laziness and general rack and ruin" and its people were "slow-witted, lacking in spirit, densely ignorant and constitutionally lazy." In contrast to this "rotten product of a decayed oriental civilization," in Japan there was "cleanness, good order, industry and general prosperity." The good news was that Japan had finally undertaken to stop the process of decay in Korea.[23]

In July of 1905 Roosevelt acceded to the Japanese takeover of Korea. Secretary of War Howard Taft and Prime Minister Katsura reached an agreement in Tokyo by which the U.S. gave Japan a free hand in Korea and Japan disclaimed any interest in possessing the Philippines, a meaningless pledge over the long term. Roosevelt within a few days wrote Taft that his conversation with Katsura was "absolutely correct in every respect." Far Eastern scholar Tyler Dennett made the Taft-Katsura agreement public knowledge in 1924, calling it a "secret pact."[24]

The Roosevelt Administration ignored six Korean pleas for help and closed its consulate in Seoul.

The True Start of the Korean War

By Way of Introduction

"For Americans, the war began with a thunderclap in 1950. For Koreans, it began in 1945."

— Bruce Cumings

The triumph of the Chinese revolution in 1949 secured the Manchurian rear of Kim Il Sung's Democratic People's Republic and brought it the bonanza of scores of thousands of battle-experienced troops. Koreans, who had been sent by Kim to fight in the Chinese People's Liberation Army against the Kuomintang, came home, bringing much equipment with them, and they were soon integrated into the new northern army.

That year of 1949 North Korea responded defensively when South Korean troops provocatively crossed the 38th parallel on the Onjin peninsula. But when the south crossed again in the same area in 1950, as substantial evidence indicates, North Korea struck all along the parallel in what turned into an attempt to unite Korea by force. By then the southern plunge had gained Stalin 's acquiescence.

In his comprehensive two volumes on the origins of the Korean war, Bruce Cumings offered three mosaics as to how the 1950 war started, adding that a conclusion was both impossible and not all that important. But in Pyongyang in 1987, Cumings got into a heated discussion with North Koreans and he at length remarked that he thought that "the war in 1950 was intimately linked with the near-war in 1949, but because crack soldiers were not back from China, the North did not want to fight in 1949, even if the South did. In 1950 the expeditionary force had returned, and perhaps then the North awaited the first southern provocation to settle the hash of the Rhee regime. This was met with a memorable eloquent silence, as the officials exchanged glances and hard faces suddenly turned soft. They said nothing more about it."[1]

Whatever the particulars, the assault of June 25, 1950, did not begin the Korean war. The war started in 1945 and it was begun by the United States.

When the U.S. XXIV Corps commanded by General John R. Hodge landed at Inchon that September 8, it found already in place and thriving a Korean People's Republic organized and led by jubilant patriots who had emerged from a strong, broad underground with a sense of historic mission. The U.S. was thus involved from the first day. Allying itself with Korean collaborators, the Japanese-trained police, youthful terrorist groups, the dominant landlord class and returned rightist exiles like Syngman Rhee, the United States occupation brought about the destruction of the People's Republic and its supportive newborn organizations—trade unions, peasant associations, and all sorts of cultural groups. Cruelties beyond count led to the establishment in 1948 of a separatist southern regime sponsored by the U.S.-dominated United Nations and headed by Rhee, who began many trips to the podium with the promise to invade the north and free its enslaved population.

The repression in South Korea was not a local American military aberration. Some particulars aside, it was the realization of an anti-Communist, counterrevolutionary policy decided in Washington and embraced by the CIA and by Douglas MacArthur in Tokyo. Key State Department appraisals recognized the strength of the anti-Japanese movement in Korea and foresaw a revolutionary upsurge in the vacuum created by Japan's defeat. The U.S. insistence on a postwar trusteeship—Roosevelt thought it should last 30 years—reflected that. Trusteeship was a relatively civil, unmilitary way of containing the Soviets by including them in relationships largely controlled by Washington.

Washington, through MacArthur and Hodge, instructed the Japanese government in Korea to continue to exercise authority until relieved, and leaflets dropped in Korea told the people not to demonstrate against the Japanese and to carry on normal activities. A MacArthur proclamation addressed to the Korean people warned them that, "Acts of resistance to the occupying forces or any acts which may disturb public peace and safety will be punished severely..." In Tokyo, MacArthur told assembled officers bound for Korea that their task was to create "an anti-Communist bulwark." In Seoul just a few days later, Hodge instructed subordinates that Korea "was an enemy of the United States" and therefore subject to the terms of the surrender.[2] His second, oft quoted appraisal, was that Japanese and Koreans were "the same breed of cat."

The first days of the American occupation foretold the future. Japanese troops fired on a large demonstration in Inchon welcoming the Americans, killing two and wounding many. Hodge retained the Japanese government in authority until Korean outrage forced a reversal. But the repression was not eased and the role of the Korean collaborators was enlarged. In the north the Soviets disarmed the Japanese, many of whom fled south, and recognized the People's Republic.

The official rhetoric and most accounts in the media portrayed the Rhee quasi-dictatorship, realized in 1948, as a praiseworthy young democracy valiantly confronting a despotic Soviet puppet in the north. But the CIA told the real story in internal documents. It said that South Korean politics were dominated by a small class that virtually monopolized the wealth and education and exercised control over the political structure through the national police, which had been "ruthlessly brutal in suppressing disorder." It continued: "The enforced alliance of the police with the Right has been reflected in the cooperation of the police with the Rightist youth groups for the purpose of completely suppressing Leftist activity. This alignment has had the effect of forcing the Left to operate as an underground organization since it could not compete in a parliamentary sense even if it should so desire."[3]

Rhee's inflammatory rhetoric and the organized terrorism of his associates alarmed and troubled important American officials, largely for pragmatic reasons, and moves to shift to a centrist regime were considered and briefly explored. But as elsewhere, among the deterrents was a serious uncertainty, the possibility that centrism might slip over to a left success. In the fall of 1946 an official told Mark Gayn of the *Chicago Sun-Times*, "last spring Washington finally came through with a policy of moderation. But you must've found out that we honor it here only in the breach. To this day our allies are boys like Rhee to whom moderation is anathema." The United States clung to Rhee and to the dictatorships that succeeded him.[4]

General Hodge played a key negative role, telling General Wedemeyer in 1947 that he thought a coalition government would turn Communist quickly. While he found Rhee personally distasteful, he could be counted on to support the far right. He summarized his right-wing politics in a January 1948 letter to William Randolph Hearst that he didn't mail:

> "The fight against Communism is an all-American fight here and elsewhere. As the U.S. commander in Korea, I have been heartily engaged in that fight since September 8, 1945, not only fighting against Kremlin Communism and its propaganda supplied directly from the Soviet North Korean

Occupation Forces, but handicapped by a lot of false and misleading information put out by the Communist, pink and idealist liberal press of the United States.

When we arrived here South Korea was in control of Kremlin Communists... we are now eliminating the danger of control through educating the people to its dangers and cracking down on illegal activities."[5]

My Korea Notes of 1947 include this estimate of Rhee: "Syngman Rhee is tough, ruthless and fanatic. He understands perfectly his dependence upon American support and material aid. But, like Chiang Kai-shek, he has assessed the situation and made up his mind that the U.S. must support him for the purposes of anti-Communism no matter what he does. General Hodge, who tapped him on the wrist now and again, privately called him a would-be dictator. Rhee told Hodge, 'You will not be here long.'"

Bruce Cumings thus summarizes the events that made up the early stages of the 1950 war: "The basic issues over which the war in 1950 was fought were apparent immediately after liberation, within a three-month period, and led to open fighting that eventually claimed more than a hundred thousand lives in peasant rebellion, labor strife, guerrilla warfare, and open fighting along the 38th parallel — all this before the ostensible Korean war began. In other words, the conflict was civil and revolutionary in character, beginning just after 1945 and proceeding through a dialectic of revolution and reaction. The opening of conventional battles in June 1950 only continued the war by other means."[6]

Cumings used as an epigraph Chang Kyong-mo's more emotional statement about much of this: "Koreans shared with other peoples in Asia and Europe released from Japanese or German control a joyous anticipation of a new age, a new destiny. We were suddenly free of the hated alien rule.... To be released from these hardships, to see Koreans walk tall and proud again, to have the jail doors swing open and our patriots come out into the sun, to speak our own language, to plan and hope for a new Korea...these were the ecstatic aspirations of our freedom on August 15, 1945. But Korea was not freed from foreign control...and liberation was an illusion sanctified into a myth."

Memories of the Beginning

Still in naval uniform, I was in Seoul briefly in October 1945, when Syngman Rhee, accompanied by a prominent OSS activist, arrived on one of MacArthur's planes to be warmly welcomed at a ceremony organized by the Americans and their Korean collaborator friends. Rhee was provided with quarters in the Chosen hotel and with a huge slush fund and ready access to the radio.

I stumbled into a sense of what the U.S. was up to then. With other junior naval officers in Seoul we delighted in a visit to the old Korean royal palace and then turned to looking up Marine Corps officers who had studied Japanese with us at the University of Colorado. We found them in a small red brick building within an easy walk of the Bando Hotel, our quarters. Teamed up with Japanese intelligence personnel, they were monitoring telephone calls. On the table in front of them was a typewritten manual titled something like "Communist Suspects in the Seoul Area."

I returned for substantial stays in 1947 and 1948. In l947, I feverishly reported on the destruction of the above-ground left, and in 1948, with Pierre Doublet of Agence France Presse, I worked to get at the truth of the farcical election that elevated Rhee to power.

Left-oriented educated Koreans had been misled into believing that if American correspondents were amply supplied with the facts they would use them to get the truth out. The result was that very many nocturnal hours were spent in preparing detailed papers on a score of subjects. The English was flawed (a scholar who became a friend spoke Shakespearean English) and some of the facts were hearsay, but they were a powerful, numbing recitation of the brutalities that frustrated the aspirations of a long-suffering people. My copies are among my Korean papers at the University of Chicago.[7]

A small sampling:

> • A paper charging that Koreans who had served the Japanese remained high up in U.S.-occupied Korea offered these numbers: Six out of 11 in the police leadership, 11 out of 15 in the Department of Law, 5 out of 6 in the administration of the Legislative Assembly. About 5,000 police of all ranks had been kept on the job. Cho Pyong-ok, national police director, served in Japanese war effort organizations and in a 1941 speech said that "We have gathered here as the subjects of our empire. The Korean people should ask for nothing, uniting our war efforts unconditionally. We must march for the final victory and create the Greater East Asia Co-Prosperity Sphere."

• A 42 page paper offers 67 quotations on the trusteeship controversy in newspapers, various right and left organizations, leading
politicians and U.S. and Soviet spokesmen. But they do not make
entirely clear that the rightists, by bold distortion and American
help, prevailed and doomed trusteeship, seen as an obstacle to a
separate southern government.

• A paper titled "List of Persecutions in the Fields of Culture and
Arts in South Korea" covering the period from November 1945 to
October 1947 describes 151 incidents in 16 legal size pages. They
have to do with arrests, beatings, confiscations of poetry antholo-
gies and other books, breakup of presses, slashing of paintings,
banning of plays and exhibitions, seizing of photographers as
their cameras clicked, terrorist invasions of dramas in progress.

• Violations of freedom of speech and the press are detailed in 18
incidents in a six-page paper. Punitive U.S. regulations are quoted
and newspapers banned one after another are listed with such
official explanations as were made. Secretary of State Acheson is
quoted ironically as stating that in South Korea honest criticisms
are welcomed rather than regarded as crimes as the United States
upholds the freedoms of speech, press and assembly.

My Shakespearean scholar friend, who contributed to at least one
of the papers and whose fate was to become a disappearance, gave me
some idea of what took place in the countryside during the first weeks
of the American occupation. In Elizabethan English he told me that he
had gone to his ancestral village outside of Seoul and joined in the
exhilarating first moves toward democracy and social reform. An
American unit commanded by an officer named Ross arrived and, acting on the complaints of village elders, arrested alleged Communists,
including him. My scholar informant argued with Ross, got others and
himself released and even received an apology. "But in many places
where there wasn't someone like me who spoke English and argued,
sad things happened."*

When I met him in 1947, he had abandoned Shakespearean schol-
arship and, going from place to place in Seoul and in the provinces,
recorded instances of arrests and terrorism and, when he could, doing
something to help the victims. In fear of arrest and attack himself, he
had moved from one house to another five times in the past year. A
year later, in 1948, I could find no one who knew where he was.

In the American Military Government in Korea some officials of
lesser rank, not many, were disturbed by the repeated violations of
democratic norms. I cherished, and found useful, those I ran into who
could not keep their distress to themselves. Late in 1946 or early in

*Complete text is the first appendix.

1947 I was visited in the Tokyo Correspondents Club by a medium-ranking AMG official who poured out his reasons for profound disillusion. On the train from Pusan to Seoul an agitated doctor told me he could not wait to get out of Korea. Screams from the jail next to the clinic in which he worked had got to him. And then there was Burton Martin, called Tony, chief adviser to the Seoul municipal government, who protested the abuse of students who had taken part in the 1947 May Day celebration. He was put down as a trouble maker and transferred hurriedly to a post in Japan. He said in his protesting memo:

> "Should the police be allowed, as at present they are being allowed, to torture school children? By torture I mean: pulling hair (especially girls), beating on all parts of the body, kicking shins and groin, pushing lighted cigarette butts into the lips, tying hands together and slamming elbows on the edge of tables and chairs, water treatments...pulling up girls'skirts and hitting their bare legs and around the pelvis."[8]

I will always have a warm feeling for a certain American economist in Seoul. I was sitting in front of his boss's desk, being fed a lot of official malarkey on industrial productivity and economic progress, when this man, unable to stand it any longer, burst out from nearby, "This is nonsense, nonsense." He proceeded to give me a mini lecture on the reality, with facts and figures. The division chief just sat there.

Press Coverage

"Among the calamities of war may be justly numbered the diminution of the love of truth by the falsehoods which interest dictates and credulity encourages."

—SAMUEL JOHNSON, 1758

"Don't tell the press anything. When it's over, tell them who won."

—ADMIRAL ERNEST KING

Even Americans who have a sharp sense of what happened in Vietnam do not think of Korea as a precedent, as a deadly parallel. The press coverage of Korea—sometimes excellent, often mediocre or worse, the product of handouts and briefings—was certainly partly responsible. Korea was frigidly Cold War and many of those who went to their typewriters knew who they were writing for and naturally kept their self-interest in mind.

In the prewar period the regular Seoul press corps consisted of Richard J. H. Johnston of *The New York Times* and wives of American Military Group personnel who served the Associated Press and United Press as stringers. Journalists stationed in Tokyo now and again came for a look around and editors of leading publications dropped in from the States on chaperoned junkets.

Later, the regulars included a *Saturday Evening Post* correspondent suspected of working for the CIA and a Hearst feature writer, Ray Richards, who received half his salary from Rhee's Tokyo ambassador.[9] In September 1947 Rhee sent a radiogram to William Randolph Hearst saying "we are so happy to have him (Richards) to present the situation to the American people." Richards was killed by enemy fire early in the war, in July 1950.

I will relate later the experience of a young International News Service (Hearst) reporter who filed a brief, circumspect report of one of the horrors and was rebuked for falling for Communist propaganda.

Correspondents taken on a tour of the countryside, much of it in turmoil, late in 1946, were told by an American intelligence officer that "We like correspondents to visit us, but not for news… The American people are too dumb to understand what's going on here. We can't wait until they wake up to our problems. The Army will tell the American people what they ought to know."[10]

Similarly, at breakfast the day after my arrival in Chonju, North Cholla Province, in mid-August 1947, the American doctor, a captain, told me that I ought to go talk to the commanding colonel first thing. "They're suspicious as hell of newspapermen here. If your uncle is in the newspaper business, you've got to explain."

Bruce Cumings relates, in his first volume on the origins of the Korean war, how Johnston of the *Times* effectively maligned Pak Honyong, the Communist leader, who held a press conference on January 5, 1946, following the Moscow Decision. Johnston "quoted Pak as advocating an extended Soviet trusteeship over Korea to be followed by the incorporation of Korea into the Soviet Union," though other reporters present "claimed that Pak wanted nothing more than a Korea run by Koreans for Koreans." Internal AMG accounts supported the view of these other reporters, saying that Pak had advocated "complete independence" and that his remarks had been misrepresented. But General Hodge described as "interesting" the falsifications of his favorite correspondent.[11]

On January 27th representatives of nine Korean newspapers asked that Johnston be recalled by the *Times*. Sgt. Robert Cornwall, one of the reporters who heard Pak, confirmed that he had been misquoted by Johnston. But a widely distributed leaflet published by the rightist Korean Democratic Party cited Johnston and persuaded many that Pak was a Soviet stooge.

The United Nations Commission, created to realize a separate southern government, was welcomed at a huge rally in Seoul stadium when it arrived in the spring of 1948. The crowd was organized by the police, block leaders and rightist youth organizations, but a group of leftist students broke in and tossed leaflets in the air. They were savagely beaten by rightist youths as the police watched. A correspondent on the speakers' stand shouted "This is murder!" but was just stared at. Later the police did intervene and the injured were taken to a hospital. Two correspondents, including the one on the stand, went to the hospital to see them and told me later what they saw: a student who had lost an eye, another whose ear had been gouged off. The wounds of others had been painted with iodine but not washed and they were lying in bloody clothes. One correspondent voiced surprise that more treatment had not been given. Later, back in his hotel, his phone rang, and a general said he understood that "you have lodged a complaint about the care given the wounded." The correspondent denied it. "Well, how was the treatment?" the general asked. The correspondent began, "Well, they did have iodine..." "You see," said the general, "they did get good treatment—much better than we can usually persuade the authorities to give leftists—and I want you to be sure to stress how good the treatment was in your story."[12]

In the 1950 war the number of accredited correspondents in the first weeks was about 70. This gradually increased to 270. Korean reporting was pre-television, so apart from newsreel cameramen, all were print journalists, but far fewer, sometimes only several dozen, were there at any one time. They got needed information and help from many officers but met with undisguised hostility from others. An article on General Edward M. Almond, MacArthur's chief of staff and commander of the X corps, was titled "The Man Who Hates Correspondents." Eleven correspondents (12 by another count) were killed in action, five were taken prisoner, and 20 were wounded. Of those killed, seven were the victims of misdirected U.S. Air Force bombings.

At the beginning of the war censorship was voluntary. Some correspondents welcomed it because it protected them against breaches of security. But when General Ridgway took command of the Eighth Army late in 1950, censorship was enforced. One reporter was moved to write new words to the music of *The Battle Hymn of the Republic*:

> *Mine Eyes Have Seen the Censor with*
> *My Copy on His Knee;*
> *He is cutting out the passages*
> *that mean the most to me;*

"This sentence hurts morale as it's defined in Section 3..."
glory to the censor; glory, glory
to the censor;
Glory, glory to the censor;
This passage must come out."

Many correspondents settled for officialese and banalities, but Korea was the subject of consistently admirable reporting by Mark Gayn of the *Chicago Sun-Times*, Walter Sullivan of *The New York Times* and Pierre Doublet of *Agence France Presse*.

Others, among them the one woman correspondent, Marguerite Higgins, often got important realities into their reports. As she writes in her book, *War in Korea*, Higgins believed that the North Koreans moved on the south because South Korea appeared to be turning into "an anti-Communist show place."[13] But her battlefield reporting was excellent.

Han Suyin, there as a columnist, noted in her diary that "There are two hundred American correspondents in this theater. Most are keen on chasing up stories of personal heroism, but few spent any length of time here. I feel proud of our little British group, English and Australian."[14]

The agency bureau chiefs in Tokyo, Howard Handleman of International News Service, Ernest Hoberecht of United Press, Russell Brines, Associated Press, and Roy McCartney, Reuters, were more or less in MacArthur's pocket and largely managed by General Courtney Whitney. Correspondents called them "the palace guard." Handleman and Hoberecht in particular were several times called in and given slanted stories that in essence were Macarthur's astringent comments on key issues, such as the Taiwan controversy. In 1953 Hoberecht wrote specious articles supporting Syngman Rhee's finally vain challenge of the truce, even asserting that Asians in general were on Rhee's side.

What made the home media particularly averse to critical reporting was that the Korean War then was also the heyday of Senator Joseph McCarthy and rabid anti-Communist inquisitions. Book publishers were as ignoble as most newspapers. Twenty-eight American publishers and a number of British ones rejected I. F. Stone's *The Hidden History of the Korean War*, which, eventually published by the *Monthly Review*, first exposed the falsifications. Many publishers also refused to publish an American edition of Reginald Thompson's eloquent *Cry Korea*, and even the British edition was not sold in most bookshops in the U.S. or bought by most libraries.

In the spring of 1952, Robert C. Miller of the United Press, returned from Korea and addressed editors and publishers at a conference in Nevada. He said that "There are certain facts and stories from Korea that editors and publishers printed which were pure fabrication. You didn't know that when you printed them. Many of us who sent the stories knew they were false, but we had to write them because they were official releases from responsible military headquarters and were released for publication even though the people responsible knew they were untrue."

James Cameron of the *Picture Post*, London, was sickened by the sight early in the war, a few yards from U.S. Army headquarters in Pusan, of skeletonized, manacled prisoners on their way to execution. But the issue containing his story and graphic photos was suppressed as the magazine was going to press, presumably at the request of the government. Cameron protested, some of the staff revolted, and *Picture Post* eventually ceased publication.[15]

Han Suyin recorded a similar sight, also in the Pusan area: "Truckloads of political prisoners taken up a lonely road to be shot. Jammed kneeling in a truck, groaning, crying. Coming back last night long after curfew I came across a long file of two thousand people being taken to prison. Four across, one hand tied to a long rope, other hand clutching the shirt of the person in front. Quite a lot were women, some with babies on their backs. A horrifying spectacle. Policemen with bayonets on their rifles every ten yards on either side."[16]

Several reporters, notably Hearst correspondent Howard Handleman, staunchly supported American officialdom in withholding and distorting information about the truce negotiations at Panmunjam, but so many of the correspondents did their practiced best to report reality that all sorts of prohibitions were imposed. According to Philip Knightley, the correspondents were "forbidden to speak with the UN negotiators... were prohibited from inspecting documents presented at the negotiations and were allowed to see only those maps specially prepared for them by the United States Army's public relations section. The picture the correspondents received in this manner—which they faithfully reported to their public—was a mixture of lies, half-truths, and serious distortions."[17]

Eventually the better correspondents began to turn to Wilfred Burchett and Alan Winnington, reporting on the Communist side, for accurate information, regularly visiting them in their press tent and sharing with them what they called "anti-freeze." Ridgway then formally banned contacts between UN and "Communist" correspondents, condemning "excessive social consorting" and "trafficking with the enemy." The ban was ignored and a press delegation sent to Tokyo that induced Ridgway to withdraw the order.

The correspondents learned from Burchett and Winnington that, contrary to what they had been told, the Communists had proposed that the actual battle line be the truce line. The UN spokesmen insistently denied this. So Burchett and Winnington presented their Western colleagues with a copy of the official English language statement detailing the proposal.

Dwight Martin, head of the *Time* Far Eastern Bureau, reported the situation in the magazine this way: "Since summer, UN newsmen have been faced with a dilemma. They have found the Communist newsmen, whom they see every day at Panmunjam, are often a better source of truce-talk than the sparse briefings by UN's own information officers. From such men as Alan Winnington of the London *Daily Worker* and Wilfred Burchett of Paris' pro-Communist *Ce Soir*, UN correspondents have extracted Red reaction to UN proposals even before the UN negotiators announced that the proposals had been made. And high-ranking UN officers have frequently asked correspondents what the Red reaction seemed to be."[18]

The effort of the American military to control what correspondents reported at Panmunjom was not to deceive the Communists, who of course had to know perfectly what was going on, but to deceive the American people.

The Little Switch of wounded and ill prisoners in April of 1953 resulted in some of the most twisted reporting by American correspondents. Associated Press reported that "American soldiers returning from the Communist prison camps told a story today of generally good treatment." That was in the beginning.

Soon the word came down that the bottom line had to be horror and that became the theme. The United Press Tokyo office got this instruction from New York: "Need only limited coverage of returning POWs except for tales of atrocities and sensations." *Time*'s correspondent reported that "Somehow a headline hunting competition for 'atrocity' stories had started." Army Counterintelligence went to work on the returned prisoners to get them to remember atrocities.[19]

Reginald Thompson of the *London Telegraph* observed that "Most of the war correspondents carried arms, and it seemed that every man's dearest wish was to kill a Korean. 'Today,' said many of them as they nursed their weapons, 'I'll get me a gook.'" Thompson said also that MacArthur "had tried to expel a total of seventeen journalists for their criticisms," and this had closed the journalist ranks against him.[20]

When I arrived in Seoul in April, 1948, I found that I was lucky to be there. The Public Information Office had given General Hodge a file of my 1947 articles and his reaction was to deny me clearance. But he changed his mind. I was not told why, but I think perhaps James Stewart, who I had known in Chungking where he was the AP correspondent and who was then the foremost former correspondent employed by the occupation, suggested my exclusion would be unwise. Harold Noble, adviser to Rhee and sometimes his speech writer, and Colonel Watlington, head of G-2, shouted insults at me, but in general I was either ignored or treated civilly if not cordially. One employee in the cultural field was sternly warned not to meet with me, I learned later. I found I was surprisingly well known. I observed in my notes that "at cocktail parties people I have never seen before greet me by name."

Mark Gayn in Tokyo learned of a Japanese Foreign Office list of "Dangerous Correspondents." On it, in addition to him, were Joseph From, *U.S. News and World Report*, Bill Costello, CBS, Gordon Walker, *Christian Science Monitor*, Margaret Parten, *New York Herald Tribune*, and me.[21]

Leadership Racism

When I was in Chonju, capital of North Cholla Province, in August 1947, during a period of repression of leftists, a retired police chief from St. Louis serving in the American Military Government told me that "Orientals are accustomed to brutality such as would disgust a white man." A torment favored by the police, he said, was to "put a gas mask on a victim and then shut the breathing tube." A British cabinet officer who visited the strife-ridden prisoner of war camps on Koje explained that Koreans are "prone to violence." Such were the clichés that enabled Americans and others to feel less uncomfortable about— and keep silent about—the horrors they could not help discovering.

Bruce Cumings has conveniently gathered examples of racism in high places: Hanson Baldwin, military editor of *The New York Times*, likened Koreans to "the hordes of Genghis Khan." He remarked that to the Korean "life is cheap. Behind him stand the hordes of Asia. Ahead of him lies the hope of loot." He hoped that "these simple, primitive, barbaric people" would be convinced that Americans were friends.

President Truman, with a penchant for schoolboy history, similarly denounced "the inheritors of Genghis Khan and Tamerlane, the greatest murderers in the history of the world." On another occasion he called them "pagan wolves." Former President Herbert Hoover was among the isolationist-inclined commentators who nevertheless feared another threatening wave of "Asiatic hordes."

MacArthur believed that the Oriental dies stoically because he thinks death is the beginning of life. Dying, he "folds his arms as a dove does its wings." He also said often that Asians respect nothing as much as demonstrations of authority, that "the Oriental follows a winner." Russians, he told Carl McCardle of the *Philadelphia Bulletin.* "are Orientals, and we should deal with them as such—they are mongrels."[22]

Ridgway advocated and helped to bring about the integration of blacks in the Army. But, visiting a prisoner of war camp, he commented that "these prisoners are in appearance but a shade above a beast." He called them "human canaille."

Edgar Johnson, head of the Economic Cooperation Administration in Korea, called the North Koreans "half-crazed automatons" in the orbit of "a monolithic slave-and-master world."

British journalist James Cameron took his eyewitness account of the brutal treatment of South Korean prisoners by the Rhee authorities to the United Nations Commission and was told, "Most disturbing, yes; but remember these are Asian people, with different standards of behavior...all very difficult."

An American who had served in the occupation wrote in the *Far Eastern Economic Review* that Korea was peopled by wild men, scoundrels and semi-barbarians. He cited missionary opinions that too much inbreeding had led to "an arrested mental development."

General Willoughby thought that the worst aspect of the war was that "simple coolies," "half-men with blank faces" were killing highly civilized American high- school boys and college graduates.

Willoughby had long been an avowed racist, who believed that white men must combine against what he called the "world of color." Defending the Italian conquest of Ethiopia in his *Maneuver of War* (1939), he wrote: "Historical judgment, freed from the emotional haze of the moment, will credit Mussolini with wiping out a memory of defeat (Adua) by reestablishing the traditional military supremacy of the white race for generations to come."

The Repression Was American-Made

An early American commitment to repression was demonstrated by the selection of Syngman Rhee as the top man. In the first months of 1942 the COI (Coordinator of Information), precursor of OSS, explored ways of engaging in sabotage and subversive activities in Korea, screened Korean exiles in the U.S. and decided that Rhee would best serve it and U.S. interests. But the American military in China protested that "playing the Korean card" would offend Chiang Kai-shek and so the COI had to back off.

But in mid-October of 1945 M. Preston Goodfellow, experienced in clandestine activities in Asia and a former deputy director of OSS, brought Rhee to Seoul and helped to place him. During the next years Goodfellow was in and out of Seoul. The OSS became the CIA in 1947 and he had steady work in Korean-American businesses (OSS and CIA covers), in links with the Taiwan nationalists, and efforts, unrealized, to initiate a guerrilla movement on the mainland. He was an influential member of Rhee's "kitchen cabinet" where he supported the establishment of a separate southern government with armed forces.[23]

Early directives from Washington urged the American Occupation to foster democracy and freedoms so as to embarrass the north and counter the appeal of Communism. But Hodge could do nothing of the sort. Even half-way democracy and freedom of speech and the press would have solidified the power of the left and frustrated General Hodge's efforts to build a presentable right. His decision to repress the left seems to have been made even in advance of the arrival of the American forces from Okinawa, and it began immediately after Hodge arrived in Korea.

The popular Korean People's Republic and its leader, Yo Un-hyong, were denounced by General Archibald Arnold, just appointed governor general, at a press conference in October of 1945. In Korea only a few weeks, Arnold lashed out harshly at Yo, whose work for Korean independence had won him three years in prison and enormous popularity, because he had refused to join an appointed advisory council largely consisting of Japanese collaborators and extreme rightists. The journalists at the conference unanimously criticized Arnold's statement. A Korean newspaper that declined to publish it was shut down—the first victim of American restrictions on press freedom.

A quotation will reveal the character of Arnold's remarks: "If the men who are arrogating to themselves high-sounding titles are merely play acting on a puppet stage with entertainment of questionable value, they must immediately pull down the curtain.... If behind the curtain of puppet shows, there are venal men holding the strings who are so foolish as to think they can exercise any legitimate government functions, let them pinch themselves and awaken to reality...."

In March, 1946, the U.S.-U.S.S.R. Joint Commission met to consult Korean organizations regarding formation of a provisional government for all of Korea and the U.S. had to confront the problem that as G-2 reported, the left "represents the majority of the people of South Korea."

Hodge's response was to prod the fractious right to simulate political power and to step up the repression of the left. The police and their terrorist youth group allies were to do it, and to give them an appearance of legality he directed the American Military Government to issue ordinances listing a 100 or more punishable offenses.

Ordinance 72 listed 82 such offenses, among them attempting to influence official actions of the occupying forces by use of force, duress, threat, promise or boycott, communicating information possibly harmful to the security or property of the occupying forces, and unauthorized communication with persons outside the occupied territory (that is, in North Korea).

Also prohibited were support of or participation in any organization or movement "contrary to the interests of" the occupying forces; "publishing, importing or circulating printed, typed or written material which is detrimental or disrespectful to the occupying forces," and organizing or attending any public gathering for which no permit has been granted.

An especially restrictive ordinance was Number 55—Registration of Political Parties. It required any group of three or more organized for political purposes to register and to provide names of officers, lists of members, and financial accounts and lists of financial contributors. As it was designed to do, it gave the police any number of reasons or excuses to fill the prisons and outlaw organizations.

One Seoul newspaper claimed that Ordinance 55 "was worse than the Japanese Peace Preservation Law," but General Lerche told Korean journalists that the provisions of Ordinance 55 "were the usual provisions for regulating political parties in democratic countries and under circumstances such as obtain in Korea."[24]

The American courts relied on the ordinances in victimizing great numbers of Koreans brought before them. Colonel A. Wigfall Green served as Judge Advocate in Korea and as president of the Board of Review for the Trial of Koreans. He was affronted by the violations of real trial procedures and became a whistle blower when he wrote his book *The Epic of Korea*, stating that the courts were instructed to convict, or, more subtly, a general would "express an interest."

General Hodge's headquarters went so far as to instruct the Board of Review to approve all trials perfunctorily. Many Koreans, including children, Green wrote, were sentenced to long prison terms for minor offenses, often on the basis of flimsy evidence. The Board of Review did disapprove some convictions, despite orders, but in 90 percent of such cases, Hodge rejected its findings.[25]

E. Grant Meade, serving in the military government in South Cholla, wrote later that "The provost courts were principally a method of removing opponents of military government from circulation. Numerous cases were tried; there were no acquittals.... Important cases were decided in advance by the tactical commander."

Later Korean courts were set up but the American governor thought they were too lenient with leftists and ordered "a series of arrests of judges and prosecutors." Cases of known leftists were assigned to provost courts. A result was that "It was not uncommon to find twelve prisoners occupying quarters intended for four."[26]

The reactionary ordinances and the vigilante courts, all violations of the U.S. Constitution, have been ignored or passed over lightly in most American accounts of the U.S. performance in Korea. As a reminder of what the U.S. military is capable of, they ought to be preserved under glass just as the U.S. Constitution is.

Elections of sorts were held in October 1946, as the Autumn Harvest Uprisings, the ill-fated resistance of the left, were being crushed. Hodge restricted the vote to property owners and village elders, continuing the four-level electoral process used by the Japanese to choose members of advisory councils. Widespread irregularities and fraud further corrupted what were officially hailed as real elections. In the city of Taegu the moderately leftist People's Party found on election day that every single party worker was in jail. Many newspapers supporting leftists were banned. In Kangwon Province the elections were actually conducted not by officials but by Rhee's party, assuring that only Rhee candidates could be elected.

Mark Gayn observed in the *Chicago Sun* of November 11 that "the secret ballot assured in the ordinance was a myth. In countless villages the names of candidates were filled in for the voters by obliging village head men.

"In other villages voters were even spared the trouble of going to the polls. Instead, messengers went around collecting name seals which then were stamped on ballots filled in by officials."

A Military Government officer summed it up for Gayn: "This is quite an election. First, they let Syngman Rhee's boys decide the procedure. Second, to make sure nothing slips up, they hold the election in a series of four levels so that undesirables might be eliminated.

Third, they let only family heads or heads of ten families vote. They put all the possible opposition in jail or drove it into the hills."[27]

E. Grant Meade reported that in February of 1946 the chief of the Bureau of Information in South Cholla "during a trip to Seoul was informed verbally by the high command that elections were planned for the fall, and that while the State Department expected Military Government to continue to operate under a facade of neutrality, the Americans were expected to make every effort to secure a rightist victory."[28]

They were excessively successful. Supporters of Syngman Rhee won 43 of the 45 seats in the 90-seat assembly. Hodge appointed centrists to most of the other 45 seats in an effort to appease Kim Kiu-sic, an American-educated moderate, but Kim's comments on the elections were harsh.

The brutalities, injustices and illegalities of the repression of the popular left are described in the generality of American historiography, if mentioned at all, as if the Americans were outsiders who viewed painfully the horrors taking place. The reality is that what took place was a planned, integrated effort of the American occupation and its rightist allies.

The Autumn Harvest Uprisings

> *An American officer described his two days at a police station jammed with rebellious peasants to Mark Gayn: "I saw cops crack men's shins against sharp-edged wooden blocks. I saw men put burning wooden slivers under men's nails. I saw more men than I care to remember get the water treatment… I saw cops beat a man and then hang him on a metal hook under his shoulder blades."*

American troops and tanks played an important role in the brutal suppression of the strikes and rural uprisings in the fall of 1946.

An effective strike of railroad workers in Pusan on September 23 led quickly to strikes in many industries and institutions elsewhere. In Seoul 295 enterprises were struck by workers numbering about 30,000. Some 16,000 students walked out of the schools in support. Violent clashes took place as the police, allied with rightist youth gangs, assaulted the strikers.

The strikes were followed by uprisings in the countryside, most of them in provinces such as South Cholla where the people's committees, the local organizations of the People's Republic, were strongest and where Red Peasant Unions had existed in the 1930s. The uprisings did not begin at the same time, but in a kind of ripple effect—an uprising in one place touched off one in a neighboring area. This reflected the fact that while some localities were strongly led, the overall left leadership was incapable of directing a concord of strikes and rural rebellions. Arrests had already weakened it.

The police were attacked everywhere. Many were killed, often after torture, and their homes were raided and smashed. County offices were occupied and grain collection records and the like were seized and burned. Evil or big landlords were targets, their opulent homes ransacked. Searches uncovered hoarded grain, which was distributed. Speakers called for restoration of the people's committees and for the release of all political prisoners.

The rebels were mostly peasants, but with them were wage laborers, peddlers, merchants, and students. And in some areas miners joined. They had few firearms and fought with farm tools, bamboo sticks, spears and clubs, as their fathers had in the Tonghak rebellion of the last century.

General Hodge reacted with the usual banalities. He told the press that outside agitators, directed from Pyongyang or Moscow, were responsible. He had been a worker, he told the strikers, and was sympathetic but had to warn them they were "misled into blind alleys by those who make great promises of something for nothing." Why were police being assaulted? Because they were defenders of law and order and the natural enemies of agitators trying to stir things up. So the agitators "work up a great hate campaign."

As few Americans in the field understood, the reality was that the strikes and uprisings were an enraged response to injustices and abuses that had both a history extending back to the Japanese era and continuing on into the painful experience of the American occupation. The People's Republic and its committees had given the countryside hope and their abolition had gone hand in hand with police brutalities, arrests, confiscatory grain collections, fall off in jobs, and inflation. While landlords hoarded rice, villagers went hungry. A letter presented to a local Military Government official by 700 young people said "We must save people who are starving and weeping." The striking workers only infrequently made revolutionary demands. They were after wage increases in line with the inflation, job security, various benefit improvements—and, the central issue, union rights, an end to American supported union bashing.

A leaflet that was circulated said that "Now our young patriots have risen in an effort to protect our fatherland from the danger of recolonization! It is their aim to clear this land of bad policemen who repress our true patriots, bad officials who extort excessive quotas of rice, and pro-Japanese traitors who are behind them."

The effective repression was the work of a triumvirate—the police, their youthful rightist allies, and American troops and tanks. The American contribution included firing on demonstrators as well as unquestioning support of everything the police did. Often Americans arrived just in time to prevent a police station from being overrun.

Mark Gayn's on-the-spot account of the Autumn Harvest Uprisings in *Japan Diary* was far and away the best and remained so for years. This is what he and a companion learned, despite official discomfiture, in the National Police Division of the Military Government in Seoul: [29]

> "We were taken to an enclosure, where copies of American police reports were being kept. There was a huge wall map, with little labels showing near the trouble spots. The labels were grouped in three clusters: one near the 38th parallel, in the areas we visited; another in a city called Taegu, in the heart of our zone; and the third in the extreme south, around the city of Pusan.
>
> "For the next two hours we scribbled feverishly. What we had before us, in the form of laconic two- and three-line reports, was the face of revolution. It was a face covered with blood, and contorted with pain and agony. As most revolutions: this one was based on deep distress—on a hunger for land, food and justice.
>
> "It was a full-scale revolution, which must have involved hundred of thousands, if not millions of people. In Taegu alone a third of the 150,000 inhabitants took part in the uprising. It was here that the fuse of the revolution was set off last month. The railroad workers went on strike, followed by the phone and metal, textile and electric workers. As each strike was suppressed by the police, another took its place. Students went out into the streets to demonstrate, and then the whole city was aflame.
>
> "From the city, the revolution spread into the countryside and was taken over by the sharecroppers. The farmers refused to surrender their rice to the police. They attacked the homes of the landlords, and then the police stations. They tore off jail doors to release arrested sharecroppers, they burned the records and stole the weapons.
>
> "Arrayed against the revolution were the police, the rightist organizations, and the U.S. Army. In one town after another, right-wing leaders offered their aid to our local commanders, or actively participated in the mass roundups of suspects. As for us, we did far more than just transport the Korean police to the trouble spots, or supply arms, or maintain preventive patrols. Our troops—come here as liberators—had fired on crowds, conducted mass arrests,

combed the hills for suspects, and organized posses of Korean rightists, constabulary and police for mass raids.

"It was amazing to recall again that despite our active involvement, no harm had come to a single American. To me it was a remarkable stroke of luck or an indication of stern discipline in the ranks of the rebels. The revolutionists wanted no trouble with us. They were merely settling their scores with the men and forces which had oppressed them under our rule, as they did under the Japanese. By today, about 75 policemen have been killed, and 200 to 300 were missing."

For all the weaknesses and mistakes of the rebels (one error was excessive vengeful brutalities), they might have prevailed if the Americans had not got into it. Certainly the struggle would have been protracted. In the opinion of Bruce Cumings, "Had Americans not been on the scene in the fall of 1946, Korea would have been thrown into civil war then instead of four years later." He said also that the fact that the repressive apparatus "had to have recourse to United States Army support on so many occasions during the autumn of 1946 attests as much to the success as to the failure of communist and leftist organizers."[30]

The actuality was a crushing of the strikes and uprisings which had a shattering effect on the left-oriented Chonpyong unions and ended what had remained of the authority of the people's committees in the rural provinces. More than 200 policemen had been killed but the national police emerged triumphant and strengthened. Very many leaders of the organizations of the left were either dead, in prison or underground. In the countryside peasants had no organizations to turn to for aid and for the moment were intimidated.

Korean National Youth and Yi Pom-sok

In general the American occupation did not provide organization for the Koreans but, instead, was an ally of Korean rightists who were undertaking that. The principal exception was the U.S. direct sponsorship, counseling, financing and supplying of the Korean National Youth, a fervently anti-Communist and semi-military organization that grew swiftly to a claimed membership of 800,000. It contributed importantly to the rightist success in developing a mass base and later to the formation of the army.

In May of 1948 Pierre Doublet and I visited the Korean National Youth leadership training school in Suwon, a decayed feudal town and former capital with ancient gates and crumbling wall a few miles south of Seoul. We allowed ourselves pleasant hours of visiting a temple to the martial gods and nearby pagodas and pavilions, but then got to our main purpose, an inquiry into the Korean National Youth. We were fortunate enough to meet and be guided about by the head of it, Yi Pom-sok (rendered Li Bum Suk during the Occupation) himself. A man of about 50, well-built, with a lean bespectacled face and close-cropped hair, he arrived in his polished blue jeep.

We had already read about him. In his years in China, Yi had been intimate with Kuomintang rightists. He served in the military, Chinese and exiled Korean, and concurrently in Tai Li's vast, reactionary intelligence network. After Tai and the OSS reached an accord, he went to work for the Americans. He was involved for a time with Chiang Kai-shek's San Min Chu I Youth Corps and also was linked to the Blue Shirts, a group that was as close to fascism as Chiang got. His experience with them had a lasting influence, apparently dictating the blue color of the Korean National Youth uniform and his jeep.

According to the semiofficial biography distributed by Korean National Youth, in China "he organized a Korean Revolutionary Death Band and put to death the enemy spies and betrayers. It is said at that time even small boys kept back their tears when they heard the name of Chul Gi, the general's pseudonym. Nevertheless, seized with ruthless hunger, cold and cruel thoughts, he suffered daily with tearful agony."[31]

Four days after Japan surrendered he was flown into Korea with an OSS team of 12 Americans and five Koreans. His biography does not mention the OSS, relating that he "returned to his Motherland with his followers and landed at Inchon, where he had planned a scene of bloodshed had the Japanese not surrendered."

General Hodge quickly assigned Yi to organizing right-thinking young men into a youth movement. The American Military Government provided him with an initial subsidy of $330,000, a generous supply of trucks, jeeps, cots, shoes and gasoline, and a U.S. adviser—Colonel Ernest Voss—for internal security.

In an early interview, Yi said that "We base our instruction on the German youth movement because the Germans are the only people who really know how to organize young men." After an interview with a *Time* correspondent caused him and the Korean National Youth embarrassment, he learned to speak cautiously for publication.

The Korean youth are backward and need direction and guidance, Yi told us. Every applicant was screened and had to be vouched for by three sponsors. Members were free to discuss political questions provided that they did not express leftist ideas. As we talked, a unit of blue-uniformed youths passed us on their way to lunch, singing their rousing song:

Within us runs the blood of one direct dynasty
Die and die again, this will remain
The land of our brethren
We alone can save the thirty million
We alone can save the thirty million

On their Prussian-style caps was the Korean National Youth emblem, a circle of stars with what Yi described as a male symbol in the center. Behind them an obelisk, another male symbol, pierced the sky, proclaiming "The Nation Above All, the Race Above All."[32]

Members of Korean National Youth were viewed as boy scouts by the more credulous Americans, and the Korean National Youth indeed performed all sorts of good deeds, improving roads, building bridges, supervising playgrounds, cleaning up neighborhoods, helping refugees, etc. But G-2 reported that in the strongly leftist province of South Cholla, it was engaged in terrorism.

Members of Korean National Youth were eager workers. In the separatist elections held May 10, several were elected to the national assembly, and Yi served in Rhee's cabinet variously as defense minister, premier and home minister. Rhee apparently needed him but perceived him as a likely rival and handled that by bringing about the absorption of Korean National Youth into a broader youth organization that Rhee controlled.

In the Korean war Yi Pom-sok was an organizer of an anti-Communist youth league that controlled a number of prisoner of war compounds on Koje Island and which, with the help of torture, sought to persuade prisoners to refuse repatriation to China or North Korea. When the British Minister of State, Selwyn Lloyd, and an aide, William Stevenson, sought to enter a particular cmpound at Koje, an American general moved to dissuade them. "The Anti-Communist Youth League wields discipline here and punishes anyone who gets out of line," he explained. What is the youth league, Lloyd inquired. It "was modeled on the Hitler Youth by South Korea's last Home Secretary, Lee Bum Suk (Yi Pom-sok)...."[33]

Assault on the Unions

As the Japan-China correspondent for Allied Labor News, New York, I gave particular attention to the plight of unions in South Korea. In Seoul and elsewhere, in 1947, I observed the general assault on the unions and the next year I encountered only remnants and victims.[34]

An official American report written by Stewart Meacham of the Labor Department gives part of the evidence. On June 18, 1946, when the U.S. occupation of South Korea was less than a year old, a Labor Advisory Mission sent from Washington submitted a report to the American Military Government in which it noted "the widespread suppression of union activities" and in cautious phrases recommended changes.

It found that the only real unions were those affiliated with the National Council of Korean Labor Unions (called Chonpyong), which it said was not Communist-dominated though "leftwing." On the other hand, it reported that the All-Korea National Independence Labor League (called Nochong) "operates under the guise of trade unions without performing any normal union functions." It was financed by Syngman Rhee and employers and is said to use "hired gangsters."[35]

The Meacham report and my report of it to Allied Labor News gained the attention of General Hodge. He wrote a lengthy criticism of the report which he sent to MacArthur in Tokyo. He also sent the report itself, but advised MacArthur not to bother reading it, explaining that "It follows the Roger Baldwin—Mark Gayn—Hugh Deane line."[36]

The American Military Government and General Hodge personally held to the view that Rhee's Nochong was the "constructive " labor group. The extermination of genuine unionism was achieved with important U.S. help.

An article in the (U.S.) *Monthly Labor Review* in April 1949 titled "The South Korean Wage Earner Since Liberation" did suggest some of the unpleasant realities: "Maintenance of order and the prevention of demonstrations which might endanger the security of the Occupation was a major goal of the United States Military Government. Police permission was required for meetings. It was not customarily granted to, nor often sought by, labor groups suspected of being in sympathy with the Communists. In addition, the police carried on an active campaign of surveillance against groups which were considered actively or potentially dissident, and a number of the labor unions were included in these categories."

In 1947 I several times visited the headquarters of the Chonpyong unions. It has been raided by terrorist youths and at the entrance to the modest premises were tubs of broken bricks and stones and a pile of staves for use in case of a serious attack. The leaders I interviewed had struggled for decades to organize workers and their scarred faces and twisted limbs were evidence of what they had endured.

They made clear to me that they were mainly absorbed with rice and *kim chi* (fermented cabbage with peppery additions) issues in organizing and dealing with employers. Inflation was rampant and Occupation policy made them victims. In January 1948, with the year 1936 as 100, prices were as high as 149,381 and wages only 18,715. A chart published by the American Military Government in November 1946 revealed comparable statistics: Using June 1937 as 100, by November 1945 wages were 2,000 while prices had jumped to 8,000. A half year later, in January 1946, the AMG froze wages but not prices, creating a desperate situation for the population. Soaring inflation led to hoarding and speculation as well as suffering. Japanese houses were torn down for firewood. The caloric intake fell to about 1,500 in 1946. Pleas and petitions for relief for the workers went unanswered.[37]

I interviewed Mun Un-jong a number of times in 1947 and 1948. His story is that of the union hopes and the union sadness in microcosm.

Some GIs who were prisoners of war might remember Mun, the shabby baggage cart puller in the Seoul railroad station who slipped them rice cakes and cigarettes when the guards weren't looking. Mun then thought of Americans as something like knights in shining armor. "Whenever I saw a B-19 fly over," he told me, "I'd want to shout a welcome, even if a bomb were to kill me the next minute."

Mun had devoted his whole life to the labor movement. He started organizing when he was 18, still a student. A seaman and railroad worker for six years, he kept up the struggle for the related goals of a free labor movement and an independent Korea. He and his comrades, most of them Communists, had some organizing successes, especially in the 1920s. A three-month strike in Wonsan shook the Japanese and led to a crackdown which drove unions underground. Mun was imprisoned three times by the Japanese for a total of nine years.

After Japan's defeat, becoming director of general affairs of the Chonpyong federation, Mun took part in the mass organizing of workers which brought more than a quarter of million into unions in about eight months. After the first major crackdown on the young unions in the fall of 1946, he and his colleagues had to operate clandestinely as they had under the Japanese.

When I saw Mun, he was working too hard, eating too little, and was very tired. He and other top union leaders were in bad health from their years in prison. Many had tuberculosis and some showed the marks of torture. They were living the lives of hunted men, always looking for terrorists, moving from one sleeping place to another.

Two days after we talked, on August 9, 1947, Mun went to the police station to protest a new ban on demonstrations and was immediately jailed, for the third time since the U.S. Army brought its brand of law and order to south Korea.

A year later I saw Mun again and didn't recognize him. His face was swollen and his fingers were puffy. He told me he had spent four months in a police jail and four more in a regular prison. In the jail he was tortured regularly in an effort to make him confess that unions were involved in an alleged Communist plot to stage uprisings and sabotage.

Mun said he was beaten so badly that he was unconscious or semiconscious much of the time. He was repeatedly hung by the heels and given the water cure. His face was smeared with human excrement and ashes. For a month he lost his sight and hearing. A U.S. Army doctor, discovering his condition, smuggled medicine to him at some personal risk. Mun could see again but had to wear dark glasses in sunlight.

I learned from a U.S. Army major what happened to one union while staying with the 96 Military Government unit at Chonju, North Cholla. The major was talking over a drink at the officers' billet. "Yes," he said, "We had a strong longshoremen's union at Kunsan once. It was leftist. Hell, it got so we had to pay through the nose to get a drum of oil ashore.

"So we called in a smart young rightist named Kim and suggested that he start a rival union. Kim had a financial interest in the stevedoring business and also was politically ambitious. He got busy.

"Well, there were a number of clashes and then last September (1946) our boys went in and smashed that union so you could hardly find the pieces. That just about wound it up."[38]

I later learned that an indirect casualty of that union busting was a Kunsan newspaper that reported the story straight. It was looted by terrorists and forced to cease publication.

In March 1947 a delegation from the World Federation of Trade Unions, which then included the CIO and British unions, arrived in Seoul. The WFTU had provisionally recognized the Chonpyong unions at a meeting in Prague and the mission of the delegation was to inspect them to ascertain if they merited full membership. The visit was a succession of horrors.[39]

"In South Korea we saw fascism in action," a delegate told me. Soon after starting their drive from the airport, the delegates met a dusty throng of banner-carrying workers who were walking to the airport to welcome them. Louis Saillant, general secretary of the WFTU, asked that the cars stop so that the delegates could shake hands with the leaders. The American officials refused and the cars sped on.

During the delegation's first day in Seoul, police arrested a number of union officers and members, and the delegates learned that the chairman and a vice chairman of the Chonpyong unions could not greet them because they were serving six-month jail sentences for holding a meeting in a private house instead of in their headquarters. The delegation did meet eight of the 25 members of the Chonpyong central committee, learning that those they interviewed had spent a total of 52 years in prison.

On the second day the delegation went to inspect the Kyung Bong textile factory. The company director refused to permit an inspection as long as the delegates were accompanied by three Korean union members. While they were talking, company guards began to push around the union members until Saillant intervened. Leaving for their car in frustration, the delegates saw two union members bearing welcoming leaflets running toward them. Guards, later identified as members of Rhee's pseudo-union, beat them and kicked them in the face.

Saillant asked that the injured men be placed in his car to be taken for treatment. This was refused. As police and armed youths gathered around the delegates and rifles were cocked, the delegates felt themselves "in a state of complete insecurity." They drove off amidst epithets and threats and called on the military governor, General Archer L. Lerch, who, they said, "was kind enough to give us a minute and a half of his time." The delegates shortly thereafter learned that Chonpyong delegates trying to distribute a statement welcoming the WFTU visit had been arrested.

The delegation described its experience in South Korea in detail in a statement addressed to Lerch, concluding with eight demands. Among them were release of those arrested, legal guarantee of trade union rights, the security of Koreans accompanying the delegation, and punishment of those responsible for the brutalities. In its later report to the WFTU the delegation said that the brutal incident at the textile factory was "only conceivable in a country where the most extreme reaction reigns."

Delegates Willard Townsend (CIO) and Ernest Bell (British labor) signed, making the protest unanimous. But press interviews of delegates in Tokyo made internal differences and bickering evident, presaging the imminent breakup of the WFTU and the formation of the anti-Communist Confederation of Free Trade Unions.

A young correspondent for Hearst's International News Service filed a brief, cautiously phrased account of the WFTU's experience in Seoul and was rewarded with a rebuke and admonition from across the Pacific: "Don't be a sucker for Communist propaganda."

What happened to the once strong union at the Seoul Electric Company is very largely what happened to all unions in South Korea.

In March 1947 about 95 percent of the Seoul Electric Company workers took part in a short general strike called to protest right-wing terrorism. Sixty of the striking workers were arrested along with 30 union functionaries. Then Rhee's Nochong pseudo union began a campaign of terror. Within two weeks 200 of the workers had been summoned one by one to the phony union's room in the plant and beaten with a wooden club which was inscribed "Correct one's mental attitude."

On April 10th the Department of Labor, which had American advisers, announced that an election would be held to determine the collective bargaining unit. Twenty workers were in the hospital being treated for beatings and others had quit under pressure. So the union boycotted the election.

Despite no opposition, the pseudo-union intensified its terrorism. Squads visited workers' homes, pressuring them to promise to vote for it. Those who did not immediately agree were told that their names would be turned over to American counterintelligence.

On April 19th the election was held at the company's main plant. At the entrance were 80 police in uniform, 20 to 30 more in plain clothes, and three truckloads of young terrorists. Microphones blared. Terrorists lined the stairs to the polls which were on the third floor.

Those coming to vote saw that the Nochong union had been given three-quarters of the ballot page. The bottom quarter was for those who wanted no union. Few dared to be seen writing on the bottom of the page but a handful turned their ballots upside down and voted against the pseudo-union, which got 3,805 votes out of 4,291 eligible voters.

Three months later, on July 27th, a contingent of Seoul Electric Company workers, carrying the real union's banners, joined the rally on South Mountain to support the U.S.-U.S.S.R. Joint Commission, then meeting to negotiate formation of a provisional government for all Korea. The police raided the company soon after, seizing 32 men and seven women and taking them to Won Hyun Palace, a terrorist youth headquarters, where they were beaten. When workers at the plant gathered in protest, the police dispersed them and arrested six. The beaten workers and others were fired.

For some months a strong underground union struggled at the Seoul Electric Company. It was gradually weakened by brutal episodes. Some survivors fled north across the 38th parallel.

The Nochong unions were the only unions recognized during the early dictatorships in south Korea. Their task was to keep wages low so that South Korean enterprises could compete in the world market. But increasingly they were moved by painful events and younger leadership to become real unions.

The Moscow Decision

Placing Korea under four-power (U.S., Soviet Union, Britain and China) trusteeship was a U.S.-initiated and long insisted on proposition. The Soviet Union readily acceded both to trusteeship and division of the peninsula, but in hard bargaining with the U.S. at Moscow in December, 1945, it did succeed in limiting the duration of trusteeship to five years and subordinating it to formation of a provisional Korea government.

The accord was soon forsaken by President Truman, who thought it was too conciliatory of Moscow—it was "babying the Soviets." Two years later Truman gave himself credit for scrapping the Moscow Decision and hardening American policy.

And the accord was promptly sabotaged in Seoul by Rhee and associates as well as General Hodge and the American command. The shaping of the south into an anti-Communist bastion had made just about any deal with the north unwelcome. A flood of falsifying propaganda (including Richard J. H. Johnston's distortion of the views of Pak Hon-yong, reported above) made trusteeship and Soviet control of Korea seem synonymous and that helped to create a rightist mass movement that gave Rhee real muscle. In Bruce Cumings' view, the Soviets saw the overnight collapse of the Moscow Decision "as a double cross and a sign that cooperation with the Americans was possible only on American terms."[40]

U.S. intransigence operated effectively in frustrating negotiations of the U.S.-U.S.S.R. Joint Commission, established to realize the Moscow Decision, thus clearing the way for the establishment of the separate southern regime that had already been decided on. In April 1946, a Soviet concession apparently brought the parties very close to agreement, but at the next session, two days later, the U.S. abruptly toughened its position.

When the Joint Commission was reconvened in May of 1947, the U.S. once again acted to make sure an agreement was impossible. The Joint Commission was instructed by the terms of the Moscow agreement to consult only parties and organizations supportive of it, including trusteeship and formation of a provisional government. This made Rhee's collection of extremist parties and organizations ineligible. Since Rhee's elimination would have given the left and center the majority view, Rhee divided his forces in two, assigning one to claim to go along with trusteeship and apply to be consulted. Choi Kyu Seul, a Rhee publicist, explained to the press that "parallel tactics" had been adopted "to fight trusteeship within and without the Joint Commission." Rhee himself was quoted as likening these parallel tactics to "the two sides of the same shield."[41]

In my 1947 Korea Notes I wrote that the Rhee right had scored its most impressive success. "It eats cake and has it too."

During the last two weeks of June, Rhee's anti-consultation bloc became increasingly strident and threatening, and on June 28 General Hodge wrote Rhee warning him to desist from any intended acts of violence. Rhee replied curtly, and on July 4, in a public address, declared: "The situation impels us to take independent action. I hope all the people understand this and that all the political parties and social organizations will push ahead."

Colonel Robinson of G-2 told me that rightist acts of terrorism had steadily increased from one or two instances a week to four or five a day. He said the leftists had often attacked police but were temporarily "on good behavior."

The Soviet side understandably termed Rhee's "parallel tactics" a subterfuge and demanded the exclusion from consultation of 24 parties of Rhee's pro-consultation bloc, but the U.S. insisted that these sudden converts to trusteeship be consulted. The Soviet delegation held firm and the Joint Commission ended in a failure that was congenial to the separatist American policy.

The Death of Yo Un-hyong

The year 1947 advanced American preparations for a separate southern regime, headed by Rhee and militantly anti-Communist. In the spring the U.S. saw to it that the second session of the U.S.-U.S.S.R. Joint Commission adjourned in failure and in August it intensified its assault on the left, ending its above-ground presence. And it could not but be relieved by the assassination of Yo Un-hyong (his name rendered Lyuh Woon-Hyung by the American Occupation and correspondents) on July 19th. A rightist hit man jumped on the running board of his car as it was taking him to an appointment and pumped bullets into his head.

I had hardly unpacked at the Bando Hotel when the news of Yo's killing reached me. I had never met him or even seen him, but he had

had a looming presence in my reading. I was shaken and in the days ahead did all I could to do right by him. An article in *The Nation* of September 6, 1947 related my findings.

Rhee and others on the right alleged that the crime had been committed by the Communists and Richard Johnston hinted that might be so in his dispatch to *The New York Times* but everyone with sense understood that the right had done it. Korea's most revered and popular political figure, the only one with the stature to take on Rhee, had been eliminated as he was trying almost desperately to oppose establishment of a Rhee government.[42]

Yo said once that Marxism was "a good idea " and liked what he knew about Kim Il Sung, but his thinking had many strands to it, including the Christianity he had absorbed in a missionary school. He was a robust man, often handsomely dressed, and silver tongued and naturally gracious. He was a staunch nationalist and truly committed to profound social change, but had moderating inclinations. He vigorously challenged Communist Pak Hon-yong for the leadership of the left and that led him to keep ties with the American military Government. But he also was careful to preserve his left base in the Democratic National Front.

A few days after Yo was killed, it briefly seemed that he might achieve in death what he had sought in his last weeks. A National Salvation Committee, embracing the left, center and part of the moderate right, was formed in the first hot abhorrence of the act of terrorism. The police, acting with alacrity, outlawed it on the grounds that it had not registered and would "agitate the people" and provoke terrorism.

If Yo was killed by the right, he was honored by the left. For a fortnight his body lay in state in the headquarters of the Laboring People's Party, which he had established in May. Tens of thousands of people came to stand before the casket, paying last respects: white-clad women chanting and wailing, intellectuals, students, workers, farmers. Organizations all over South Korea wrote messages on the walls in blood, pledging to continue the struggle for the People's Republic, condemning the terror, echoing the hope expressed by Yo in his last radio address that the Joint Commission would reach an agreement.

Nine attempts had been made on Yo's life since 1945. He had been beaten twice, often harassed by the police and threatened many times. In vain he asked Americans for permission to carry a weapon and to arm his bodyguards. American officers scoffed. Circumstantial evidence suggests that the Black Tiger Gang, a clandestine part of the Seoul police force, committed the assassination. Yo's daughter, Yo Yongu, was one of those convinced this was so.

On July 30, I went to Yo's Laboring Peoples Party where thousands came to view and pay homage to the body, intoning laments, and inspecting the glass cases outside filled with many photos of Yo and his blood stained clothes.

August 3, the day of the funeral, was one of the most peaceful days of the summer. Police, on foot, mounted, and in jeeps, were stationed every 50 feet along the two-mile route to Seoul Stadium, but they had little to do. Except for a few young men caught singing leftist songs, which were prohibited for the day, no one was arrested. The terrorists in Seoul took a holiday. The long procession moved gravely between the lines of white-clad, silently watching people listening to the sound of solemn music written for the occasion.

The police sought to minimize the significance of the funeral. They prohibited the closing of stores, the suspension of music and dancing, and the hoisting of mourning flags, save the flags of Yo's own party. But they could not ban politics. The solid ranks of the People's Democratic Front were a plain political statement. For the few hours of the service the left, the small center and some moderate conservatives stood united. The extreme right did not participate. Kim Ku's Independence Party disdained to offer even perfunctory regrets. A number of Rhee's associates sent a thousand yen each to the funeral committee, which the committee refused to accept. A junior officer expressed General Hodge's condolences.

Yo has a secure place in the history of Korea's struggle for independence. As Hong Nam-pyo, a leading Communist who had known Yo in China, told me emotionally, "Yo is at the heart of our history all by himself." Hong said he had known and lived near Yo for 15 years. His words for him were heroic, honest, straightforward, self-sacrificing, open minded: "I was a shadow to his sun."

Yo was born in Kyonggi Province in 1885 of no longer affluent privileged-class parents. His uncle was a Tonghak rebel. He was educated in a prominent missionary school and some Christian ideas stayed with him. He went to China in 1914, and in 1919 he joined the provisional government-in-exile in Shanghai. In 1921 he and some 30 Koreans attended the Congress of the Toilers of the Far East in Moscow and met Lenin and Trotsky. He rendered some service to Sun Yat-sen as a propagandist at the time of the Northern Expedition and recalled meeting Mao Zedong.

In 1929 he was seized by the Japanese consular police in Shanghai and taken back to Korea. He never again left Korea. After getting out of prison in 1933 he became president of the Korean language *Central Daily News* and an active sponsor of Korean athletics, which he regarded as indirect resistance to Japanization.

In 1943, Yo foresaw Japan's defeat and plunged into illegal politics. In August 1944 he was the leading organizer of the underground Korea Independence League, which along with the vigorous Communist Party became the nucleus of the later Korean left and which had branches in Manchuria and elsewhere in China and contact with Koreans in Yanan.

A year later, on the eve of Japan's collapse, he was approached by the Japanese Governor General's office and asked to help prevent violence. With its agreement Yo formed the broad Committee for the Preparation of Korean Independence (CPKI), the twofold mission of which was to minimize disorder and organize independence. Negotiating with the Japanese, Yo successfully demanded that all political and economic prisoners be released and that there be no interference with organizing for independence. The CPKI almost overnight became a powerful force in the countryside as well as in the cities and towns. On September 6, 1945, on the eve of the American arrival, the Korean People's Republic was proclaimed in the Kyonggi Girls' High School.

For a brief period after the liberation, Yo was the virtually unchallenged leader in South Korea. He was the de facto head of the People's Republic; even part of the right, momentarily frightened, yielded to him, and for a time it seemed that he would establish himself as Korea's Sun Yat-sen. When General Hodge and the 24 Corps came in, the Americans did what they could to break him, insultingly, clumsily, but effectively. Many Koreans remember a fatuous statement by General Archibald V. Arnold, after only four weeks of Korean experience, suggesting that Yo and others prominent in the People's Republic were "foolish or venal men." And General Hodge insulted Yo to his face at their first meeting and, managing to ignore all the evidence to the contrary, put down Yo as "a well-indoctrinated Comintern Communist."

This is Yo's own account of his first meeting with Generals Hodge and Arnold, published in 1947: "About the middle of October 1945, after the elapse of more than a month since coming to Korea, General Hodge and General Arnold condescended to receive me. After shaking hands, the first question General Hodge put to me was 'What connections have you with the Jap?' Answer: 'None.' Then he asked 'How much money did you receive from the Jap?' Answer: 'None.' I was completely taken aback by his questions and his unfriendly attitude. Luckily, I had a prepared statement with me. I handed the same to him. I started to leave, but General Hodge asked me if I would accept membership in the Korean Advisory Council. I said 'Very willingly.'"[43]

But arriving to attend the first meeting of the council, Yo saw that the other nine members were reactionaries, some of them prominent collaborators. He resigned.

For a period Yo was beset with uncertainties. He kept thinking that perhaps American errors were due to misinformation, that perhaps the United States was really intent on democratizing South Korea, that perhaps with patience he could influence American policy. And distancing himself from the Communists, he needed Occupation connections. When, in December, 1946, the majority of his People's Party, together with the Communist Party and the New People's Party, formed the Labor Party, Yo refused to go along, charging Communist domination. He joined with a number of ex-Communists and others in forming the Laboring People's Party in May.

Yet in every crisis Yo almost automatically stood with the left. He refused to be a minority figurehead in an abortive "political unification" committee selected largely by Syngman Rhee. He never had anything to do with anti-trusteeship politicians. To his death he remained on the presidium of the Democratic National Front, though it was dominated by the Labor Party. So weak was the center, so compelling the pull to the left, that even his Laboring People's Party, designed as a non-Communist force, shortly began negotiations to enter the People's Front.

Yo was left-oriented with pragmatic and moderate ideas on how to achieve needed change. He saw the usefulness of a center and participated in the aborted Occupation-sponsored coalition maneuver, entering into discussions with the prominent moderate centrist Kim Kyu-sik and others. He sometimes seemed to lean one way, sometimes the other, but his basic politics were democratic and anti-right. The Labor Party said of Yo's death that "The tragedy of Yo is the tragedy of the people." Much can be read into this. An aspect of the tragedy is that Yo's most profound convictions and hopes were being devastated by the U.S.-Rhee alliance. Another aspect was that Yo was temperamentally a kindly man with a distaste for the violence all about him.

Three years after Yo's assassination, friends and admirers held a memorial meeting. Rhee had 97 of those attending arrested.

Today, as Bruce Cumings has observed, Yo is the sole eminent Korean honored in both the Koreas. Many members of his family took refuge in the north and a daughter rose to prominence in the northern regime.

The Repression Systematized: 1947

The left resorted to guerrilla warfare only when its above-ground organizations were systematically demolished. By the fall of 1947 that had been achieved by General Hodge, the police, and the terrorist youth groups. Ho Hon, a founder of the People's Republic and chairman of the South Korean Workers Party, whom I found one of the most impressive of the left leaders, told me in a few sentences that the Workers Party was unable to act freely. "We cannot expect any freedom of movement in South Korea because the pro-Japanese have infiltrated the Military Government and the police forces."

Roger N. Baldwin, director of the American Civil Liberties Union, visited South Korea in June and reported about his trip to a press conference in New York. He described South Korea as a police state and said that "he found political leaders who were afraid to sleep in the same bed two successive nights, trade union leaders with whom he had an appointment unable to keep the date because they had been thrown in jail, and another important figure lying in a bed in an American hospital because he was, as he put it, 'politically ill.'"[44]

Late that same month G-2 reported that "the power of the left wing is steadily increasing in South Korea."

These are excerpts from my 1947 Seoul diary, published in *The Nation*, November 1, 1947.

> "JULY 27: Fifty thousand people carrying banners of the People's Front climbed South Mountain to celebrate the reconvening of the U.S.-U.S.S.R. Joint Commission. This was destined to be the last authorized political assembly of the left. Major General A. E. Brown and Colonel General T. F. Shtikov, chiefs of the American and Soviet delegations to the commission, addressed the gathering. General Brown explained that the American "concept of democracy" and "the right of the individual" forbade exclusion of "certain large rightist parties" from consultation. A Korean speaker who followed him said: "General Brown spoke of individual rights. But do we have such rights in South Korea today? In South Korea there is brutal terrorism and oppression of the people." This man was arrested by the police as he stepped from the rostrum, before the eyes of the Soviet general. General Brown had left when it started to rain.
>
> "The meeting broke up in a monsoon downpour. As the crowd thinned out, terrorists waylaid the participants in the alleys and beat them up, saying, 'You have been to South Mountain. We know because you are soaking wet...'

"JULY 28: A G-2 report described how other People's Front meetings had been broken up:

"In Yonan the police chief announced that he had arrested forty-two students attempting to organize a left-wing meeting. In Paekchon police announced the arrest of forty students for attempting to organize a leftist meeting. In Kangning no meeting occurred, possibly because of the presence in jail of 200 left-wing leaders. In Cochiwon an orderly pro-commission meeting was held by 700 Communists. In Ochwon police broke up an unauthorized meeting of 5,000 leftists. A group of 3,000 refused to disperse. Police broke it up, killing five and making several arrests.

"AUGUST 5: The police announced the discovery of a Communist plot in the Seoul radio station. Fourteen employees had been arrested and the informer was in protective custody. On August 12 James W. Browitt, American adviser to the station, told me that the Communists had had a three-point program—working propaganda into the programs, spying on American personnel, and causing mechanical breakdowns during rightist broadcasts. A police official charged that the Reds planned to blow up the station 'if worse came to worst.'

"AUGUST 11 TO 15: Large-scale arrests throughout South Korea, coupled with intensified terrorism, drove the left underground. The Americans had in effect given the police a blank check in conferences of high officials. One American official said later, 'G-2 did not know how far the police would go and frantically tried to find out what was going on. But the line was to back the police whatever they did.'

"All offices of leftist political parties, trade unions, the farmers' union, and similar groups were raided and closed by the police. Roughly 2,000 arrests were made; about half were released within a few days. A few arrests were also made by the American Counter-Intelligence Corps.

"Most of those arrested were leaders or staff workers of the twenty-four parties and groups affiliated with the People's Front. A great number of key leftists escaped, however, thanks to long-standing precautionary measures. Many liberal teachers, writers, artists, newspapermen and lawyers were rounded up, among them the co-chairman and general secretary of the Civil Liberties Union....

"During this period right-wing terrorists in Seoul and elsewhere searched homes, beat up leftists and suspected leftists, confined and tortured leftists in private prisons and looted leftist headquarters and newspaper plants. On the fourteenth a group of leftist newspapermen were arrested as they left a Soviet press conference. By the fifteenth about half of the leftist press had suspended publication. On August 13 Kim Kok-tong, member of the central committee of the centrist Socialist Democratic Party, was kidnapped. His body was found in the gutter on the fourteenth.

"After August 15, arrests continued on a lesser scale; terrorism subsided to the high level which had prevailed before the eleventh. By the nineteenth several leftist papers were able to resume publication...

"AUGUST 20: Cho Pyong-ok, the police chief, told me that a plot involving the entire People's Front had been discovered, directed from North Korea. 'Of course we can prove little connection with North Korea; naturally they keep these things secret.' He cited various acts of leftist terrorism: seventy-eight policemen in all had been killed, 60 in the Taegu riots of last October, and 494 rifles had been stolen."

Interviews with three leaders of the National League of Peasant Unions, called Chonnong, in mid-August, informed me that repression also characterized the situation in the countryside. Kim Chin-yong, in charge of general affairs and the chief spokesman, told me that unfair grain collection and terrorism on the part of the police and rightist youth groups were at the heart of peasant grievances. "The extortion of harvested grain exceeds even that under Japanese rule," he said. "For failure to give quotas many peasants have been arrested—in North Cholla 22,842 peasants have been arrested, two of them killed." Despite losses in the Autumn Harvest Uprisings, he said that Chonnong had three million members and influenced as many as ten million. But most of his particulars were about setbacks.

Kim, about 40, graduated from an agricultural college in Hokkaido, Japan, was a founder of Chonnong and had been jailed five times. Of the others, Paik Yong-hu, 74, had been organizing peasants since 1919 and had spent nearly eight years in prison under the Japanese. Yi Ku-hun, 38, had spent 19 years in prison, half his lifetime, and in recent years had been active in the northern province of Hamgyong.

On August 22 General Hodge held a conference for the foreign press that I attended. He asserted that the discovery of the plot to blow up the Seoul radio station had led to the exposure of a broader conspiracy 'of a revolutionary nature.' Only that day, he said, a police raid had unearthed a cache of weapons. Later I was told that Japanese weapons, deteriorated to the point of uselessness, had been dug up in the backyard of a house belonging to a member of the Socialist Democratic Party. Hodge said also that the Communists were instigating riots and interfering in grain collections in order to cause starvation and so create unrest. He expressed surprise that the Soviet Union should protest, since such activities "were directed from North Korea."

On August 21 one of Rhee's jubilant spokesmen, Y.T. Pyun, later foreign minister, urged that the Soviet maritime provinces be turned over to "Great Korea." "It is a Japanese myth," he added, "that Koreans are incapable of ruling or fighting…. Doubtless we shall make finer troops than either the Japanese or Chinese."

The Uprising on Cheju

> *A Dutch seaman shipwrecked in 1652 on Quelpart (Cheju) wrote that the island is "quite surrounded with rocks but abounds in horses and cattle. Yet paying great duties to the king, the natives are very poor and are despised by the inhabitants of the mainland."*
>
> —HENRY KAMAL

The people's committees on the volcano-made island of Cheju, off the southern coast, survived longer than those on the mainland but when punishment of the villagers for their left temerity came in 1947 it was brutal. The police and their allies in the Northwest Youth Corps savaged the villages and the hatreds thus engendered led to riotous demonstrations that climaxed in an island-wide rebellion of 1948-1949.

That April, when the rebellion began, two Catholic missionaries told correspondents: "Hardly a family on this island but has had at least one member beaten by the police. And when the people pick themselves off the ground, they are leftist—or at least getting even with the police has become one of their chief aims in life."[45]

The Cheju rebellion was civil and revolutionary. It was the Korean war of 1950 in microcosm.

The United Nations Commission on Korea served the U.S.-Rhee alliance in making critical decisions but one of its reports made some of the rebellious realities evident: "Destruction was on a vast scale. Village after village was burned down and the damage to houses, livestock and crops was estimated at many billion won. Eighty police stations were attacked, burned or damaged. The police seem to have been a particular object of attack, over 100 of them were killed or wounded."

The American military supported the crushing of the rebellion, in one instance reportedly by firepower, but the early American Military Government information was that the island had been subjected to an official campaign of terrorism for months. It said the governor was an "extreme rightist" who was "ruthless and dictatorial in his dealings with opposing political parties"—meaning all those opposed to Syngman Rhee. The year 1947 was characterized by beatings and crowded jail cells and by a succession of unauthorized grain collections.

The rebellion of a huge number of the 250,000 islanders that began the next year was a response to police and Youth Corps brutalities and also to the scheduled May 10 elections that were to create a southern government and put Rhee in power. A demonstration against the planned elections on March 1 was broken up with the arrest of 2,500 young people, at least three of whom were tortured to death. The rebellion began on April 3 with attacks on 11 police stations (policemen were speared, hung by their heels and decapitated), destruction of bridges, and severing of phone lines. Demonstrators urged unification with the north and denounced the elections, the holding of which was accompanied by as many as fifty demonstrations, attacks on rightists' offices and houses and three government buildings, and the burning of ballot boxes.

A guerrilla appeal: "Dear citizens, parents, brothers and sisters! Today, on April 3, your sons and brothers have stood up with arms in hand. We oppose the country-selling separate elections to the death, and have risen up in order to liberate the people, unify the fatherland, and achieve independence. We have stood with arms to get rid of the American cannibals and their running dogs, to destroy them, and to stop them from killing people. We have stood up to avenge your grievances for you! You should also rise up to help us fight for final victory!" According to John Merrill's comprehensive account, "The strength of the main guerrilla units was about five hundred men. Half were armed with rifles while the rest carried an assortment of swords, sickles, sharpened bamboo spears, homemade grenades, explosives, and picks and shovels. Besides the estimated three thousand persons who accompanied them down the mountain, the guerrillas gathered additional supporters in the coastal villages. Government forces on the island consisted of an under-strength constabulary regiment, 450 police, and several hundred members of right-wing youth groups. The guerrillas set upon the police and members of right-wing youth groups with great ferocity, but left the American military government company on the island undisturbed. Stretched thin, the police and rightist youth groups were ineffective in coping with the attacks. By moving swiftly and concentrating their initial raids on the northern coastal villages, the guerrillas were able to easily overpower their opponents. In the first wave of attacks, they killed thirty police and youth group members while losing only four of their own."[46]

On April 20th the 3,000-strong 11th constabulary regiment was sent to Cheju, but for some weeks took little action. The relationship of the constabulary and the police on the mainland was strained and the constabulary commander on Cheju blamed the police for the uprising. The Cheju constabulary, locally recruited, included many who sympathized with the abused villagers. Some were infiltrated Workers Party members. On April 29 many members of one company defected and executed a number of police, but then were encircled by constabulary loyalists and nearly all killed or captured.

The constabulary and the rebels did seek a peaceful resolution but each side made demands the other could not accept. Kim Ik-yol, constabulary commander, himself met with Kim Sam-dal, one of the three rebel leaders, and in a report published in the August 11 and August 13 issues of the *Seoul Times* said that "we imagined that the commander of the rebels must be a man of unkempt hair and ill-looking, but to our surprise he was a young man as handsome as a movie actor. His forehead was broad enough, his eyes twinkled just as sky stars in the long night, and he was dressed in modern style."

The constabulary demanded what amounted to surrender and Kim Sam-dal countered with six blunt demands: opposition to formation of a separate southern regime, guarantee of people's freedom, disarmament of the police, dismissal of the island's high officials, punishment of guilty officials, and prohibition of the entry of youth groups from the mainland.

Kim Ik-yol apparently was recalled to Seoul for being overly soft on the rebels. He commented in the *Seoul Times* that he was not in a position to accept the demands of the rebels, but was greatly surprised by the decision of the constabulary command to mount a general attack on them.

General William F. Dean, the military governor, flew to Cheju on May 1 to inspect the situation and try to reconcile police-constabulary differences. He brought with him an army camera crew that produced a propaganda film featuring burning villages, said to have been fired by the Communists, and showing many dead, alleged to be victims of the Communists.

By June the rebellion had spread. Two regiments of guerrillas were operating from mountain bases. The Americans counted their total strength at about 4,000, one out of 10 possessing firearms. An escaped prisoner of the rebels told G-2 that ordinary rebels were armed with bamboo spears, that leaders of seven-man squads carried Japanese rifles, and that the overall commander had a Japanese revolver and a dagger. Recruits at this camp, the informant said, were given Japanese army uniforms, rubber shoes and mess kits and told that the guerrillas called each other comrade instead of by their individual names. They were given lectures on communism and the government.[47]

Interrogators found that the South Korean Workers Party, Communist, had cells in most towns and villages with a total membership of many thousands. In overall command was Yi Tok-ku, a poor fisherman who became a Workers Party activist. In 1947 he had been arrested and tortured for three months.

The rebels, called the People's Army, operated in fast-moving units of 80 to 100, taking advantage of the tall grass nearly everywhere and caves and tunnels dug by the Japanese during World War II. A well-organized system brought the guerrillas food from the villages—sweet potatoes, millet, fish, seaweed.

An American colonel, Rothwell H. Brown, reported that the rebellion had brought about "the complete breakdown of all civil government functions," that two constabulary commanders had refused to work with the police, and that island "blood ties" made obtaining information extremely difficult. He ordered suppressive action and a long-term program to offer proof of the "evils of communism" and the superiority of the "American way."

American military involvement, according to Bruce Cumings, included "daily tutoring of counterinsurgent forces, interrogating prisoners, and using American spotter planes to ferret out guerrillas."[48]

The press alleged that American troops were in action at least once in April. It reported also that Japanese had been brought to the island to provide help of some kind, possibly in connection with the extensive defenses constructed during the war.

In August of 1948, following the monsoon rains, insurgent and counterinsurgent activity grew. Attacks on police stations and the homes of rightists increased. Guerrillas roved at will through central Cheju and only short coastal strips remained safe for non-rebels.

In October, the Yosu uprising heartened the rebels and they gained a number of successes. In February they attacked a convoy returning Japanese rifles that had been exchanged for M-1 carbines. They captured 100 rifles and killed 17 soldiers. According to an American report at this time, "Losses among the armed forces have been relatively heavy, considering the minor inroads they have made on guerrilla concentrations to date. However, many of the army casualties can be attributed to the failure to follow the tactical suggestions of the U.S. advisers..."[49]

But in the spring of 1949, the tide turned. Four Korean army battalions arrived and joined the toughened constabulary units (Northwest Youth terrorists were recruited into them) and police in expanded repression. Strategic hamlets, fortified villages surrounded by high walls, were established. The cleansed constabulary and police and the youth group toughs conducted massive sweeps. Mountain villages were burned. Screening centers sought to weed out guerrillas. An offer of amnesty persuaded many thousands to turn themselves in.

Rebel chief Yi Tok-ku was killed in June. His body, mutilated with spears, was hung on a cross in front of the administration building in Cheju City. Four other leaders were killed in April. Kim Sam-dal escaped to North Korea where he joined the Kangdong Political Institute and was placed in command of a battalion of guerrillas. South of the parallel, this band was reduced to a handful and kept on the run in the mountains. In March of 1950 Kim was believed to have been killed. His head was placed in a pan of gasoline and brought to Seoul for identification. But even officers who had known Kim when he was a student at Nippon University in Japan or had met him at the truce conference in Cheju were unable to make a positive identification.[50]

Members of the United Nations traveled on the island in a controlled tour and testified that indeed peace had been restored. They did take note of the widespread destruction and the heavy loss of life.

Some 70 percent of the villages were burned (of 400 villages, 170 survived) and about 40,000 homes destroyed. Also destroyed were 34 schools. Estimates of the number of dead vary widely but may have totaled 30,000, about ten percent of the island's population. In July some 350 "unrepentent Communists" were sentenced to death and in October 250 were executed after Rhee himself reviewed the sentences. Thousands were sent to mainland prisons, where some succeeded in organizing other inmates into Workers Party cells. But many were massacred early in the 1950 warfare when they were likely to be freed by advancing North Korean troops.

Atrocities ended the lives of many. Boatloads of rebels and suspects were taken out to sea on barges and dumped. Right-wing terrorists slaughtered many with bamboo spears and went on to gain control of the newspapers and seize businesses and eventually become wealthy.

Signifying that the rebellion had been suppressed, Syngman Rhee flew in for a few hours' visit on April 9, 1949.

Some villagers (perhaps as many as 40,000) fled to Japan. A community of them in Osaka kept alive the memory of the rebellion by regularly publishing accounts of it that stressed that it was truly Cheju, born of Cheju injustices and not shaped or directed by outsiders.

Seoul policy later was to make the island a tourist attraction by opening inns for honeymooners, casinos and whorehouses.

Southern Resistance: Guerrillas

*That terrorism must be answered with terrorism has now
become a truth that people in southern Korea have clearly
grasped from their own experience. They have come to
the conclusion that unless terrorism is answered with
terrorism, they are destined to suffer once more the
prospect of being a nation without a country, the permanent slaves of the aggressors.*

—HO HON, 1948

The Autumn Harvest Uprisings, not well led, were savagely crushed
and the losses to the left were heavy. But survivors and those turned to
the left by events were drawn to violence as they resisted.

The brief Yosu rebellion took place in October 1948 with the
refusal of elements of two constabulary units, which had been infiltrated by leftists, to go to Cheju on counterinsurgency orders. Some
2,000 mutineers, soon joined by civilians, seized Sunchon to the north,
the port of Yosu, and a number of nearby localities. They rounded up
rightists and just about anyone who was well dressed, executing
policemen and others, flew the North Korean flag and called for
national unification. The People's Committees were then restored in
Yosu and some other localities.

The civilian rebels included at least 70 teachers. The head of the
Yosu People's Committee was Song Uk, principal of the Yosu Girls'
Middle School—the girls were described as "redder than the inside of
a watermelon" and proved it when, armed with Japanese rifles, they
fought in the vain defense of the city.

In Sunchon some police were summarily executed, but others
were tried by a People's Court. While some were found innocent or
merely castigated, most were beaten and then executed. The police
chief got the worst of it. His eyes were plucked out and he was
dragged by car along the streets. Shot, his gas-drenched body was tied
to a pole and set on fire. Some 900 people, among them 400 police,
were killed in Sunchon by the rebels.

The uprising shook the newly established Rhee regime and got
international attention. Foreign correspondents came to get the story; a
State Department spokesman denounced the "barbarity" of rebel behavior. American officers joined in assessing and planning to crush the
rebellion and some took command of loyal constabulary units—secret
protocols gave them covert authority over Korean military forces.

The rebel resistance was courageous but disorderly and was overwhelmed in a matter of days. Retribution was merciless and made victims of many who were innocent, reported the American G-2 and several of the correspondents. Carl Mydans, reporting for *Time*, saw some 5,000 in detention being "beaten with bars, iron chains, and the butts of rifles." Stripped to their underwear, cowed, many were executed. James Hausman, an army counterinsurgency expert who helped to organize the suppression, reported that so many loyal civilians were killed that "people are beginning to think we are as bad as the enemy."[51]

Yosu was defended house-to-house and the city suffered devastating damage. The entire city "is in ashes, still surrounded by horrors and terrors," according to a graphic account. "All kinds of notices cover the walls of the town in the form of orders, appeals, and threats issued by both sides. Dead bodies and broken furniture are scattered over the rice fields and house lots…. Many groups of beggars are digging in the ashes for whatever they can find…. The police station and martial law headquarters are crowded with suspects awaiting trial…. We learned that more than 1,200 persons were killed as of November."[52]

Syngman Rhee declared that Korea had "never had as many traitors in its history" and seized the opportunity to get a repressive and conveniently vague National Security Law enacted. Immediately aimed at what remained of the South Korean left, from the beginning it victimized also many thousands without left links or thoughts. All major organizations were scrutinized and purged. By the spring of 1950 nearly 60,000 people had been jailed, of whom 50 to 80 percent were charged with violations of the National Security Law. The constabulary was purged; over a thousand officers and enlisted men were arrested. The National Assembly was not immune. By October of 1949 sixteen assemblymen were in jail.

But the cities and towns were more easily dealt with than the countryside. A thousand or more participants in the Yosu uprising escaped into the nearby Chiri Mountains, which rose 6,300 feet and were capped by hundreds of acres of thick forest. They became part of a guerrilla war organized principally by the South Korea Workers Party that soon engulfed large parts of the south. Youthful leftists explored the mountains for the sites of bases and scoured villages for arms. A training center based on the procedures of China's Eighth Route Army and Mao Zedong's writings was established in Chungchong Province. In early 1949 the guerrillas were estimated by the CIA to number at least 3,500 and at most 6,000, but an accumulation of evidence suggests the figure was much higher.

A former American adviser explained the difficulties of getting at the guerrillas: "The mountains were thickly wooded with trees and underbrush, precipitous and extremely rocky and rough in nature, which not only provided excellent cover for the guerrilla groups, but confined troop movement to single trails on which the guerrillas could bypass and escape the pursuers. Spotting the guerrillas by air was almost an impossibility...."

The guerrillas had some spectacular successes but also suffered serious defeats, among them the discovery and capture of the headquarters in a cave in the Chiri Mountains in South Cholla. This is a description of it:

> "...there was everything, bedding piled up in the corner with comforters, women's clothes heaped up like a mountain, three pots full of beef sitting on a stove, and next to them spoons and dishes of vegetables spread over the floor. Surprisingly, there were even two sewing machines, a safe, and binoculars—all raided from villages. The walls were covered with the slogan, 'Long live the People's Army!' It was like a big home.
>
> "According to a captured rebel, their mountain life was very strict. Since there were many women guerrillas, celibacy was strictly enforced. If a man engaged in sexual relations with a woman even once, he would be punished physically or shot to death. One guerrilla who raped a woman after kidnapping her in a valley was executed with a Japanese sword. This puritanical attitude seems very strange, considering their savage behavior on the way to the mountain.
>
> "A secret file was also found there. It contained an analysis and criticism of problems encountered in the rebellion, along with operations plans, a table of organization, and a record of their movements."[53]

I began to study and reflect on the guerrilla possibilities in South Korea in 1948, and became convinced that Korea would soon resemble the civil wars in Greece or North China. As I put it in my notes, "North Korea will be accused of sending agitators and military equipment south of the 38th parallel and the Korean problem will be made to look as if it were simply southern defense against northern aggression." I thought that the guerrillas would be strongest in the two Chollas, provinces a long way south of the 38th parallel.[54]

In this instance my conclusions proved entirely correct. American commentators at the time and historians later assumed self-servingly that the guerrilla movement was a northern export. The

Encyclopedia Britannica's summary was the crudest. It declared that "Throughout 1949 and early 1950 the North Korean government took all possible measures short of overt war to create trouble in South Korea. There were frequent raids across the 38th parallel while Communist agents south of the border fostered disorder through propaganda, sabotage, guerrilla action and terrorism."[55]

A guerrilla training center, the Kangdong Political Institute, was indeed established in the north. Guerrilla units were sent south, generally to operate in the area just south of the 38th parallel.

Bruce Cumings found that the Soviets were not involved with the southern partisans and that North Korean involvement was minor "while the seemingly uninvolved Americans organized and equipped the southern counterinsurgent forces, gave them their best intelligence materials, planned their actions, and occasionally commanded them directly."[56]

Reporting on the guerrilla war in March of 1950, Walter Sullivan of *The New York Times*, one of the best of the American correspondents, wrote: "Large sections of South Korea are darkened today by a cloud of terror that is probably unparalleled in the world... Nights in the hundreds of villages across the guerrilla areas are a long, cold vigil of listening." The listeners, he said, were village guards crouching in straw shelters. Summary executions of captured guerrillas and of villagers suspected of aiding them were a normal occurrence.[57]

The peasant rebels in China and Vietnam were protected in some measure by forests, jungles and mountain ranges to which they could retreat, but guerrillas in southern Korea had fewer and smaller such havens. Rhee's American-directed army was able to get to them in an offensive begun in the fall of 1949. Troops, kept fresh by rotation, pressed the guerrillas hard and a complementary effort to get leftists to turn themselves in persuaded many weary of the struggle to do so.

The guerrilla movement, new and still learning, suffered defeats in some areas and was held in check in others before the northern assault of June 1950. But guerrilla bands sprang up again when the Korean People's Army crossed the 38th parallel. The number of southern guerrilla casualties (perhaps including eliminated suspects) during the first two months of the war (July and August) was double the number of Americans killed in the entire war.

The UN Umbrella Over the Separate Elections

The U.S. took advantage of its then domination of the United Nations—by 1949 it had a decisive voice even on UN hiring and promotion—to use it to give respectability to the establishment of a South Korean government headed by Syngman Rhee. It took the Korean issue to the United Nations on September 17, 1947 and readily brought about the formation of a Temporary United Nations Commission assigned to overseeing and approving elections that came to be held on May 10, 1948.

Eventually, and on all important matters, the commission did as it was bid. It anointed the Rhee regime and went on, two years later, to hoist its blue flag over the American intervention in the Korean civil war. But especially in the beginning, before the elections were held, the U.S. had to deal with recalcitrance, questioning, and resentment within the commission. Of course some delegates, those from El Salvador, the Philippines and China (Taiwan) were flunkies. But the delegates from Canada and Australia and some members of the other delegations were shocked and dismayed by the repressive, anti-democratic realities in Korea and made their doubts known, their reward being put down by the occupation military as covert Commies.

Arriving in January, the commission learned immediately that nearly all of the political spectrum were opposed to a separate election and separate state, that support of them was virtually a Syngman Rhee monopoly. A few weeks later, on February 7, what remained of the battered left launched a strike expressly aimed at the commission. These were the results as reported to the commission by the U.S. authorities: "Between 7 February and 19 March...there were 139 attacks on police boxes, 28 police killed and 53 wounded, 19 non-rioters and 78 rioters killed, 53 railroad locomotives sabotaged, 10 rail lines cut, and 106 cases of sabotage of communication. On 26 February 1948 the Director of National Police was reported to have stated that the total number of persons arrested in consequence of the outbreaks was 8,479."[58] The refusal of the north to participate in the UN elections added to the number of critics, but insufficiently to affect the outcome. Both Canada and Australia cast no votes when on February 26 the Interim Assembly approved the U.S. proposal to go ahead with the elections in the south by a vote of 31 to 2, with 11 abstentions. Twisted arms cast many of the 31 yes votes.

I knew firsthand of India's performance. The original chief delegate from India and chairman of the commission was the left-oriented intellectual K.P.S. Menon. I was invited to the Indian embassy in Tokyo to offer my information and views to Menon and found he hardly needed them. He indicated publicly that he was opposed to unilateral elections and a separate southern government, stating on February 20, that "The commission has received a mass of evidence about the restrictions on, or deprivation of, civil liberties in the United States zone of South Korea. This raises the question whether elections could be carried on in a free atmosphere."

In his report to the United Nations General Assembly, Menon put the elections in broad context: "Deep down in the heart of every Korean, whether in the north or in the south, is this longing for unity. I feel that if only the Koreans are left to themselves—not merely in name but in reality—they will work out their own salvation and establish their own democratic government... What has obstructed progress is the 38th parallel. If a government in South Korea cannot be national in a geographical sense, it cannot also be national in a political sense, that is, in the sense that it can normally defend itself against aggression without foreign assistance."

But in March 1 was informed by an upset member of the Indian embassy that the State Department virtually blackmailed India into voting with the U.S. on February 26. The American ambassador in New Delhi informed Nehru that the Indian action on Korea would affect the U.S. attitude toward the Kashmir dispute. Nehru cabled orders to India's commission delegation to refrain from criticizing American policies in South Korea and to vote with the U.S. Menon, who said he was too ashamed to return to Korea, did so briefly and voted as instructed but in mid-March resigned and departed. He was replaced by a diplomat of lesser rank, Bahadur Singh, so that India could relinquish the chairmanship of the commission.

I had had friendly relations with Singh in Tokyo and he welcomed me aboard the commission's special train in Pusan so that I traveled to Seoul in comfort and style and drank burgundy at lunch. But the U.S. had his votes in its pocket. I also got along with a French delegate, Olivier Manet, with whom I visited the ancient Silla capital of Kyongju. We were quickly taken in hand by Rhee supporters, shown the indeed impressive Silla sights—one of the first astronomical observatories, tiered pagodas, tombs, palace and fortress ruins, and standing granite sculptures. We were overfed several times, most elegantly at the Purple Temple, and told that all was going well in the election campaign. I rode in a jeep with the police chief who kept his hand on the revolver in his pocket. The police station was fortified with sand bags.

Manet was a firm conservative with a somewhat compensating habit of cynical observation. He regaled me with tales of evenings in

Kisaeng houses (geisha equivalent) with Cho Pyong-ok, chief of national police, and he told me that Syngman Rhee had a slush fund of six or seven million won to be spent for amusing the members of the UN commission.

Left and centrist parties and groups, and some anti-Rhee rightists, were vehemently determined to boycott the elections but, in February, the UN Commission decided to try to show its impartiality by inviting the left leadership to a consultation session. It invited the chairmen of the trade union federation, the South Korea Workers Party, the People's Republic Party, the All-Korea Peasant Union and the Women's Democratic Alliance, but had to observe that "Taking account of the fact that the above persons were either in prison, under order of arrest or under some form of police surveillance" the U.S. authorities had to be asked to grant them temporary immunity. That was granted but all the invitees refused to appear. [59]

In April the opposition to the elections climaxed. Fifty-six North and South Korean parties and social organizations attended a seven-day conference in Pyongyang where it was agreed to unanimously oppose the elections scheduled for May 10 and the establishment of a separate southern government. They called for the simultaneous withdrawal of Soviet and American troops. Rightist Kim Ku and Moderate Kim Kyu-sik attended, though Kim Kyu-sik merely took part in negotiations, absenting himself from the general gatherings.

Along with a throng of Korean and foreign correspondents I went to the parallel to greet and interview the returning southern delegates, who generally verified the unity achieved in Pyongyang. Kim Ku and Kim Kyu-sik issued a joint statement that set forth this "basis of national unity" envisaged by the conference:

"1. Withdrawal of the two occupation armies from Korea.

"2. The organization of a provisional government by a national political conference immediately after the withdrawal of troops.

"3. The adoption of a national constitution and the formation of a united national government by representatives to be elected through a national election."

They commented: "Human hunger cannot be satisfied by the first mouthful; the unity program in itself cannot be the final fulfillment. The ultimate achievement of our purpose will depend on the joint struggle of our people with the weapons of our past experience."[60]

But the very broad unity was not as impressive as it appeared, for differences and qualifications began to develop soon afterward. Most important, Rhee, not they, had organizational clout based on the police and the youthful terrorists. The preparations for the elections were hardly affected.

In despair, Kim Kyu-sik (graduate of Roanoke College and Princeton, 1903), long an active exiled nationalist, announced retirement and held a final press conference at which he denounced the American Military Government and the separate government it was setting up. I was moved to take careful notes. He demanded that foreign powers get out of Korea and stay out: "If we Koreans are to suffer, let it be by our own hands. If we are to prosper, let it be by our own efforts."[61]

A second Pyongyang conference, somewhat weakened by rightist defections, was held from June 29 to July 5. It supported the establishment of a government in the north and the holding of delegate elections, direct in the north, underground in the south, on August 25. The underground elections were dismissed as merely propaganda in most accounts, but John Merrill, an informed commentator, concluded that "…U.S. sources indicate that the SKLP (South Korean Labor Party) did organize a signature-gathering campaign in the summer of 1948 to select delegates to the conference that established the DPRK. As many as 25 percent of the rural population may have participated…"[62] The southern parties thereafter were indeed represented to a limited extent in the new northern regime.

By the month of the elections the police force had grown to 35,000, triple that found necessary by the Japanese, and the prison population had risen to 15,000, three or four times what it was under the Japanese. By December 1949, according to official Seoul government statistics, the prison total had grown to 40,000.

I covered the elections in Seoul with Pierre Doublet and Peter Kalischer, United Press. We found as I wrote in my notes on May 11th that "The entire right seems to have mobilized for the election and it was expertly organized." The youth groups both got the vote out, by coercion when needed, and managed the polling places; the police stayed on the fringes. The left was a weak presence in Seoul and nearly everywhere. We saw the usual beatings of the few who ventured some sort of protest and were told of cases where rice ration cards were taken away from people declining to vote. Nationally only a handful of the polling places were assaulted. The commission reported that 245 people were killed in the pre-election period and 44 on election day. According to another count, 589 people were killed in the six weeks before the vote.

Most of the violence during the May 8-10 period took place in the so-called Red areas—South Cholla, the Taegu area and Cheju. The UN Commission had observers only at a few polling places but estimated that 75 percent of the people voted. It was informed of a variety of violations but validated the elections with few misgivings. It detected "a real enthusiasm on the part of the people." Predictably Washington hailed the elections as a great democratic triumph.

Early in June, a few weeks after the elections, Ahn Chai Hong, American-appointed Civil Administrator of the South Korean Interim Government, handed in his resignation and agreed to a private interview with Pierre Doublet of Agence France Presse. Ahn had impeccable nationalist credentials—his periods in Japanese prisons added up to eight years—but he was a mild-mannered, usually timid moderate and he answered the first questions cautiously as was his wont, blinking his somewhat owl-like eyes. However he had some pride, some feeling for the truth, and he said he would be frank if assured that his remarks would not be published in South Korea, adding that this condition was not preposterous but for him a matter of life or death.

Assured, he said that he had not resigned in November because the appointment of the United Nations Temporary Commission on Korea had given him hope, which had not turned out to be justified. The elections? "They have served to usher in an extreme rightist regime which can only bring evil to my country. They were held in an atmosphere created by thousands of acts of terrorism on the part of the police and rightist youth organizations." Thus spoke bitterly and fearfully the top official in South Korea, made that by General Hodge. Like Kim Kyu-sik, he spent his last years in North Korea.[63]

Very much reduced in size and even less independent, the commission played a supine, sorry role when the 1950 war began. Given the task of observing along the 38th parallel, it did little, but never hesitated to echo the U.S. and Rhee assertions.

Syngman Rhee's Election at the East Gate

The East Gate District in Seoul was quiet on May 10, 1948, the day of the United Nations-observed elections. The polls were closed and, except for the patrols of the young men of the Neighborhood Defense Corps wearing armbands and carrying clubs, few people ventured abroad. Dr. Syngman Rhee was the unopposed candidate for the district's seat in the legislative assembly. In the afternoon he received the Korean press. "I wish to thank the voters of the East Gate District for giving me the privilege of serving them as a member of the legislature," he said. "I wish I had had an opponent. I have always believed in democracy and equality...."

Until May 7th Rhee did have one opponent, Choi Nung-chin, formerly chief of the detective bureau of the South Korean police. Choi was educated at the University of Dubuque, Iowa, and at Springfield College, Springfield, Massachusetts, which was linked to the YMCA. By a chance I marvel at, he was the one Korean I knew in my Springfield boyhood. Parents in our neighborhood decided their sons would benefit from athletic instruction and hired Choi, called Daniel or Danny, to teach us. He gave me my first boxing lesson. I remember also that he came to a holiday dinner at one of our houses, bringing pomegranates to present to the hostess.

As an English-speaking Korean and chief detective, Choi received considerable publicity early in the occupation, including a feature article in *The New York Times*. In Seoul in 1947, I was delighted to identify him as the Daniel of my youth. We had a happy reunion full of reminiscence.

Choi had fled south from North Korea in 1945 and become an admirer of Syngman Rhee. But events had turned admiration into dislike and he decided to run against him in the East Gate District as "a liberal and Koreanist." Three days before the election Choi was disqualified by the National Election Committee on the grounds that 57 of his 217 recommendations (200 required) were forgeries or obtained by misrepresentation.

His candidacy encountered continuing difficulties. On April 12th he brought over 300 recommendations to the East Gate District election office but the officials refused to certify them. "This is Dr. Rhee's district and only he is to run," they told him.

That evening Han Kun-cho, Deputy Chief of the Department of Justice, called on Choi. He said that Rhee had sent for him that afternoon and told him he heard that Choi intended to oppose him. "I entreat you earnestly to give up the idea," Han said.

Mun Bong-jei, chief of the far rightist Northwest Youth Corps, visited Choi on a similar mission. "President Truman agreed to make Dr. Rhee president of Korea, " Mun argued. "He has promised to give Korea money and to build up an army to march against the north."

The last day for registration of candidates was April 16th. On the 13th an American from G-2 went with several members of Choi's party in a second attempt to register. The officials declared that no business was being conducted that day, that an official had taken the seals away and wouldn't be back for three or four days.

On the 14th Choi called on Dr. Harold J. Noble, a G-2 official and an adviser and speech writer for Rhee. Choi explained that he wished to bring the case to the attention of Military Governor General William F. Dean and the United Nations Commission. "Why go to the UN?" Noble asked. "Do you want to make propaganda? General Dean is the proper authority."

Choi and I went to see General Dean on separate occasions. I remember the amused expression on the faces of Dean's clerks in the outer office when I said that my name was Deane and I wished to see General Dean. The military governor assured me calmly that steps would be taken to enable Choi to register. But I learned later that Dean had authorized the Korean police to deputize bands of so-called loyal citizens into Community Protection Organizations—soon known as Rhee's goon squads.

On the 15th Choi again took his recommendations to the district election office and things seemed to go smoothly. But a few hours later goons from the Northwest Youth Corps attacked Choi's campaign workers, seized the bags containing the recommendations and fled. The police were able to arrest only two—both Choi's men.

On the next day Choi again saw General Dean, who phoned an order to the National Election Committee to complete the registration even though Choi had not been able to replace all the stolen recommendations. Nevertheless, the district election office refused to accept a verbal order and added a series of requirements and objections and in the end, after a pointed inquiry by a Rhee representative, denied Choi's registration.

On the 17th Choi saw General Dean who told him not to worry. On the 18th Choi and friends obtained additional recommendations to make the total 217. On the 19th Choi appealed his case to the municipal election committee and on the 20th he was registered.

Pierre Doublet of Agence France Presse and I soon discovered that Choi's problems were not all solved. Choi was unable to rent an office in his district or even to appear there. When his helpers put up posters, youth corps members tore then down or the police covered them over with safety regulations. Choi moved in with a friend, guarded by about 20 young men.

On May 6, Doublet in a jeep followed two truckloads of Choi's student campaign workers into the East Gate District. The trucks stopped a few times and the students gave short speeches and threw out leaflets. The police came and said the trucks would have to keep off the main streets. On side streets the trucks were at first stalled by police taking an interminable time to read their permits. Then both trucks were found to be overloaded and unsafe, and the contents were thrown in the gutter.

The police arrested the four men in charge of the trucks and turned them over to youth corps members who held them overnight and beat them, in the morning turning them over to the police again, who beat them. Two had to be taken to the hospital.

Choi complained to the National Election Committee which referred him to the police. Choi wrote to Police Chief Chang Taek-sang but received no reply.

The police and youth corps members investigated those who had signed Choi's recommendations. Some said they had signed for wives or relatives and some said they had not really known what they were signing. Still others said they were shown photos of Rhee and Pak Hon-yong, the Communist leader, asking them if they meant to vote for Pak against Rhee, "our national leader."

Asked about the Choi case at a press conference on May 8, a National Election Committee spokesman stated, "We tried to be fair. We even gave Mr. Choi several days grace to complete his registration. But having ascertained by scientific methods that 57 of the recommendations were spurious, we had no alternative but to void his candidacy."

Choi took the case to the United Nations Commission and the American command. General Dean appointed a committee of three to investigate. By late May it reported it found that 18 of Choi's recommendations were spurious, reducing his number to 199, one less than the minimum required.

Rhee was inaugurated president on August 15, having been elected by the legislature. General MacArthur arrived for the ceremony, bringing the entire Tokyo press corps with him, and in a speech rich in hyperbole, declared that the "artificial barrier" of the 38th parallel "must and will be torn down." As he walked away with his arm around Rhee, he was overheard to promise to defend the new regime.[64]

For me the occasion was a welcome opportunity to hurriedly look up the friends who earlier had done their best to inform me.

Rhee had Choi arrested and charged with sedition. Specifically, he was alleged to have been the leader of a plot to overthrow the government on the anniversary of the Bolshevik revolution. He was among the many executed on the eve of the fall of Seoul to the North Korean forces.[65]

The 1950 War
in the Making

Northern Beginnings

There may be various ways and means of accomplishing national unification. But whatever may be the concrete ways and means, the country must in any case be unified independently by the Korean people themselves and it cannot be otherwise. Korean unification is an internal affair of the Korean nation.

—KIM IL SUNG

The Soviet occupation of the north began with a disgrace—Soviet troops behaved atrociously in the initial period. I was told so by responsible left journalists who had come south. And according to Bruce Cumings, "the Soviet troops who entered Korea committed depredations against the Japanese and Koreans, including rape and looting, on what appears to have been a wide scale..." In effect, the Soviets made partial amends by quickly recognizing the people's committees linked to the Korean People's Republic and by supporting reforms generally. But they supported Kim Il Sung as he gradually converted fairly autonomous committees representing a variety of views into a more or less centralized state firmly in Communist hands. At the same time the Soviets permitted, indeed promoted, far-reaching revolutionary changes, disarming to some extent those offended by the top-down decision making.

By the time the brief Soviet occupation ended, North Korea was becoming an independent commandist state. It was not a satellite, even in its formative stage, though careful of relations with its two great neighbors. In a number of respects it was modeled on China—copying some of the achievements of the Chinese revolution but emulating also its greatest defect, the failure, eventually corrosive, to realize real democratic exchanges between leaders and the led.

The historic China-Korea ties fostered revolutionary relationships. Kim Il Sung had been a member of the Chinese Communist Party in his youth and he waged a hard-bitten guerrilla war along the Korean-Manchurian border like that characteristic of the Chinese party's struggle for power.

A number of Koreans who rose to prominence studied under Zhou Enlai and Guo Moruo at the Whampoa Academy in Guangzhou and one is known to have made the Long March. A Korean military-political school was organized at Yanan by the Korean Emancipation League with Chinese assistance. Many of the League's some 2,000 cadres slipped back into Korea as the war drew to a close to join local resistance groups in anti-Japanese activities and to begin organizing the People's Republic.

As noted, many thousands of Koreans fought in the Chinese civil war, not only in Manchuria but as far south as Hainan, there acquiring expertise in the envelopment and flanking tactics that surprised and bedeviled American forces during the first weeks of the 1950 war. Throughout the Chinese civil war North Korea was a rest and recuperation area for the People's Liberation Army. A study in late 1949 revealed that of 1,881 "cultural cadres" in North Korea, 422 had experience in China's Eighth Route Army.

But Kim was selective in his emulation of the Chinese. He borrowed heavily from Mao without naming him when he made speeches and was stimulated by the Great Leap Forward while ignoring its evident excesses. He generally sided with the Chinese party in its ideological struggle with the Soviet Union. But he stayed clear of the Cultural Revolution, which he saw as threatening alienation of the people. He supported an earlier decision to eliminate Chinese characters from use in the Korean alphabet—such use would be symbolic of flunkeyism, he thought.

Kim boldly rejected Soviet pressures to turn the Korean economy into an appendage of Comecon, the integrated Soviet-Eastern Europe economy, arguing forthrightly that its decisions might well subordinate Korean interests. He gave priority to swift economic development energized by Jurche (creative self-reliance) and Chollima (winged horse symbolizing rapid growth) while at the same time succeeding in extracting aid from the Soviet Union and China. In 1955 he declared that, "Although some people say that the Soviet way is best or that the Chinese way is best, have we not reached the point where we can construct our own way." In 1975 he took the Democratic People's Republic into the Non-Aligned Movement, distancing it from both Beijing and Moscow.

Kim's cult matched Mao's—Mao was the Red Sun in Our Hearts, Kim was a Beautiful New Red Star in the Sky. In one respect Kim emulated Chiang Kai-shek rather than Mao, like Chiang naming his son, Kim Jong Il, his successor. The cult of Kim necessitated distortions of history. The Korean revolution is asserted to have been brought to victory by the Kim-led guerrilla struggle; the impressive and heroic contributions of the underground in Korea proper get less attention. Similarly China's enormous aid both in the war and in postwar reconstruction is de-emphasized.

But the standard demonization of North Korea includes disinformation.[1] Pyongyang positively carried out an effective land reform, eliminating private ownership entirely by 1958. It succeeded in expanding literacy and education, introducing 11 years of compulsory education by 1975. It lavished money on cultural opportunities, often politicized. And it took full advantage of what had survived of the economic and infrastructural development realized by the Japanese and pressed ahead with industrialization, thus creating many thousands of jobs and expansion of technical knowledge.

Many northerners must have felt stifled by the top-downism, the lack of critical give and take between the leadership and the governed, and the limitless adulation of the leader. But they knew also that the standard of living was rising and that the regime had powerful enemies with selfish motives to the south and abroad.

North Korean statistics are scant in some areas and generally need to be assessed cautiously but make evident swift economic development and successful industrialization. In 1946 the share of industry in national income was 16.8 percent contrasted with the agricultural share of 63.5 percent. By 1965 the industrial share had grown to 64.2 percent while agriculture's had fallen to 28.3 percent. By 1963 technical and industrial workers comprised 65 percent of the work force.[2]

Critical differences—essentially the differences between revolution and counterrevolution—separated the north and the U.S.-Rhee south. Indeed they had different names; the south called itself Tae Han internally; the north stayed with the more usual Choson. In contrast to the Chinese and Korean revolutionary experience of the military in the north, the southern army was initially commanded by Koreans who had been officers in the Imperial Japanese Army and were proud of it. Their Japanese swords were hung above their desks or in their quarters. Some had served in units trying to extirpate Kim's guerrilla force, some were guilty of World War II crimes.

A favorite of Syngman Rhee was Kim Sok-won, known in the Japanese army as Kanegawa Skakugen, who commanded the special detachment pursuing Kim Il Sung in Manchuria. He was decorated by Hirohito with the Order of Merit for services in the war against China. I watched with dismay from the sidelines in June 1948 when he led several thousand veterans of the Japanese army, wearing their old uniforms, along the streets of Seoul.

The guerrillas were both a revolutionary legacy and a continuing North Korean asset in both north and south. They were an important help to the drive of the Korean People's Army across the 38th parallel in 1950. Late in the year, following the northern retreat, U.S. intelligence counted some 60,000 guerrillas operating as far south as Pusan.

In the 1950 war the North Korean forces never practiced a scorched earth policy either in the south or in the north, whereas the South Koreans and the Americans did so everywhere, almost invariably. And whereas the North Korean troops usually fought well and gained American respect, the South Korean forces sometimes performed valiantly but more often didn't.

In their occupation of the south, the North Koreans did what they could to revive the people's committees abolished by the American Military Government, began a land reform that had some lasting effect, and promoted trade unions and various mass organizations.

But in the immediate aftermath of the war Kim Il Sung obtained what he thought was conclusive evidence that leading southern Communists and Koreans returned from China and the Soviet Union were preparing to challenge his virtually absolute authority. His response was forthright. A purge of the southern Communists began just a week after the armistice. They were scapegoated for the failure of the 1950 drive south, and those at the top were victims of trials like the Moscow trials. Pak Hon Yong, leader of the South Korea Workers Party and later foreign minister in Pyongyang, was charged with treason and espionage and executed in December 1955. In 1956-1958 Kim persecuted leading Koreans who had returned from China or from the Soviet Union, and from then on was secure at the head of a narrowed regime.

Anna Louise Strong, who was my neighbor in the Press Hostel in Chungking in 1940-41, was in North Korea while I was in the south. She wrote me to suggest that we exchange notes, which we did. Her letters to me in Tokyo were intercepted by U.S. intelligence and included in General Willoughby's pernicious file on the "Communist Far Eastern Ring," both of us named as Communists. I tried to get parts of Strong's report on North Korea published in Japan, but Willoughby had it suppressed by the censor.

I found Strong's report and her later pamphlet, *In North Korea*, useful but erroneous in insisting that the Koreans had no contact with the Chinese revolution. I suppose that she was overly impressed by the evidence of Soviet efforts to prevent such contact. Her letters to me were more candid in several respects than her later publication. She complained that she was told that everything was "100 percent successful" and she was an early observer of the lack of democracy. She wrote that the people were accustomed to "slave-teaching" and thought that "all government comes from above." But she failed to repeat these observations in her pamphlet.[3]

Strategic Change Inclines the U.S. to War

The day will come, and possibly sooner than we think,
when realism will call upon us not to oppose the reentry of
Japanese influence and activity into Korea and Manchuria.
This is, in fact, the only realistic prospect for countering
and moderating Soviet influence in that area…

—GEORGE KENNAN, **1949**

When the anti-Japanese war merged into World War II, the Roosevelt administration looked to China, specifically Chiang Kai-shek's China, to take the place of a presumably defeated Japan as its pivotal ally in Asia. So it poured money and arms into China, sent Marshall to China to try to negotiate a civil peace that would favor Generalissimo Chiang, and, as the State Department's 1949 White Paper admitted, did everything it could short of sending troops to prevent the success of the Communist revolution. The White Paper was in the main an explanation of what came to be known as the loss of China, but it also gave notice that Washington was turning to the Japanese substitute. The United Press reported from Washington the unanimous view of "diplomatic observers" that "the White Paper has highlighted the U.S. need for a strong Japanese ally and that suitable measures would be forthcoming."[4]

Civil war raged in China during the first years of the American occupation of South Korea and the occasional view of it from MacArthur's office in the Dai Ichi building in Tokyo tended to be somewhat complacent. In March 1947 MacArthur told astonished diplomats over dinner that a combination of American air power and increased supplies of American arms would quickly end the Communist threat. But some months after the establishment of the separate southern government in South Korea and the inauguration of President Syngman Rhee, the great battle of Huai Hai destroyed the last of Chiang's American-equipped divisions and made painfully evident that a Communist triumph was inevitable. MacArthur told interviewing correspondents that his thoughts were much more on China than Japan.

The essence of the strategic revision that emerged from discussions and papers was that Japan had to be turned into the principal

U.S. ally in Asia, and that required that the Japanese collection of small islands be assured of markets and access to raw materials. That meant that a politer version of Japan's prewar Greater East Asia Co-Prosperity Sphere had to be created and that gave the American policy makers who advocated rollback, not mere containment, but a much stronger case.

Hanson W. Baldwin summed up for the public in *The New York Times* of December 22, 1950 what was already a policy being realized: "If a counterpoise is to be created to balance the mass might of Russia and Red China in the Orient, Japan will have to provide the bulk of it.

"The renaissance of Japan as a great power—a great power politically, economically and militarily—is essential to any long-term stabilization program in the Orient."

The change in basic American policy began in 1947 as the possibility of a Soviet takeover of Japan was taken seriously and as the Chinese Nationalists were seen to be weakening. It was essentially completed in 1949, in time for the Korean war. By then some of the pleasant chaps in striped trousers had been converted to the rollback policy. An October 1949 draft of the highly classified policy document NSC 48 described the island chain including Japan and Taiwan as "our first line of defense and, in addition, our first line of offense from which we can seek to reduce the area of communist control, using whatever means we can develop, without, however, using sizable U.S. armed forces." In the final version of NSC 48, the critical phrasing became "to contain and where feasible to reduce" Communist power in Asia.

As time went on, thoughts of a rollback were taken to the public. Speaking on NBC's Meet the Press program on February 10, 1952, John Foster Dulles said "I think that in the long run you cannot keep an absolute barrier between Japan and the mainland, and the solution which we ought to seek and which the Japanese would like to join us in seeking is to change the character of the mainland."

American deliberations and planning focused on Northeast Asia and that made Korea much more important. It was a "dagger pointed at the heart of Japan" as well as vice versa, a corridor linking Japan to Manchuria, and itself possessing, in its north, industries and ferroalloys.

Japan had ruled Korea and Manchuria (its Manchukuo) and dominated much of north China. The strong Japan Washington had in mind was thought to need some restoration of an economic presence in the area.

The swiftly growing, semi-independent CIA was among the first to expound on the new strategy which it was soon helping to implement by the presence of agent Goodfellow in the Syngman Rhee entourage, as well as by espionage and dirty tricks in Korea and China.

The dirty tricks included the disabling of a Chinese cable below the Yellow Sea and a simulated pirate attack on a Norwegian vessel to seize medical supplies and Indian doctors and nurses on their way to China; the doctors and nurses appear to have been executed. And an American Indian agent code named Buffalo was one of several offered a "grand prize" and sent to Pyongyang to assassinate Kim Il Sung.[5]

In China, according to a Taiwan-based agent, the CIA's role was to do what it could to impede government control. Goodfellow's dream was to organize a serious guerrilla movement on the mainland. That never got out of the dream stage, but the CIA did set up something of an espionage net and did carry out nuisance raids. Before the Korean war began, the CIA's covert activities had 302 employees, a budget of $4.7 million and seven foreign stations. By 1952 the covert operation had 2,812 direct employees, many more in deep cover, a budget of $82 million and 47 foreign stations.

In mid-1948 the CIA argued that "The key factor in postwar development in Japan is economic rehabilitation. As in the past, Japan, for normal economic functioning on an industrial basis, must have access to the Northwest Asiatic areas—notably, North China, Manchuria, and Korea—now under direct, indirect, or potential control of the USSR." It added that integration of these areas could provide the largest industrial potential of any area in the Far East."

Late in 1948, a paper by an Economic Cooperation Administration official described North China and Manchuria as the one area on the mainland "of vital importance to the U.S." It said that "without the resources of this area, there would be literally no hope of achieving a viable economy in Japan."

The particulars of how to remedy this situation were part of the ongoing debate in Washington and gave obvious credence to a rollback. Japan could hardly regain a presence in Northeast Asia without it.

The U.S. needed a Korean war. Straight forward aggression across the 38th parallel was unacceptably disadvantageous but positive scenarios could be imagined and translated into planning. The CIA's Goodfellow several times articulated one scenario with the happiest of endings. American policy, he said in effect, was to be ready to take advantage of a North Korean assault. If it occurred, the southern forces would pull back, far back. The U.S. would intervene in great force and the enemy would not only be halted but driven back north and conquered. Not only MacArthur but others could look across the Yalu and envisage a rout of the Chinese revolution and an American presence in Manchuria and beyond.

Kim Il Sung in Pyongyang had to consider strategic as well as peninsular realities. He had to take into account the U.S.-Japan rapprochement and see it as an obstacle to Korean unification. And he had to suppose that MacArthur's crushing of the Japanese Communists and the crackdown on unions in the spring of 1950 might be the equivalent of a clearing the ship for action.

In the early years of the Japanese and Korean occupations, the two were often contrasted—in Japan extensive reforms, in Korea repression and reaction. In the spring of 1950 the difference ended as the U.S. acted to make certain the continuing political dominance of the Japanese right. On May 2 MacArthur issued a statement suggesting the possibility of outlawing the Communist Party and a few weeks later took advantage of a minor clash between demonstrators and police to begin his crackdown on the unions and the left.

On June 6 he purged—stripped of all political rights—the 24 members of the Communist Party's central committee and the next day similarly purged the 17 top staff members of *Akahata*, the party newspaper. On that day Japanese police began a week of raids on Communist offices, universities and left unions. Ultimately several hundred Communist and leftwing publications were suppressed. Mass organizations shrank, abandoned by the intimidation. During the previous September MacArthur had outlawed the League of Koreans in Japan, most of whose members favored the north, thus perpetuating the subjection of this minority.

A major consequence was the weakening of the formidable populist peace movement. As I wrote at the time, "… in the belief that the peace movement in Japan would not survive the excision of the Communists, MacArthur applied the classic principles of generalship and struck hard at the left flank of the enemy."[6]

Public meetings and stated opinions of peace champions indeed were adversely affected.

In Korea, south as well as north, many feared the consequences of a stronger Japan allied with the U.S. Those with long memories thought a repetition of the early 1900s might be Korea's fate—when Washington supported Japan's seizure of it. In Pyongyang the consequences for Korea had to be seriously weighed. Kim Il Sung had to consider that perhaps for unification and the north it was now or not for a long time.

For Washington, intervention in the Korean civil war was imperative if it was to seriously heed its ambitions in northeast Asia and in Asia generally. The decision to intervene was presaged in papers at least a year old.

Equally imperative was the virtually automatic decision to cross the 38th parallel in October 1950 and undertake to roll back Communism. The crossing of the parallel from north to south in June of 1950 had been magnified into a justification for U.S. intervention, but when crossed from south to north the parallel became to Acheson and others a mere "surveyor's line."

The Truman Administration and most liberals—among them O. Edmond Clubb, John Paton Davies, John Carter Vincent, and the Americans for Democratic Action, headed by Francis Biddle—cheered the decision to realize a rollback as heartily as MacArthur and Willoughby.

And the Defense Department remained mindful of the conviction that the U.S. needed Manchuria as well as a controlled Korea. It observed on behalf of the Joint Chiefs of Staff that unification of Korea "might induce Manchuria to gravitate away from China and that in turn might cause Peking to question its current alignment with Moscow."

John M. Allison, director of the Office of Northeast Asian Affairs in the State Department and in charge of studies concerning future Korea policies, agreed vehemently with that thinking. "When all the moral and legal right is on our side why should we hesitate?" But Washington's strategic scenario clashed bloodily along the Yalu with a triumphant great revolution, and among the consequences was the revelation of the illusionary character of Washington's Manchurian-Northeast China aspirations.[7]

Both the Korean and Vietnam wars took place on the China periphery and looked forward to changing China. And both were shaped by the necessity of assuring Japan as well as the U.S. of Asian markets and raw materials. Despite the lack of success of the American military and the resulting failure to get into China's Northeast, Japan and also South Korea were strategically served and the U.S. design in part realized. Japanese economic strength was restored and modernized by enormous U.S. military purchases that rewarded Tokyo for serving as a rear base and privileged sanctuary for the American war effort. The year before the beginning of the Korean war the Toyota Motor Company, close to bankruptcy, dismissed 1,600 workers. By the end of the war it reportedly had earned 10 billion yen in profits from repairing U.S. Army trucks and bulldozers and manufacturing its own trucks.

The U.S. continued to pour money into Japan for years, compensating it for the loss of Manchuria and for Washington's prohibition of Japanese trade with China, which lasted into the early 1970s.

The Vietnam war, in which Koreans fought as mercenaries, similarly gave vast help to the economic transformation of South Korea. Its leading conglomerates got their start there in military construction.

The reversal in Japan was accompanied by related changes in Washington's Asian policy. Overall NSC-68 launched a major military buildup, the decision to deny Taiwan to the mainland hardened, and in May economic and military aid to the French began. By June 1950 Beijing and Washington saw each other as enemies.

The San Francisco signing of the peace treaty with Japan in the second year of the Korean war, in early September 1951, formalized and solidified the conversion of Japan into an American military base and a subordinate ally with a revived Asian mission. It restored to authority in Tokyo Japanese who had cruelly ruled Korea and directed barbarous aggression in China. Addressing the Tokyo Correspondents Club MacArthur, according to my notes, had explained away a lot of history by describing Japan as merely a poor country that had erred in "reaching out to get resources."

Kim Il Sung, Stalin and Mao

Publication of many Chinese and Soviet books, articles, memoirs and documents have added to our awareness of Soviet and Chinese foreknowledge of Kim Il Sung's determination to unify Korea by military means if necessary, and also has amplified understanding of how and why China got into the Korean war.[8] But important questions and uncertainties await the study of still closed archives.

In 1949 Stalin was persuaded that South Korea was stronger than the north and therefore was fearful of a southern assault on the north, a worry intensified by the frequent southern violations of the 38th parallel. In September he reacted negatively to Kim Il Sung's proposal that the north undertake a limited offensive, at the same time urging expanded preparations to do so. By the winter he had become more optimistic about the chances of a northern drive south and let Kim know this.

Stalin possibly discussed Kim's invasion idea with Mao during Mao's winter visit to the Soviet Union. Khruschev recalled that Mao was informed and also approved, but years later Mao said he was kept in the dark at that time. In the spring, despite misgivings, both Stalin and Mao acquiesced in what seemed to promise a Korean revolutionary success that also served their national interests.

Stalin commented that Kim "will listen to the voice of his ideas, not the voice against his ideas; he was really young and brave."

Kim visited Stalin in April of 1950 and probably saw Mao in May, informing him that the decision to send his army across the 38th parallel at an unspecified time had been made. About that time Mao received a telegram from Stalin informing him that, in view of changes internationally, he had consented to a military assault on the south. Kim came away persuaded that he had Mao's consent also. Kim's timing obviously had to with peninsular considerations, but the U.S. turnaround in Japan, an evident threat, may have helped to decide him.

As noted, Kim Il Sung waited for the return of tens of thousands of Koreans—entire divisions with equipment—who had served in the People's Liberation Army during the Chinese civil war. In 1949 two People's Liberation Army divisions comprised largely of Koreans and several smaller units were returned to North Korea with equipment . They became the KPA's 5th and 6th divisions. Early in 1950 another 23,000 Korean soldiers returned and became the 7th division.[10]

The situation south of the 38th Parallel offered both negative and positive considerations. On the one hand, the guerrilla movement had suffered defeats and was no longer a threat to the Seoul regime. On the other hand, the second national elections in South Korea on May 30 turned out badly for Syngman Rhee. Despite the built-in obstacles, a substantial number of anti-Rhee centrists and independents were elected to the National Assembly by disenchanted voters. Kim Il Sung sent three northerners south to confer with the victors. Rhee had them arrested and evidently executed.

John Foster Dulles conveniently pointed his homburg across the 38th parallel. In Seoul he predicted that some day the Communists would lose their hold on North Korea. He met with Rhee and promised U.S. aid. On June 20th he was quoted in the Seoul press as believing that "Korea is a qualified member of the free democratic nations… Korea will not be isolated."

Five days later Kim Il Sung alleged the untruth that the south had struck along the 38th parallel. Whether or not it had struck just in the area of the Onjin peninsula remains uncertain. But it quickly became evident that the "really young and brave" Kim had launched an effort to unite the peninsula by military force.

The Onjin Beginning, 1949 and 1950

An unadmitted shooting war…is in effect today along the thirty-eighth parallel…It is smoldering throughout the territory of the new Republic of Korea…only American money, weapons, and technical assistance enable the Republic to exist for more than a few hours.

—JOURNALIST ARCHIBALD STEELE

A series of clashes along the 38th parallel in the spring and summer of 1949, most initiated by the South, had an evident civil war character. Units as large as battalions were sometimes involved and the casualties were substantial. Syngman Rhee, his self-confidence enhanced by the suppression of the Yosu and Cheju rebellions, called publicly for conquest of the north. Students organized by the regime demonstrated in front of the U.S. Embassy demanding "give us arms."

In May of 1949, in the area of the Onjin peninsula in the west, the South launched a four-day engagement in which its troops advanced several miles into the north. Some 400 North Korean border guards and 22 southern soldiers were reported killed. South Korea had committed six infantry companies and several battalions to the engagement; to its consternation two of its companies defected to the north.

In Pyongyang, in October of 1997, I conversed with Lieutenant General Kang Tae Mu, who had commanded one of the two defecting companies. He told me he had early joined the left-dominated All Korea Farmers Union but soon enlisted in the constabulary, the force that became the new southern army. He had risen in the ranks, received leadership training and thus commanded a front-line company in 1949. He had become increasingly hostile to the Rhee regime and resentful of the authoritative American role in the army, which was engaged in suppression of guerrillas. "They were nominally advisers but their advice was in truth a command." He listened to the Pyongyang radio and, with others, was persuaded to defect. He wasn't certain how he would be received, but Kim Il Sung embraced him as a patriot and he was immediately taken into the northern army. He was made a general at age 29.

In August of 1949 fighting continued for days on Unpa, a strategically placed mountain just north of the parallel. The occupying South Korean forces were routed, two companies wiped out. The response of Rhee's generals was to demand an invasion of the north. But the local commander, a Captain Shin, heeded the American military advisers and refused to attack.

A memorandum by U.S. Ambassador Muccio spelled this out: "Captain Shin stated that the reports from Onjin reaching military headquarters in the morning of August 4 were most alarming. These reports indicated that the (South) Korean forces on the peninsula had been completely routed and that there was nothing there to stand against the northern assault. He went on that...the military were insistent that the only way to relieve pressure on Onjin would be to drive north. The military urged an immediate attack north..."[11]

As Muccio added, both Rhee and Premier Yi Pom Sok criticized Captain Shin for refusing to take the offensive. South Korean naval forces became aggressive, however, sinking four northern vessels and capturing one and shelling shore installations.

By the end of August Muccio wrote that "There is increasing confidence in the Army. An aggressive, offensive spirit is emerging... A good portion of the Army is eager to get going. More and more people feel that the only way unification can be brought about is by moving north by force. I have it from Dick Johnston (*The New York Times*) that

Chiang Kai-shek told Rhee that the Nationalist air force could support a move north..."

Also at the end of August, Gregory Henderson, Third Secretary of the American Embassy, conversed over dinner with Colonel Kim Paek Il, commandant of the School of Arms, and three other colonels. Kim said that "the morale of the troops, especially of new troops, was generally very high but this feeling was based on the feeling that they were coming into the Army to get the job of unification done."

Colonel Min Ki Sik had this to say: "One usually hears that the Army never attacks North Korea and is always getting attacked. This is not true. Mostly our Army is doing the attacking first and we attack harder. Our troops feel stronger."[12]

Rhee himself at this time made one of his explicit statements threatening to invade the north. Writing to his admiring supporter Robert Oliver on September 30, he said he felt strongly that now was the most psychologically advantageous time to move on Pyongyang. "We will drive some of Kim Il Sung's men to the mountain region and there we will gradually starve them out."

The August success of the Korean People's Army was its most impressive to date and Kim Il Sung reacted by deciding to try to seize the Onjin Peninsula and the nearby city of Kaesong. These were militarily serious targets since in southern hands they would facilitate an offensive to capture Pyongyang, just to the north. But Kim seems to have been thinking of a takeover of the entire south. If the offensive to seize Onjin went well quickly, the objective could readily be enlarged. But Stalin was not persuaded. On September 24 the Soviet Politburo disapproved of Kim's proposal, finding that military and other preparations for it were incomplete.

Kim's disappointment was eased by Moscow's reasons—which focused on the state of preparations. He pressed ahead with preparatory efforts and ordered a limited action near the parallel that resulted in ferocious fighting on October 14.

In January, Kim renewed his request for approval of a northern offensive and found Stalin more receptive, again stressing preparations and the need to minimize risk but also offering to be helpful. He said he would always be ready to receive Kim and discuss matters. In April, Kim spent some weeks in Moscow and received Stalin's unequivocal approval of his planned military offensive.

Just when Mao learned of this is uncertain. He complained later that he was not enlightened when he was in Moscow, that the talk on Korea then was simply about ways of strengthening Kim's regime. But on May 14 Stalin informed him in a telegram that "in the light of the changed international situation" he had agreed to the proposed

Korean move toward unification. Stalin did not explain what he meant by changed international situation. Presumably the 1949 triumph of the Chinese revolution and the reactive U.S. decision to ally itself with Japan were central factors.

A Soviet listing of arms supplied to North Korea in advance of the war included 100 military airplanes with assorted functions, 100 T-34 tanks, 57 armored cars, 102 automatic cannon, 44 landing craft, plus quantities of rifles and ammunition.

Kim Il Sung asserted on June 26, 1950, that the south had started the war by a general assault across the 38th parallel. I found out in Pyongyang in 1997 that it still makes that claim which has no basis in fact. Actually the war started locally in the area of the Onjin peninsula and spread west. Kim Il Sung ignited it, turning border clashes into a general civil war. He waited and hoped for a southern provocation and perhaps got one—possibly raiding southern troops crossed the parallel that June as they certainly did several times in 1949.

The southern 17th Regiment, a special unit of anti-Communist zealots nearly as large as a division, was conspicuously in the strategic Onjin area. Commanded by former officers in the Imperial Japanese Army, northerners who had fled south, it had a reputation for military provocations and braggadocio. Kim Sok Won, a Japanese Army veteran who commanded a division in the area, boasted that he would "breakfast in Haeju, lunch in Pyongyang and have dinner in Wonsan."

An early report of the 1950 fighting widely published in the American and European press declared that in the Onjin area the 17th Regiment had taken the offensive and captured the northern city of Haeju, important because it was rich in rice, because it was occupied by South Korean Labor Party exiles, and because it was a jumping off point for northern agents with southern destinations.

According to top secret maps in General Willoughby's office in Tokyo, Haeju was held for two days. It was then abandoned as surviving elements of the regiment fled south. Was Haeju seized in a counteroffensive or was it the provocation Kim Il Sung had hoped for?

Robert Oliver and Harold Noble, both Rhee partisans, said that South Koreans indeed had occupied Haeju, as did the United States Armed Forces Radio Service, reporting from Seoul on June 2. The *New York Herald Tribune*'s account said that the Southern troops "captured quantities of equipment."

In his article "How Did the Korean War Begin?", Karunakar Gupta observed that North Korean troops drove across the border at Onjin and captured the southern city of Kaesong, adjacent to the border, within five hours of the start of the invasion. The South Korean forces had been pushed back and were in retreat and he found that a South Korean counteroffensive to seize Haeju at this point "inconceivable." "The hypothesis cannot be excluded," he wrote, "that the South Korean onslaught on Haeju from the Onjin area took place before 4 p.m. on June 25, and that there must have been an element of surprise in this attack."[13]

Shortly before the start of the war Rhee told John Foster Dulles that he was prepared to invade the north even if it led to a general war. With Dulles when the conversation took place was William Matthews, editor of the *Arizona Daily Star,* and he reported that Rhee "is militantly for unification of Korea. Openly says it must be brought about soon… Rhee pleads justice of going into North country. Thinks it could succeed in a few days."[14]

Ambassador Muccio's first cable on the outbreak of the war said uncertainly that "Korea Army reports partly confirmed by KMAG field advisers" asserted that the north had attacked in the Onjin area. In an oral statement later Muccio said that continuous incidents along the 38th parallel for which both sides were responsible "made it so difficult to determine what was going on…the morning of the 25th." But Washington's adroitly selective use of Muccio's statements converted the uncertainties into certainties and succeeded in getting the United Nations to fly its blue banner over the American intervention.

As Bruce Cumings has observed in one of his admirable summations: "Whatever happened on or before June 25, it was immediately clear that this war was a matter of 'Koreans invading Korea'; it was not aggression across generally accepted international lines. Nor was this the point at which the civil conflict began. The question pregnant with ideological dynamite 'Who started the Korean War?' is the wrong question. It is not a civil war question… Americans do not care any more that the South fired the first shot on Fort Sumter; they still do care about slavery and succession."[15]

Armies at War

The American Invasion

*A nation fighting for its liberty ought not to adhere
rigidly to the accepted rules of warfare. Mass uprisings,
revolutionary methods, guerrilla bands everywhere, such
are the only means by which a small nation can hope to
sustain itself against an adversary superior in numbers
and equipment.*

—KARL MARX

The Korean war of 1950 began in the rainy season. Early in the morning of June 25th northern divisions surged across the 38th parallel. It was briefly a civil war in which the forces of revolution, north and south, had victory in sight when the United States began its massive, devastating intervention.

Thousands of the northern troops had fought for China's revolution and they faced the army of a reactionary regime commanded in large part by veterans of the Imperial Japanese Army. Some southern units fought well but in the main, as General MacArthur later put it, they melted like butter.

Seoul fell in three days. After a pause northern columns pushed down the peninsula in east and west, engaging both Republic of Korea forces and the first American units being committed piecemeal. It soon was a people's war, fought by an effective combination of northern veterans and southern guerrillas.

Americans got a swift education. In the first hours MacArthur boasted that "he could handle it with one arm tied behind his back." A day or so later he said that with a single division, the First Cavalry, he would quickly have the Reds skedaddling north. Arriving in Korea, he told Marguerite Higgins that two divisions would be needed. This was far from enough, it soon turned out.

Many just arrived Americans were sure that the Korean People's Army would scatter after looking into American eyes. As David Halberstam observed, "Almost everyone, from top to bottom, seemed to share the view that the moment the North Koreans saw they were fighting Americans rather than ROKs they would cut and run. It was arrogance born of racial prejudice."[1]

A colonel in the 24th Division spread the word that only half of the North Korean soldiers had arms.

Such illusions faded quickly as then small American as well as ROK units were out generaled and out fought. In a war fought in steaming heat and intermittent rain, the Americans were forced into a succession of retreats by skilled envelopments, even double envelopments, determined assaults and guerrilla ambushes.

The guerrilla movement was immediately reborn in the south. It gave timely aid to the Korean People's Army in the early battles and often liberated southern towns before the arrival of the northerners. Police stations were a chosen target.

The most impressive northern victory was the offensive in July that seized the central city of Taejon, a geographical and communications center which Rhee selected as his capital after the fall of Seoul. It fell after 14 days of hard fighting, a triumph of people's war—river crossings, frontal and rear assaults by the Korean People's Army strongly supported by guerrillas from nearby villages.

A panorama in the central circular building of the War Museum in present day Pyongyang celebrates the victory.

The U.S. 24th Division commanded by General William F. Dean was seriously mauled and replaced on the line of battle. Dean himself, injured in a fall, was made prisoner after several weeks of wandering in the mountains. Dean said later that his division consisted of troops who "had been fat and happy in occupation billet, complete with Japanese girl friends, plenty of beer and servants to shine their boots."[2] The division lost a third of its strength in three weeks of combat.

Marguerite Higgins' pertinent phrase for the warfare in the south she observed was "circular front." South Korean General Paik Sun Yup's phrase for it was "200 miles of Hell."

Han Suyin, with the Americans in retreat, summed it up this way in her diary on July 14: "On the American side, there's been a hopeless underestimation of the opposition; old fuddyduddy generals, the sort the British army always had to get rid of during the first two years of war, always at the same cost of thousands of men killed; inexperienced ill-trained troops, who've never been under fire before, let alone taken part in a retreat… Men so nervy they think every Korean is an enemy, firing at, and sometimes killing refugees. And then the good men, calm and steadfast…"

Two weeks later she wrote in her diary: "The Americans are not making many friends in Korea. Part of the journey yesterday I traveled in a train containing American troops. Before the train left, a major announced in the coach: 'Men, this train is only for American troops. If any Gooks try to get on, kick them off.' Day after day with their aircraft the Americans are laying waste towns and cities, killing fifty civilians for every one soldier."[3]

In terms of weaponry, the North Korean advantage in the early fighting was some 150 T-34 Soviet tanks. Used effectively in defense of Moscow, the T-34 tank was heavily armored, had broad treads and mounted one 85 mm gun and two machine guns. Soviet military aid delivered in advance of the start of the war included quantities of armored vehicles, landing craft, artillery, several hundred planes and various kinds of ammunition. But the newest kinds of tanks and artillery were withheld.

As early as July MacArthur offered this revised assessment of his foe: "The North Korean soldier must not be underestimated. He is a tough opponent, well-led, combines the infiltration of the Japanese with the tank tactics of the Russians of World War II. He is able to march and maneuver and to attack at night with cohesion..."[4]

The general publicized his lack of confidence in the Republic of Korea (ROK) troops. In Suwon he saw long lines of retreating southern troops and "did not see a wounded man among them."

But after capturing Seoul in a few days the North Korean forces fatally paused, partly to resupply and gain artillery and in the east to avoid being outflanked. The general in command was replaced. The Americans often knew what was coming tactically because they quickly broke the simple northern codes. Even so the successful American defense of the Pusan perimeter, a 130-mile arc in the southeast, was a near thing.

The three-month northern occupation of much of the south was strongly revolutionary and, until chaotic defeat set in, relatively tolerant and forbearing.

Along with unification, Pyongyang had two priority tasks in the south—restoration of the people's committees which the American occupation had eliminated in 1945 and a thorough land reform. Thousands of cadres, among them many exiled southerners, were sent south to realize these tasks even as guerrillas were mobilized to coordinate war efforts with the Korean People's Army. People's committees, cadres were told by the Interior Ministry, were "an unprecedented new form of sovereignty," populist organs "set up by the people with their own hands, spontaneously."

Provisional committees were formed in the first days of the northern presence. Elections to regularize them were held in July and August and were completed or nearly so in about half a dozen provinces before Inchon. Composed largely of the poorer peasants along with some Workers Party members, among them many women, the committees were each made responsible for administering 2,000 to

5,000 people. A later American study, made for the Air University and based mainly on interviews, found that all sorts of services were initiated, and that great numbers of peasants held some post or other for the first time in their lives. The cadres intervened only infrequently and discreetly to further prime objectives.[5]

The land reform program was hastily organized in the first days of the occupation and was similar to that carried out in the north. It took land from the landlords, a majority of whom had fled, and gave it to the landless and the peasants with small plots, the size determined mainly by family labor power. Land reform implementation committees and the people's committees cooperated in handling the distribution. Warmly welcomed, the reform was realized to such an extent, despite the short time, that it cleared the way for the palliative land distribution carried out at U.S. insistence by the restored Rhee regime. It did so by just about destroying the landlord class, which had successfully obstructed an earlier weak land reform effort.

Pyongyang ordered land reform in the south as early as July 4 of 1950: "Agrarian reform measures will be carried out in southern Korea, in accordance with Article 7 of the Constitution of the Korean People's Democratic Republic, in order to transform speedily the backward rural economy and give freedom and a better standard of living to the peasants of south Korea… Agrarian reform will be based on the principle of confiscation without compensation and distribution without charge."[6]

The occupation of the south also tried to reestablish the mass organizations that the Americans and their Korean allies had broken. Chongpyong unions were revived, as were peasant, student and women's organizations. Students in Seoul and elsewhere were the most fervent supporters of the occupation regime, volunteering readily for all sorts of tasks. An especial effort was made to draw members into the Women's League, organized at various levels. Success was limited, but in Seoul, according to an American study, "women held jobs of honor, worked at employment usually denied them, sometimes went around calling each other comrade."

A variety of ad hoc committees and other organizations were quickly formed to deal with war and reform problems, and an enormous number of meetings and rallies of all sorts were held. A radio announcement invited those with a guilty conscience to come to the local police station to confess and thousands did. Criticism and self-criticism were practiced daily and at meetings people rose to talk about their past and repent errors. A campaign against illiteracy was centered in the schools, which were also political forums. Many of the small number of southern moderates and liberals, including some 60 members of the National Assembly, stayed on in Seoul and 48 of them at a meeting pledged allegiance to the Democratic People's Republic. Some were appointed to judgeships and other offices. According to his son Philip, Kim Kyu Sik "made a few speeches" but did not join the government.

Northern tanks, entering Seoul, smashed the gates of the main prison, freeing prisoners who had survived recent mass executions. Acts of vengeance by the freed followed, but were quickly forbidden. Some night arrests took place; prominent Rhee officials and "pro-Americans" were incarcerated, but the policy of the occupation was to unite as many as possible and was generally forbearing. People who confessed were told they had "a second chance." Generally the cadres from the north were courteous and given to offer explanations when they confiscated property or insisted on corvee labor.

Seoul was defended long enough after the successful September American landing at Inchon, the capital's port, to enable a retreat both of northerners and anti-Rhee southerners. Among those going north were Kim Kyu-sik (reported to have died in Pyongyang in August, 1951), Ahn Chai-hong and people associated with Yo Un-hyung, including his brother Yo Un-hong. Involuntarily taken north were hundreds of ROK army and police personnel and rightist youths. Others were just executed in Seoul—about a thousand, according to a CIA estimate. The killers included local students. Reginald Thompson saw "the corpses of hundreds slaughtered in the last days by the Communists in a frenzy of hate and lust."[7]

On September 15th MacArthur skillfully handled his Inchon leapfrog—completing the conversion of the civil war into an American invasion. Contrary to established wisdom, the Communists were not surprised. The Chinese as early as July had foreseen it as a likely possibility, but one that could only have been countered by substantial nonexistent sea and air forces. A huge armada of 262 ships (it secretly included a Japanese mine-sweeper flotilla manned by former Japanese navy personnel) landed some 70,000 troops at Seoul's port, confronting a noticeably sullen population.[8]

But the recapture of the capital did not come easily. Fiercely defended by students and others as well as northern units, gutted by American artillery fire and bombings, the city fell on September 28 after 10 days of street fighting. Half the population had fled the city. "The battle involved house-to house, cellar-to cellar, roof-to-roof fighting of the most vicious sort," Marguerite Higgins reported. "We had to burn down many acres of the city with artillery and flame-throwing tanks."[9]

Joseph Alsop's report was similar: "Set high in the surrounding hills, heavy U.S. artillery poured sheets of fire into the city. Thousands of civilians died in the brutal crossfire, and when it was over much of the city lay in smoldering ruins. So our conquering force received a perfunctory welcome."[10]

Pravda reported on September 23 that "Cement, streetcar rails, beams and stones are being used to build barricades. The situation is very serious. Pillboxes and tank points dot the scene. Every home must be defended as a fortress. There is firing from behind every stone."[11]

MacArthur claimed that Seoul was taken on September 25 when the fighting was still fierce. The following day the U.S. suffered 185 battle casualties, on the next day 182, on the next 183. The Associated Press was unusually caustic: "If the city has been liberated, the remaining North Koreans did not know it."

Reginald Thompson concluded his dispatch to the *London Telegraph* on the recovery of Seoul with a comment on what the people of Korea faced: "It is inescapable that the terrible fate of the South Korean capital and many villages is the outcome of a new technique of machine warfare. The slightest resistance brought down a deluge of destruction, blotting out the area. Dive bombers, tanks and artillery blasted strong points, large or small, in town and hamlet, while the troops waited at the roadside as spectators until the way was cleared for them. Few people can have suffered so terrible a liberation."[12]

Inchon was "MacArthur at his finest," many said and indeed it was a brilliant stroke. To Dean Acheson Macarthur was "the sorcerer of Inchon." But overall MacArthur in Korea was at his worst, the victim of his ethnocentric bias, his utter ignorance of the Chinese revolution and of Chinese tactics and strategy, and his reliance on the intelligence provided by the bigoted General Charles Willoughby, "my little fascist," as MacArthur sometimes called him.

The Rhee regime is known to have executed some 1,200 Communist suspects between the outbreak of war on June 25 and July 14. It ordered a blood bath in the southern regions retaken from the north after Inchon in the fall of 1950 and later, its task simplified by the discovery of signed statements of contrition or cooperation during the northern presence. Some 500 were tried conspicuously for show, condemned to death and executed. Thousands were rounded up in localities reputed to be leftist and executed. Gregory Henderson estimated in his *Korea: The Politics of the Vortex* that probably more than 100,000 were killed without any trial whatsoever when soldiers and the Counter-Intelligence Corps recaptured areas where the left was known to be strong. He said the story of the killings "has nowhere been written, but scars remained."[13]

In December *Time* reported that "Since the liberation of Seoul last December, South Korean firing squads have been busy liquidating 'enemies of the state'—Korean civilians accused of sabotage or collaboration with the Communists. With savage indifference, the military executioners shoot men, women, and children."[14]

Corespondent Don Greenlees reported to his paper, the London *Daily Mirror*, that a single Seoul court had handed down 84 death sentences in a six-day period. He said the trials were held in groups of 40 and that in the more than 100 cases he watched no defense witnesses appeared. He said the number of those executed in the area exceeded 600. The cells he saw were so crowded the prisoners could not lie down.[15]

U.S. Marines Capture Seoul

Andrew Geer's THE NEW BREED: THE STORY OF THE *U.S.* MARINES IN KOREA *includes an eloquent and comprehensive account of how the Marines captured Seoul. Excerpts follow.*

"In any small unit battle the outstanding behavior of a few men is always discernible over the others. The moral balance which decides a hotly contested battle is a delicate thing. On the one side is flaming courage and victory; against this are irresolution and defeat. The scale is tipped by a few—by the ten percent—who rise to the heights where the enemy and death can be met without a hesitant step. When the final assault was ordered, the Marines of Smith's company knew what was facing them... Of the forty-four men available, thirty-three would form the skirmish line while the remainder came on later with machine guns and ammunition.

"Korean terrain posed a constant problem of determining positions in view of the fact that the maps were not accurate. In the case of Jaskilka's advance on Hill 72 there was some doubt at the battalion OP as to where he was and if he was moving onto the right target. Visibility was hampered by intervening hills, distance and haze from enemy smoke pots.

"At this time Stevens and Able Company was the sole remaining rifle company commanded from the brigade. Of the eighteen platoon leaders who led their units into action in southern Korea, four had been killed and thirteen wounded. Of the twenty-four officers involved, twenty-two were casualties before 50 days of combat had been completed.

"The circle was a litter of stones, bricks, timbers, antitank gun mounts and the enemy dead. The buildings around it were on fire and the black, turgid smoke cut down visibility to a few hundred feet. Wounded of the 1st Platoon began to drift back and there was the cry for "Corpsman" heard over the slamming of shells and the ricocheting whine of bullets. A shortage of stretchers developed and Chaplain Otto Sporter tore metal shutters from street windows and utilized these as litters… Easy Company passed through the dead and wounded and hard-hit platoons of Fox and carried on the attack. After a sharp fight the enemy broke and ran. Many were killed.

"The barricades became more imposing structures as the middle ground of the capital was reached. Stretching from one side of the street to the other, they were composed of fiber sandbags five to eight feet thick at the base. The process of overcoming these roadblocks was tedious, efficient and costly… The average time to break through such a barricade was forty-five minutes. Three or four hundred yards along the street the process had to be repeated. The work of breaking through the hurdles of Seoul would have been much slower and more costly had it not been for Marine and Navy Corsairs.

"Shooting the machine gun from his hip, Bowen blasted a hole in the side of the house to provide a firing aperture, He got the gun into action and began firing along the street in the direction of Independence Gate. The fire fight by this time was general along the length of the company with all units engaged… Breen directed Sartwell to take his platoon into the assault on the prison grounds. The unit was hard hit… It was slow work as the enemy was using automatic weapons fired from the upper stories of the buildings lining the streets.

"The fight for and capture of Seoul proved to be one of the most difficult in the history of the Corps. The division suffered 2,430 casualties, of which 414 were killed or died of wounds. Of these casualties, 1,064 were sustained in the five-day period when the Marines were fighting in the outskirts and streets of Seoul… Losses inflicted on the enemy were by far the greatest he had suffered since the beginning of hostilities."

Operation Rat Killer

The war in the south was not over. Guerrillas, joined by fragments of northern divisions, had experienced a surge of growth and effectiveness. Scores of guerrilla bands verying from a few hundreds to several thousand were operating throughout the UN occupied areas. U.S. intelligence estimated that nearly 30 percent of the UN troops were defending against them, British sources said that "a vast number of guerrillas" was still at large in the south and that sniping occurred even in the Seoul-Inchon area. According to an official estimate, a minimum of 40,000 guerrillas remained in South Korea. Others thought that number existed in South Cholla alone.

A captured diary of a southern guerrilla conveyed this information about guerrilla thinking and practice: "Bandits plundering rich farmers shall be taken in and trained to fight against the enemy." Criticism and self-criticism are stressed. Questions to be asked and thought about: "Have you inflicted losses on your country through following your own interests?" Resolve: "Let us bear each other's agony and show more love toward our fellowmen with whom we live and die...never damage anything belonging to the people." But "kill unconditionally all those who work for the enemy. Divide their property among the poor."[16]

The Kochang killings in February 1951 were a notable instance in which the South Korean counter guerrilla forces slaughtered villagers thought to be aiding the partisans. Some 600 men and women of all ages were herded into a narrow valley and cut down by machine guns.

In 1950 General Walker gave the U.S. IX corps the task of countering guerrillas in southwest Korea but very little success was achieved. So in December 1951 General Van Fleet, aggravated by an increase of guerrilla raids in November, detached two ROK divisions from the front, the Capital and 8th, and sent them to the two Cholla provinces and nearby areas in the deep south to suppress the guerrillas. Placed in command of what was called Operation Rat Killer was South Korea's perhaps ablest general, Paik Sun Yup.

This is how Paik described the activities of those he was assigned to destroy: "The guerrillas conducted rear-area harassment missions throughout the southern districts of the Republic of Korea, seriously impairing law and order and taking a toll on the UN Command transportation and communication lines as well. The guerrillas grew so adept at blowing up roads and rail lines that even the main rail link between Seoul and Pusan was unsafe. Guerrilla control was so strong, especially in the mountainous, interior areas of the south, that a popular saying of the day had it that 'It's the Republic of Korea during the daytime. But it's the People's Republic of Chosun (North Korea) at night.'"[17]

Paik might have observed that police stations were a favorite guerrilla target.

Allied with Paik and his two divisions were National Police regiments, a squadron of ROK air force Mustangs, and a team of 60 Americans, most of them experts in various aspects of counter guerrilla warfare. The senior officer, Lt. Col. William Dodds. had served under Van Fleet when he warred on Greek guerrillas after World War II and was especially selected for the mission by him.

The priority task was an assault on Mount Chiri, which arose from a concentric circle of rugged, wooded peaks and which was the principal guerrilla base. The ROK forces moved up the mountain on all sides, finding, killing or capturing an increasing number of guerrillas, squeezing remaining guerrillas to the top where many were the victims of bombings and ground troop action. Follow-up sweeps in nearby mountains inflicted additional guerrilla casualties.

Operation Rat Killer generally ended in February 1952. ROK army records state that 5,800 guerrillas were killed and 5,700 captured. ROK casualties are not mentioned. The U.S. Army claimed that the ROK and the National Police together had killed 9,000 guerrillas. Paik was surprised by the number of North Korean soldiers who had found refuge with the guerrillas after Inchon. Those his troops captured snarled defiance. Other captured guerrillas were members of the South Korean Workers Party but many were simply local villagers.

Paik admitted that the guerrilla movement was not entirely destroyed and in March Ridgway's headquarters estimated that some 3,000 guerrillas were still in the area. An informed American declared that "There is evidence that major guerrilla activity continued, suggesting the persistence of widespread opposition to Rhee's government and support for Communist rule in the ROK."[18]

Graphically supporting that were the photos taken in the Chiri Mountain region by Margaret Bourke-White and published in the December 2, 1952, issue of *Life*. She found that as many as 10,000 guerrillas, many of them women, were still in the hills and fighting a force of 5,000 police and 11,000 "young volunteers" (read members of the terrorist youth groups) in "the savage, secret war." The task of suppressing the guerrillas was "only half done."

What totally ended the guerrilla struggle in the south was the end of the war. In its last months it was no longer militarily significant.

In the north the Americans made some effort to organize guerrillas but had almost no success. The reason was basic: Their natural allies in the countryside were those opposed to change and reform. They did organize a number of partisan groups on the small islands off the west coast which, after the truce, were inducted into the ROK army.

Rollback: MacArthur's Drive to the Yalu

Within a few days after escorting Syngman Rhee back to Seoul, MacArthur sent troops north across the 38th parallel—ROK troops first, then the First Cavalry—initiating the first ever rollback campaign. American opinion was generally enthusiastically supportive. Diplomat George Kennan was prominently in the minority warning against the move.

State Department releases and newspaper editorials forecast an exemplary occupation of the north, a model of democracy. Secretary of State Acheson said that "Korea will be used as a stage to prove what Western Democracy can do to help the underprivileged countries of the world.[19]

What happened was the opposite. The UN, the State Department and the allies soon found that they were ignored. MacArthur and Rhee, the occupiers, were in command and responsible for the savage reality—the extension of Rhee's south to the north. Police and youth terrorists from the south and ROK troops "perpetuated a nauseating reign of terror," in Bruce Cumings' words.

Washington's contribution was to conceal and excuse the mass graves, looting and destruction and the assault on the positive achievements of the Kim Il Sung regime—Acheson rebuked *The New York Times* for reporting some executions. An early forecast in captured Pyongyang, soon visited by the Bob Hope show, was that the land reform would be abolished so that the land could be restored to its "rightful owners." The occupation was much too brief for such an undertaking.

U.S. forces plagued by guerrillas napalmed entire valleys of villages and turned over suspects to the South Koreans for execution.

Counterintelligence was instructed that the destruction of the communist Workers Party was a basic objective, and that targeted the membership of a mass party. Estimates of the number of North Koreans executed or turned into roped work gangs by the Rhee forces during their brief stay range up to 150,000. After reoccupying Pyongyang, the North Koreans claimed that 15,000 people had been massacred there—the bodies filled the courtyard of the main prison and 26 air raid shelters.

A horror, perpetrated by South Koreans almost certainly with American participation, took place in the northern town of Sinchon, south of Pyongyang. In 1987 Bruce Cumings visited the site accompanied by the sole survivor, Kim Myong Ja. Some 400 women and children were herded into a storehouse and a tunnel in November 1950, kept without food or water for days while they were being told to reveal the location of their husbands and older sons. When they begged for water, according to the survivor, then a pigtailed girl, a big American threw buckets of shit on them. After some days the walls were doused with gasoline and torched. Kim Myong Ja found herself alive at the top of the heap of bodies, near a ventilation hole, when it was over.[20]

Major General Kim Tae Hua, addressing me and my two companions in Pyongyang in October 1997, added some details about the Sinchon horror. When women begged for water for the children, some were given what they first thought was water but turned out to be gasoline. He told us also that his father, a farmer, was killed as he worked in a field by a strafing plane, almost certainly American. Six other members of his family were killed. Interviewed years later, Tibor Meray, a Hungarian correspondent, commented that in North Korea he saw terrible deeds committed by Americans—"peasants in the fields were often machine gunned by pilots..."[21]

In terms of scale, the worst American atrocity was probably the massacre of citizens of the major northern port of Wonsan. American and allied warships bombarded the city for 861 days, ending a minute before the cease-fire hour on July 27, 1953. Early on, according to Rear Admiral Allen E. Smith, in Wonsan "you cannot walk the streets. You cannot sleep anywhere in the twenty-four hours, unless it is the sleep of the dead." The population has been reduced to "suicide groups."[22]

At the end, according to an American account, Wonsan was "a mass of cluttered ruins." The semiofficial account of the Wonsan bombardment by two naval commanders, Malcolm Cagle and Frank A. Manson, in *The Sea War and Korea*, reports in detail the effect on the flow of military supplies to the south but does not have a word to say about the civilian killings and destruction.

Inchon did not turn into a total North Korean rout. Despite grievous losses in men and materiel, the Kim Il Sung leadership drew on Chinese experience and planned and partially realized a strategic retreat to the northern mountains, the fastnesses where Kim's guerrillas had struggled years before and which Kim had recently turned into a new province, named Chagang. In a matter of weeks it had a number of divisions in the process of being reorganized.

Surviving northern forces in the south either made their way north, divided into small units, or joined the local guerrillas. In a dispatch from Eighth Army Headquarters on February 1, 1951, the Overseas News agency reported that "The guerrillas behind the UN lines are North Korean regulars who were cut off by the UN landing at Inchon and the subsequent sweep into North Korea. Instead of disintegrating as a military force, a fate the UN command had fondly predicted, the enemy troops stayed in the hills, conserving their manpower and supplies. Today they are an active, potent military force. "Enough guerrillas have been captured in recent weeks for the UN command to determine that they operate in organized units under a central command. Most of the larger units have direct radio contact with the higher echelons in North Korea. In many places in South Korea they put out propaganda leaflets..."[23]

MacArthur's decision to divide his forces, the Eighth Army to the west, X Corps to the east, was based on guerrilla strength as well the mountainous geography, the later resulting in the former.

Week after week Willoughby, MacArthur's G-2, estimated the North Korean military as a scattered few thousand—20,000 was a favorite figure—incapable of organized resistance. In October the People's Army actually may have numbered over 100,000, but it was in the process of a frantic reorganization and could not cope with the U.S. advance.

After Inchon, Premier Zhou Enlai gave a blunt 11,000 word speech in which he said China would not sit supinely by if U.S. troops crossed the 38th parallel. General Nie Rongzhen, Acting Chief of Staff of the People's Liberation Army, said much the same thing. Secretary of State Acheson and his *New York Times* confidant James Reston were among the many who thought Beijing was bluffing. Acheson said it would be "sheer madness" for the Chinese to intervene. Mao "will hesitate to commit suicide," Reston argued on the day South Korean troops crossed the parallel. He wrote that this was the general view in Washington.

Elements in the mistaken American judgment were a contemptuous opinion of the Chinese military and the conviction that Moscow made the important decisions for China. Arguing with British Prime Minister Attlee in early December, Truman challenged his view that Beijing was an independent player, asserting that the Chinese "are satellites of Russia and will be satellites as long as the present Peiping regime is in power." Acheson agreed, saying of the Chinese that "all they do is on the Moscow pattern."

MacArthur assured Truman on Wake Island, on October 15th, that there was "very little" chance of a Chinese or Soviet intervention. If the Chinese drove on Pyongyang, he said, "there would be the greatest slaughter."[24]

"Come up to Pyongyang," he invited reporters at Wake. "It won't be long now." And he told Averill Harriman and Matthew Ridgway in Tokyo that if the Chinese intervened, he would deal them a crushing blow that "would rock Asia and perhaps turn back Communism."[25]

The supposition in Washington was that Beijing's Korea focus was on the Yalu River border and it did take some small steps to allay

Chinese worries about its national security. It instructed MacArthur to send only South Korean troops to the border (he disobeyed) and to respect China's interest in electricity plants along the Yalu. And it suggested that possibly a neutral zone could separate China and a U.S.-conquered Korea, as proposed by the allies.

MacArthur used some purple rhetoric to denounce these modest concessions, but had no need to do so. To Mao they were trivia. He had made up his mind to send troops across the river and soon.

The Chinese Cross the Yalu

We have decided to send some of our troops to Korea under the name of Volunteers to fight the United States and its lackey Syngman Rhee and to aid our Korean comrades. From the following considerations, we think it necessary to do so: the Korean revolutionary force will meet with a fundamental defeat, and the American aggressors will rampage unchecked once they occupy the whole of Korea. This will be unfavorable to the entire East.

—MAO TO STALIN, OCTOBER 2, 1950

Stalin's constant priority consideration was keeping the Soviet Union out of another great war. Some 3,000 Soviet military advisers—averaging one for every 45 Korean officers and men—assisted the North in preparing for the war and at the start of it, but, on Stalin's orders, did little after Inchon. It followed that Stalin came to look to China to take the serious risks in doing what had to be done to keep the Pyongyang regime in the war.

In the days after Inchon Mao was of course concerned about the Yalu border—he knew very well that on the Chinese side was much of the nation's important industry and he had to recall that the Japanese, having taken over Korea, had moved across the Yalu to turn China's Northeast into Manchukuo. But almost from the start of the war he had determined that China would get into it if the north was in peril. He believed that a defeat of the north would not only threaten the Yalu border but inevitably weaken China's revolution. Indeed Inchon and continuing U.S. military successes in Korea were stimulating the domestic opposition to the revolution. Hostile rumor mongering, railroad and communications sabotage, assassinations and localized small-scale uprisings were on the rise.[26]

Mao perceived the Chinese revolution, just a year in power, as a means of elevating China's global reputation and as a model that would serve other revolutions in Asia and beyond. And he and the party leadership believed that China had responsibilities and security interests in Korea and Indo-China as well as Taiwan. Korea and Indo-China had been shaped economically, culturally and politically in part by a long Chinese presence and influence. China had fought wars both in Indo-China and Korea (the 1884 war with the French, the Sino-Japanese War of 1884-85). Both Ho Chi Minh and Kim Il Sung had been members of the Chinese Communist Party and the histories of their parties were intertwined with that of the Chinese Communist Party.

The tie with the Koreans was bone deep. Several Koreans had studied under Zhou Enlai at Whampoa military academy in Guangzhou and at least one made the Long March. In the Chinese civil war the critical area of struggle was in the Northeast, the former Manchuria, and the Chinese Communists were able to prevail there in 1948 because North Korea served as their rear base. Kim Il Sung sent thousands of young men to fight in China's Fourth Field Army and battle tattered Chinese units retreated into North Korea to regroup. Some 2,000 freight cars of military equipment left in North Korea by the Japanese were turned over to the Chinese Communists, much of it without charge. Many families of Chinese Communists found refuge in Korea. For historical as well as contemporary reasons the Chinese Communist Party had formally resolved to confront American imperialism at three locations—Taiwan, Korea and Indo-China.

President Truman added to Mao's critical thinking. On June 27 Truman had not only announced the decision to intervene in the Korean war but proclaimed that the Seventh Fleet would patrol the strait between Taiwan and the mainland and prevent any offensive from either direction. The president also announced increased aid to the embattled French in Indo-China and to the anti-Huk struggle in the Philippines.[27]

The propriety and wisdom of these escalations were applauded in Washington and the American media. Only a handful of small left organizations and publications with tiny readerships—survivors of the McCarthy onslaught—were critical. Notably among them was a closely argued statement in the August issue of the then new *Monthly Review* and forthright statements issued immediately by the Progressive Party and by the Committee for a Democratic Far Eastern Policy.[28]

Mao saw American entry into the Korean civil war as continued intervention in the Chinese revolution and the beginning of an Asian offensive by American imperialism. He pointed out publicly that Truman had already violated his pledge not to intercede in defense of Taiwan and he scoffed at Truman's pledge to bar also a Kuomintang assault on the mainland. MacArthur's two-day visit to Taiwan late in July was taken as further confirmation.

Beijing had to yield to the Seventh Fleet. It abandoned plans to invade Taiwan. But it poured in aid to the Vietminh in Indo-China. Before the end of September 1950 it had delivered some 14,000 rifles, some 150 pieces of artillery, 1,700 machine guns, many tons of grain, much ammunition, medicine, uniforms, etc., and it sent some 79 war-experienced advisers, among them General Chen Cheng, a high-ranking PLA commander. Many of the howitzers and other artillery supplied then or later were American, captured in the Chinese civil war. The U.S. supplied the French lavishly but the Chinese aid changed the military balance of power in Indo-China, providing much of the weaponry that immediately made possible the liberation of the area of Vietnam bordering China and later the great Vietminh victory at Dienbienphu in 1954.

Through July and August of 1950 an uneasy and questioning PLA command was informed repeatedly that Chinese troops might be obliged to enter Korea. The priority task was to prepare. On July 7 and July 10 meetings of top commanders chaired by Zhou Enlai agreed that "it is necessary to prepare an umbrella before it rains" and decided on the formation of what became the Northeast Border Defense Army. Stockpiling of arms and other supplies began and plans were made for political mobilization.

On July 13 the Chinese Military Commission, chaired by Mao, formally instructed the new army that its main tasks were to "defend the borders of the Northeast, and to prepare to support the war operations of the Korean People's Army if necessary." On August 4 Mao told the Politburo that "We should not fail to assist the Koreans. We must lend them our hands in the form of sending in military volunteers there. The timing could be further decided but we must prepare for this."

Zhou Enlai commented that "in order to win the war, China's strength must be added to the struggle." Commanders were to be fully briefed in mid-August and instructed to be ready for action by the end of the month.[29]

Antiaircraft artillery was placed in defense of the Yalu bridges. Training exercises began; steps taken to increase field hospitals and soup kitchens; and an array of sewing machines began turning out cotton-padded uniforms. Some 2,000 Koreans living in Manchuria were recruited to serve as interpreters. Additional military attaches were sent to Pyongyang to put together war information and collect topographical data. Preparations were rushed but the People's Republic had been in authority less than a year and the difficulties and shortages were daily encounters. And many leading officials and officers, possibly a majority, while supporting preparations, were inclined to oppose actual intervention. August deadlines became September deadlines as a result of tardiness in the military buildup north of the Yalu.

On August 26 a report by Zhou to the Central Military Commission declared that China had to face up to a turn for the worse in the war. "Our duty is now much heavier, and we should prepare for the worst and prepare quickly." He warned that a planned entry into the war had to be kept secret, even from the North Koreans, so that "we could enter the war and give the enemy a sudden blow."

MacArthur's amphibious assault at Inchon, followed by the retreat of the battered Korean People's Army, though somewhat foreseen, brought the issue of Chinese intervention to a boil and decided the timing. Earlier when the war outlook seemed favorable, Kim Il Sung had rather haughtily rejected a Chinese offer of some assistance but reacted to the reversals by appealing to both Stalin and Mao for intervention by their armed forces. Stalin asked in a cable to Mao if China was prepared to send troops to aid the North Koreans. When Mao did not immediately respond, he seemed to accept loss of the war and asked if China would permit Kim Il Sung to set up an exiled government in the Northeast.

Mao had determined to get into a war turned disastrous and was insistent at a succession of leadership meetings in the first days of October capped by an enlarged meeting of the Politburo October 4-5. He prevailed finally over substantial Politburo doubts and objections. "When our neighbor is in critical trouble how can we stand by with folded hands?"

China was to get into the war on or about October 15, actually doing so on the 19th. Peng Dehuai, very experienced, was named commander of the committed troops, called volunteers. Peng arrived in Beijing from the Northwest and spoke vigorously in support of intervention, adding a presence and a voice to Mao's case.[30]

On the very next day a meeting of the Revolutionary Military Commission chaired by Zhou Enlai got down to the business of working out the particulars of the movements of the intervening troops.

Mao himself explained the decisions later finalized in his long telegram to Stalin dated October 2. He stated that Chinese troops would only combat enemy forces north of the 38th parallel. "At the initial stage, they will merely engage in defensive warfare to wipe out small detachments of enemy troops and ascertain the enemy's situation; on the other hand, they will wait for the delivery of Soviet weapons. Once they are equipped, they will cooperate with the Korean comrades in counterattacks to annihilate American aggressor troops."[31]

Warnings by Zhou Enlai and Nie Rongzhen that China would intervene if American troops crossed the 38th parallel and headed for the Yalu were somewhat disingenuous. Republic of Korea troops crossed the parallel on October 1 but the U.S. First Cavalry Division did not cross until October 7—two or three days after the Chinese Politburo voted to intervene. The North Korean plight was the controlling factor. But the Zhou and Nie statements helped to explain and justify the actual intervention and were public relations in general.

On October 8 the Northeast Border Defense Force was renamed the Chinese People's Volunteers and Mao, acting as chairman of the Military Commission, issued the order sending the volunteers to Korea:

> "In order to support the Korean people's war of liberation, repel the invasion launched by the American imperialists and their running dogs, and to defend the interests of the people of Korea, China, and all the other countries in the East, I hereby order the Chinese People's Volunteers to move immediately into Korea and join the Korean comrades in fighting the invaders and winning a glorious victory."

He went on to declare that the volunteers "must fully anticipate possible and inevitable difficulties and be prepared to overcome them with great enthusiasm, courage, care and stamina… So long as you comrades are firm and brave and good at uniting with the people there and at fighting the aggressors, final victory will be ours."[32]

Later he directed that "The Chinese comrades must consider Korea's cause as their own and the commanders and fighters must be instructed to cherish every hill, every river, every tree and every blade of grass in Korea and take not a single needle or a single thread from the Korean people, just the way we feel about our own country and treat our own people."[33]

On October 12 the CIA saw no danger of a substantial Chinese intervention.

On October 10 Stalin reneged on a vital promise—to provide the Chinese volunteers immediately with air cover. Molotov told a shocked Zhou Enlai that air cover would be delayed about two and a half months. Mao ordered all preparations for intervention halted pending the outcome of an emergency leadership meeting in Beijing but at that meeting the decision was made to swallow hard and go ahead. In Mao's view, the grave consequences of nonintervention prevailed against the losses lack of air cover would cause.

Stalin was impressed when Zhou Enlai informed him that China would intervene regardless and again and again said emotionally, "The Chinese comrades are good comrades."[34]

The Soviet Union did provide air defense of key Chinese cities and before the end of the year the Soviet Air Force did get into the war on a limited scale. Its fighter planes were restricted to an area extending some 60 miles south of the Yalu, thus reducing the risk that the Soviet pilots of downed planes would be captured. Far more important, Soviet bombers stationed in China's Northeast were a deterrent to any U.S. extension of the war to China.[35]

On October 16, a day after MacArthur assured Truman at Wake that a Soviet or Chinese intervention was most unlikely, a regiment of the Chinese 42d Army quietly entered Korea. The main Chinese force began to cross the Yalu on the cold and rainy night of October 19. When later China admitted the intervention, statements and editorials cited both the national interest and the debt incurred by the blood shed by so many Koreans in the service of the Chinese revolution. They also cited precedents of volunteer involvement in foreign wars, among them the Abraham Lincoln Brigade in the Spanish civil war and the service of Lafayette and other French in the American revolution.

Simultaneously a Great Movement to Resist America and Assist Korea was launched throughout China. It began with elaborate denunciations of American imperialism and its hostility toward the Chinese revolution. It called on the Chinese people to neither admire nor fear the United States.

The Chinese crossed the Yalu into Korea during the hours from dusk to 4 a.m. daily and then hid in the hills. They were first engaged in the brief period from October 25 to November 5. Vanguard units from a force that eventually grew to about 200,000 joined by reconstituted North Korean units ambushed and routed elements of the Republic of Korea 1st, 6th and 8th divisions in 12 days and nights of battle. The Chinese estimated they inflicted 15,000 casualties.

On October 25, the first day of the offensive, the Associated Press learned from "informed sources" that "most American troops may be out of Korea by Christmas. They said General MacArthur expects the first elements of the Eighth Army to begin moving back to Japan by Thanksgiving."

One of the eight regiments that were the hardest hit by the offensive was the Eighth Regiment of the horseless U.S. 1st Cavalry Division. The instructions were to attack only South Koreans but the cavalry regiment was caught as it replaced a ROK regiment. On November 2, some 600 of the regiment were surrounded in the Unsan mining area, in the late 19th century an American concession, and slaughtered—"an Indian-style massacre," foreign correspondents called it.[36]

A passing sergeant, looking down from a height, was more specific—the body littered scene reminded him of Custer and the Little Big Horn.

The Chinese operations were halted on November 5th, Mao, who in effect shared command with Peng Dehuai, reluctantly agreeing, because their forces had suffered substantial casualties and were exhausted and short of supplies. At a staff evaluation of the battle, Peng observed that "we routed the enemy forces more often than we annihilated them." To annihilate a regiment is more important that routing a division, he stressed. He rebuked commanders who had hesitated at envelopment.

Then and later logistical inadequacies contributed to failures to mop up surrounded enemy forces. In the revolutionary wars the Communists had reduced logistical problems by relying on the people to be suppliers of food and much else. But in Korea enormous quantities of many kinds of materiel—more than 9,000 items—had to be brought across the Yalu. Zhou Enlai was given overall responsibility for logistical development and devoted much his time to it. Nie Rongzhen, Acting Chief of Staff, wrote in his memoirs that "Comrade Zhou Enlai did everything he could to ensure supplies for the Volunteers and contributed enormously in this regard."[37]

Western sources conjectured that the Chinese paused because they had some hope that their assaults would be taken as a warning to stay away from the Yalu. Mao had no such thought. Hiding again in the hills, in the hope their numbers would not be detected, the Chinese prepared for a second and more ambitious offensive. Many more Chinese units crossed the Yalu.

U.S. intelligence, General Willoughby in particular, to some extent deceived by Chinese disinformation, continued to belittle the Chinese presence. At a high-level military conference at Wonsan he scorned more realistic estimates of Chinese strength and intent and explained away the Cavalry 8th Regiment massacre as the result of a lack of sufficient outposts. On the very eve of the major Chinese intervention the CIA forecast that it wouldn't happen.

As of November 15 MacArthur's Far East Command was conspicuously in error in its estimates of enemy capabilities. It said that the "Eighth Army is now properly deployed with reserves to contain any enemy attack." Such an attack "would probably hasten the enemy's destruction." It added that the "Eighth Army has adopted a conservative plan to make a general advance with the main effort in the center...This course of action is designed to meet any course of action which might be exercised by the enemy." Evidently no one anticipated the calamity.[38]

With the acquiescence of Washington, on the bitterly cold morning of November 25 MacArthur ordered his troops forward to the Yalu in what he told correspondents was a "home by Christmas" offensive.[39]

It began well—what was called "a giant pincer" went according to plan, a communique announced. MacArthur saw the success he expected as "Mars's last gift to an aged warrior." South Korean officers said they would soon bathe their sabers in the Yalu.

The Air Force strikes preliminary to the offensive struck a headquarters structure and killed Mao's eldest son, Mao Anyang, who had served with distinction in the Soviet army.

On November 25th the Chinese, joined by North Koreans, began their second offensive. In reinforced strength infantry wielding small arms and grenades counterattacked in both east and west from mountains that MacArthur had described as too precipitate to shelter troops. Again the ROK divisions were prime targets and badly battered but American divisions and the newly arrived Turkish brigade, part of it caught sleeping by campfires, were also successfully engaged. The ROK II Corps, the connecting link between the Eighth Army in the west and the X Corps in the east, was cut to pieces and collapsed, exposing the right flank of the U.S. 2nd Division and the 1st Cavalry. Two battalions penetrated the Eighth Army rear.

Lack of air cover did prove costly to the Chinese. Lieutenant Frank H. Armstrong, an aerial observer for 1st Cavalry, related an instance when the fog lifted and exposed Chinese troops moving in force along a dirt road. "They relied on an air warning system where teams of Chinese posted on hill tops sounded a whistle warning when they spotted aircraft... However on this day the air warning system did not work... We flew in at a low level. There seemed to be a Chinese soldier in every little ditch or gully. They had not dug their holes but were lying prone and motionless...exceptionally vulnerable to ground-skimming shrapnel..."[40]

Nevertheless, in the view of British historian Max Hastings, "Most of the Eighth Army fell apart as a fighting force in a fashion resembling the collapse of the French in 1940, the British in Singapore in 1942..."   But he reported the praiseworthy strong resistance of the U.S. Marines in the northeast.[41]

On the morning of November 29 the Eighth Army, though about equal in numbers to its enemy, began a general, disorderly retreat along roads that soon were gauntlets, fired on from the hillsides, clogged with smashed vehicles, tanks and bodies. In a few days it suffered some 11,000 casualties.

On the orders of General Walker, the retreating Eighth Army carried out a scorched earth policy upon abandoning Pyongyang and moving south. The troops burned houses, killed livestock, and destroyed rice supplies, as a result of which much of the civilian population had no choice but to flee south. General Ridgway rescinded the scorched earth order on January 4.

According to Callum MacDonald, discipline worsened in retreat. "There was an outbreak of disorder in Seoul which was quashed only by the imposition of a curfew and firm action by the military police. It took the form of looting, rape and assaults on civilians. The 'gooks' were resented and blamed for the rout beyond the Chongchon."[42]

The myth created by MacArthur's communiques, the apologetics in the Encyclopedia Britannica and some of the histories is that the force that struck at the US/UN forces and inflicted a humiliating defeat on them was entirely Chinese. In fact elements from a growing North Korean army of scores of thousands (estimated at 200,000 early in 1951) in the east engaged and pursued retreating forces through December. Russell Spurr observed in his book *Enter the Dragon*, which generally underplayed the North Korean role, that "The North Koreans had in fact astonished the Chinese by the speed at which they had reconstituted their shattered forces. Three North Korean corps reinforced the eastern flank for the coming offensive."[43] As early as October 25 American pilots saw streams of North Korean tanks moving south in the area of the refugee capital of Kanggye.

On December 18 a British military attaché observed that "for several weeks now Eighth Army have only contacted North Korean forces along their front." Throughout these weeks northern guerrillas were guiding the Chinese through unfamiliar terrain and severing supply routes. Indeed they were compelling the retreating Eighth Army to fight through them. Guerrilla conscious, the Chinese had brought two guerrilla detachments in North Korean uniforms with them.

These are the notes on the Chinese at war set down by Reginald Thompson, *London Telegraph*: "Usually at night, to wild bugle calls and using flares as signals, the attacks swooped upon command posts, eluding, killing, and capturing the weary men in the foxholes. At once withdrawal began, and the enemy, moving swiftly on the flanks of bewildered units, cut off and enfiltrated escaping troops. Each day the rearguard columns licked their wounds and awaited the hideous night... Unaccustomed to march, and clinging to their vehicles and equipment, they offered themselves as a sacrifice to the enemy. They were not short of courage, but of all the arts of war."[44]

And this is how the Communist offensive was remembered in his memoirs by General Paik Sun Yup, a graduate of the Manchukuo Military Institution and later an officer in Japan's Kwantung Army. He was then in command of the Republic of Korea 1st Division:

"On November 25 as the ROK 1st Division was fighting a seesaw battle with Chinese units south of Taechon… the enemy surrounded the ROK 7th Division at Tokjon, and the ROK 8th Division at Yongwon. Chinese forces then proceeded to destroy the two divisions. A mere one day into the Christmas offensive, the ROK 7th and 8th divisions had disintegrated… The main body of the U.S. 2d Division, complete with its tanks, artillery, and vehicles, entered a valley about nine miles long. The entire stretch of road was bordered closely by mountains on both sides. As the 2d neared Yangpyon, Chinese Army forces lying in ambush in the hills suddenly opened volley fire and pressed home a merciless attack from both flanks. The narrow road was so clogged with vehicles that those which survived the initial barrages were unable to pull free from the wreckage around them… In the brief span of half a morning the 2d Division lost three thousand killed and wounded…Its defeat was the worst recorded for the U.S. Army during the Korean War."

Paik wrote that the "God of Death himself hovered with heavy, beating wings over that road…"[45]

The fleeing GIs sang a song with many verses:

> *Hear the pitter patter of tiny feet*
> *Its old Two Div in full retreat*
> *I'm movin' on….back to Inchon*
> *I'm buggin' out fast*
> *Afore they get my ass*
> *Yes, I'm moving' on…I'm movin' on fast*
> *To where I shacked up last*
> *And I'm movin' on…*[46]

Andrew Barr, a lieutenant in a heavy mortar company, fought as long as he could when his unit was surrounded and largely wiped out by Chinese but then was in the retreat which he remembered this way: "We got overrun every night. Finally the battalion commander leapfrogged everybody back, unit by unit, to where my old mortar company's jeeps were… We climbed into those jeeps and drove south all night. We kept driving for seven straight days, and in those seven days I never went to bed, never slept except for little catnaps, never had a warm meal. The roads were crowded like a crowded highway in a big city. You'd go four or five miles an hour, in a long convoy, starting and stopping. People were falling asleep at the wheel and it would stop the entire convoy. I don't remember being afraid… There was an overwhelming craving for sleep."[47]

The Home by Christmas offensive was soon described as a reconnaissance in force which had succeeded in provoking the enemy to make a premature assault. As MacArthur's stunned command retreated, Willoughby's minimal estimates of enemy strength gave way to "hordes," prompting one war correspondent to inquire solemnly, "Sir, how many battalions are there to a horde, or is it vice versa." A more elaborate joke was widely circulated: "Three swarms equal one horde, two hordes equal a human wave, two waves equal a human tide, after which comes the bottomless oceans of Chinese manpower."

The Chinese recaptured Pyongyang on December 9 and in a few days were south of the 38th parallel. The second offensive ended on December 24 by which time, according to Chinese count, the Eighth Army and ROK divisions had suffered 36,000 casualties.

Peng Dehuai, summing up the second offensive, said the Eighth Army and ROK forces were tired and failed to dig themselves in. "Then our main force swept into the enemy ranks with the strength of an avalanche and engaged the enemy at close quarters with grenades and bayonets. The superior firepower of the enemy became useless. Overturned and damaged enemy vehicles were strewn on the road, blocking the retreating enemy troops."[48]

But Peng also observed that the Chinese volunteers were badly in need of rest. He recommended that a further offensive be postponed and was supported in this by Nie Rongzhen in Beijing. But Mao pressed for an another immediate advance and a third offensive began as early as December 31 The results apparently justified his insistence. In nine days of battles the Eighth Army was driven south of the 37th parallel and Seoul was retaken, but costs were heavier. This was the last successful Chinese offensive.

Indicating some ROK army shortage, in January the Eighth Army was directed to screen the flood of refugees and pull out males aged 15 to 40 for impressment in the ROK forces. Some 3,000 were thus impressed in a brief period.[49]

Mao was initially confident that the military strategy that had won victory in the Chinese struggle for power was applicable to the Korean war. Throughout that struggle Mao had had to conceive of ways in which inferior forces could take on and eventually defeat superior forces. "Our strategy," he had declared in *On the Protracted War* (1938), "should be to employ our main forces in mobile warfare over an extended, shifting, and indefinite front, a strategy depending for success on a high degree of mobility in difficult terrain, swift concentration and dispersal. It will be a large-scale war of movement..."[50]

Particularly relevant was Mao's doctrine of "luring the enemy in deep" which motivated Kim Il Sung's forces as they regrouped in the northern fastnesses and which seemed verified by MacArthur's plunge toward the Yalu and the disaster inflicted on it. "We have always advocated the policy of 'luring the enemy in deep,' precisely because it is the most effective military policy for a weak army strategically on the defensive to employ against a strong army," Mao said in his 1938 essay.

This appraisal was at once a summary of much of the Communist experience in the struggle for power and an inheritance from historic military thinking. This is an excerpt from Sun Zi's *The Art of War* which Mao knew very well: "War is a game of deception. Therefore feign incapability when in fact capable; feign inactivity when ready to strike; appear to be far away when actually nearby, and vice versa. When the enemy is greedy for gains, hand out a bait to lure him; when he is in disorder, attack and overwhelm him... If his forces are rested, wear them down. If he is united, divide him. Attack where he is least prepared..."[51]

Mao's rephrasings: "Make a noise in the east but strike in the west; Avoid the solid to attack the hollow."

The Chinese press referred to the "luring the enemy" statement several times in the first months of the 1950 war and the entire *Protracted War* essay was reprinted in 1951. Commentaries hardly questioned its continued relevancy. Early in the Korean war both the Korean People's Army and the Chinese volunteers indeed put to good use the fluid tactics developed in China. Yet even in victorious battles superior American weaponry raised questions about the validity of the concepts. Successfully enveloping Chinese units often found wiping out well armed trapped enemies difficult or impossible, and as Peng Dehuai stressed, routing the enemy was not enough, destruction of units was far more important. As the U.S. and allied forces retreated south, the negative factors grew in influence. Mobility was reduced in the narrower waist of the peninsula and superior American air power and artillery became far more effective. The Americans moved on wheels, the Chinese on feet. Logistics became a heavy burden as supplies had to be borne, often on backs, over lengthening tortuous routes.

Peng Dehuai concluded in his first speeches to the Volunteers Command that the mobile war strategy employed in the civil war could not be expected to work in Korea. In an address to division-level commanders and political commissars on October 14, Peng said that "Because of the enemy's situation and the topographical conditions of Korea, the mobile warfare of marching and retreating in big strides that we adopted in the civil war is not necessarily suited to the battlefield in Korea. Owing to the narrowness of Korea and some of the enemy's advantages, we must combine mobile warfare with positional warfare."[52]

Together with Mao he did combine mobile and positional warfare and he had reason to be generally satisfied with the results of the first three offensives. But in the winter of 1951, as the Eighth Army under General Matthew Ridgway became a more formidable opponent and as Chinese limitations became apparent, he was drawn by battlefield results to the conclusion that Mao's expectation of expelling the Americans from the peninsula could not be realized. In their fourth campaign, which began on January 27th and ended April 21st, the Chinese found themselves mainly on the defensive, engaged by a strongly reinforced and ably commanded Eighth Army.

China and the Undoing of MacArthur

Show me a hero and I will write you a tragedy.

—F. SCOTT FITZGERALD

MacArthur paid little attention to restraining instructions. Early in the war he ordered bombing of targets north of the 38th parallel, disobeying instructions not to do so. He did not wait for United Nations permission to send his troops north across the 38th parallel. He ridiculed and then ignored peace-minded proposals to set up a buffer zone along the Yalu and he violated orders to send only South Korean units to the Yalu. "God's right hand man," as Truman once called him, offered a variety of excuses for disobedience, when he bothered; his favorite was tactical necessities.

At the Yalu in October-November 1950 his arbitrary initiatives and provocations made evident that his goal was nothing less than war with China.

MacArthur visited China for the first and only time as a young officer accompanying his father, General Arthur MacArthur, on an inspection tour. But as he said in his memoirs, China was often on his mind. His first years in Tokyo as Supreme Commander of the Allied Powers paralleled the civil war in China, which he observed with increasing perturbation. According to an aide, "Chagrin turned to near pathological rage as he helplessly watched Chiang Kai-shek's regime being systematically overrun." He blamed Washington's Communist-coddling policies.

As late as February 1948, I was informed authoritatively, he told the Indian ambassador and other astonished diplomats at lunch that American bombers and quantities of small arms could turn the tide of battle. But "unfortunately," he cabled the House Committee on Foreign Affairs to say that the Chinese problem "has become somewhat clouded by demands for internal reform."

In Korea MacArthur saw an opportunity to remedy what he saw as the American blunder that allowed the Communists to come to power in China, an opportunity also to add even more luster to his military career by conquest of the great power of the Asian mainland. He explained his China thinking at length in a 90-minute interview with John Osborne, published in the September 25, 1950, issue of *Life*. Generalissimo Chiang's armies should be openly and fully built up, anticipating their return to the mainland. "No port, no capital, no industrial center now held by the Communist enemy, or now tempting him, would be beyond the reach of our power." Preparations for the reconquest of the Asian continent should begin now, to be undertaken when opportune.

MacArthur's understanding of the Chinese was not commensurate with his hostility. Thinking that craven policies had led to the Communist success and persuaded that squadrons of bombers and freighters full of small arms could have stopped them, he saw no need to examine seriously the military means by which they had won. His military thinking over the years helps to explain that neglect.

A clue is his citations of past battles and wars. In urging the Inchon assault, he recalled General James Wolfe's daring scaling of the Quebec heights to defeat Montcalm in 1759. He knew well Anthony Wayne's bayonet charge at Stony Point in the revolutionary war. He often quoted Napoleon and Wellington in speeches and had a statement by the Roman general Titus Livius framed on his office wall. But he was never known to have commented on the great 55-day battle of Huai Hai in 1948-1949, one aspect of which was the crushing of the last of the Kuomintang's 39 American equipped divisions, a battle in which some of the able Korean generals confronting him had officer experience. He is never known to have been curious about the Chinese military experience of Evans F. Carlson and Joseph "Vinegar Joe" Stilwell.[53] Two of his generals, Walker and Ridgway, had tours of duty in China. MacArthur is not known to have questioned them.

In August, Beijing ordered stepped-up studies of MacArthur's combat history and previous amphibious operations, but reverse studies were not initiated. If MacArthur had studied the climactic battle of Huai Hai and the likes of Carlson and Stilwell, he might have been drawn to examine the extensive military writings of Mao Zedong, and it was Mao who sat across from him at the Korean chess game. MacArthur's ignorance was shared by the entire American military establishment. Until 1954 when Mao's collected works were published in London and New York, Mao's military writings took an effort to locate. Neither the Library of Congress nor U.S. military libraries had them. A costly instance of racism in high places that led to mistakes and casualties in Vietnam as well as Korea.

Contributing to MacArthur's erroneous views and ignorance was his practice of surrounding himself with yes-men—the so-called Bataan Crowd, reverential mediocraties and sychophants who could never speak differing opinions to him. General Willoughby's intelligence invariably provided analysis confirming MacArthur's views and wishes. MacArthur did not wish the Chinese to intervene and Willoughby concluded that they wouldn't in the face of mounting evidence to the contrary.

MacArthur was oblivious to much of what was happening in the mountains south of the Yalu that fall. He minimized the Chinese presence, on November 17th informing the U.S. ambassador to Seoul that only about 30,000 Chinese were in Korea when the number was at least several times that. He had only hazy notions of what the North Koreans were up to after Inchon and announced that the Korean People's Army had been destroyed when in fact a number of its reconstituted divisions were about to take the field against him. In both south and north his command was obliged to wage a combination of positional and guerrilla warfare, but his communiqués and reports hardly ever got close to saying so.

MacArthur made little of the first clashes with the Chinese in late October 1950—as if, I.F. Stone observed, he was fearful that the Chinese would pull back and deny him an expanded war. But early in November he turned to maximizing the Chinese presence. On the 6th, at a time when the Chinese forces were still waiting quietly in the hills, he grandiloquently accused China of committing "one of the most offensive acts of international lawlessness of historic record." Then on the 7th he ordered the virtual destruction of the city of Sinuiju, on the Yalu, the first of the great blows by which American air power turned Korea into rubble and craters. Seventy-nine B-29s and 300 fighter planes dropped 630 tons of bombs, including 85,000 napalm bombs.

Certainly knowing that some thousands of Chinese were in the hills, MacArthur ordered American as well as South Korean units to drive on the Yalu on November 25—probably not by coincidence the date on which a Chinese Communist delegation would arrive at the United Nations for discussions that might lead to peace. MacArthur both promised victory—a Tokyo communiqué he wrote announced a "massive compression envelopment in North Korea" that "should for all practical purposes end the war—and contemplated the possibility of a failure which would get him the war on China he thirsted for. He told a diplomatic aide in Tokyo, William Sebald, that if the advance failed, he "saw no alternative to bombing key points in Manchuria."

The general retreat that followed the Communist counterattack served MacArthur's purposes even as it called his generalship into question. The image of Chinese "hordes" and "human waves" driving on outnumbered Americans (actually the opposing forces were about equal in numbers) in itself could make a case for taking the war to Manchuria and all of China.

But the possibility of preparing for an expanded war by evacuating the Eighth Army and X Corps from Korea soon commanded serious attention. The loud rhetoric and hullabaloo of the following months added up to a complicated dialectic—evacuation versus a strengthened military effort on the peninsula.

For some evacuation just meant getting out of the war. A poll early in 1951 revealed that some 66 percent of the people favored withdrawing and ending the war. But to others, notably MacArthur himself, evacuation was the essential precondition for extension of the war to China. Not evacuated, the American forces on the peninsula might well be trapped. Bombing of the "privileged sanctuary" of Manchuria in all likelihood would bring on Soviet as well as Chinese counterblows, including perhaps some aimed at the American "privileged sanctuary" of Japan. Soviet air and submarine activity might practically sever Japan-Korea communication, isolating and dooming UN troops on the peninsula.

The link between evacuation and a wider war was assessed in the capitals of the major allies as well as in Washington, and doubtless in Beijing and Moscow also. MacArthur was not alone in finding attacks on China attractive. The Joint Chiefs several times agreed conditionally on China attack scenarios. Truman, who usually sided with MacArthur, was tempted, though Secretary of State Dean Acheson, saw adverse possibilities.

The debate was ongoing and heated. Those for expanded war and rollback seemed close to dominance. But two related considerations were cautioning—the danger of a great war with China that would gravely weaken defense of Europe and the strong opposition of Britain and other allies to an extended war, voiced privately but forthrightly.

Shaken by the unforeseen effectiveness of the Communist assault that quickly forced ignominious retreat and abandonment or burning of mountains of supplies, MacArthur lashed out at critics and defended his actions, without exception. He insisted that the retreat had been planned and he lauded it as "one of the most successful strategic retreats in history, comparable with and markedly similar to Wellington's great Peninsula Withdrawal." Correspondents whose dispatches irked him belonged to "the disaster school of war reporting." Acheson concluded that he seemed to be in "a blue funk" and close to panic.

The editors of the *Reader's Digest* in Pleasantville had reason to panic. The subject of the lead article in the January 1951 issue, being printed, was the victory in Korea titled "The Right Man in the Right Place." A third of the 11 million copy run had been printed and had to be very carefully destroyed.[54]

But MacArthur quickly got to his remedy—extension of the war to China. He sought immediate permission to bomb a road junction on the Manchurian side of the Yalu as well as a supply depot close to the Soviet border. He warned again and again that the forces under his command faced destruction. He threatened to resign.

The immediate effect of the war in Korea was to mute the rhetoric of Senator Joseph McCarthy and others engaged in the anti-Communist purge during the Truman and Eisenhower administrations. Truman and the Democrats after all were taking on the Communists. But McCarthy soon resumed his tirade. He alleged that Dean Acheson—to him the "Great Red Dean"—had invited the Communists to attack in Korea. On another occasion he rose before the Senate to charge that Acheson was saying "let's be calm, let's do nothing" even as Americans were being killed by a half a million Communists. On still another occasion he wondered why Communists were being fought in Little Korea while Giant China was given a free pass.

In the continuing inquisition the academic, government and professional victims were often questioned on their Korean opinions by the prosecuting committees and employers working with them. Some 25,000 academic personnel and civil servants lost their jobs during the war. The FBI set up a special office in the UN to check on the loyalty of its American employees; it got suspects fired. Julius and Ethel Rosenberg were arrested just after the start of the Korean war and executed a month before the armistice. The sentencing judge told them, "I believe your conduct has already caused the Communist aggression in Korea with the resultant casualties exceeding 50,000 Americans."

A noted academic victim was Dr. Gene Weltfish, called "Germ Warfare Gene" by the redbaiting publication *Counterattack*. An anthropologist at Columbia University, she was fired for expressing the view that the U.S. was indeed guilty of waging germ warfare in Korea.[55] Several Korean-Americans were deported to South Korea where they were imprisoned and perhaps executed.

After the "Home by Christmas" debacle, a chorus of voices agreed with MacArthur that anti-China actions were necessary. Senator Paul Douglas, a Truman Fair Dealer, argued that the atom bomb should be dropped "on any military target where it would be useful," and that "in this fight for survival, I am ready to take Franco, Tito and Chiang as allies." Bernard Baruch, on his park bench, was also among those who thought the bomb should be dropped. Former

President James Conant of Harvard, Julius Ochs Adler of *The New York Times* and others with prominent names organized the Committee on the Present Danger to articulate and press for such policies.[56]

Representative Albert Gore of Tennessee declared that "Korea has become a meat grinder of American manhood." He proposed that a radioactive strip be laid to divide the peninsula.[57]

Truman's comments suggested that he was close to hysteria. He said that the Chinese "are satellites of Russia and will be satellites as long as the present Peiping regime is in power… the only way to meet communism is to eliminate it." And, he went on, the Russians only understand the mailed fist, and that is what we are preparing for them. If the U.S. were to quit Korea, "all the Koreans left behind would be murdered. The Communists care nothing about human life." Contrary to MacArthur and some of the later establishment histories, for the most part only small-scale fighting took place as the UN forces fell back to south of Seoul. The writers of the communiqués and the spokesmen at the briefings for correspondents had to stretch patrol skirmishes into battles. The speed of the retreat often outstripped the Sino-Korean advance. Gabriel and Joyce Kolko observe in *The Limits of Power* that in the three weeks after November 25 total UN casualties were 13,000, a small fraction of losses in comparable retreats.[58]

On November 30, President Truman told a press conference that the use of nuclear bombs in Korea was under "active consideration." It actually was. Since about mid-November the Army's Plans and Operations Division and the Joint Strategic Survey Committee had been studying the use of nuclear weapons in Korea. General Stratemeyer had directed that the Strategic Air Command prepare "to dispatch without delay medium bomb groups to the Far East—the augmentation should include atomic capabilities." By the end of March atomic bomb loading pits at Kadena Airfield in Okinawa were operational.

Truman made a muddle of the press conference. Not only did he say twice that use of the atomic bomb was being actively considered but he forgot for the moment that only the president could authorize its use. Pressed by reporters, he said that "The military commander in the field will have charge of the use of weapons, as he always has." The thought that MacArthur would make the decision alarmed the British, French and other allies and no doubt some Americans. *The New York Times* headline the next day was "President Warns We Would use Atom Bomb in Korea." The headline of the *Times of India* was "No, No, No."

Truman's words reached Reginald Thompson and several other correspondents when, weary and nervy from the flight south, they blinked their way into the press room at Eighth Army headquarters: "It

was a large room with two stoves, coffee, typewriters and two tele-
phones, two majors, a corporal, and two or three agency men. They were
vague about it, but it seemed there was a real chance that America would
use the atom bomb against China. Truman had made some kind of a
statement, and the news was bringing horror to mankind… We three
slumped down as if we had been shot, each with our terrible thoughts,
as the monstrous possibility drowned our senses for awhile. I know my
thoughts were how to get home, to die with Mel and the babes. It seemed
vital that we should all be together when we died. Oddly, many others,
when we sorted it out afterwards, had similar thoughts."[59]

British Prime Minister Clement Attlee, with European and
Commonwealth backing, flew to Washington in early December to
express grave concern. He had Winston Churchill's support on the issue.
Churchill rose in the House of Commons to state once again that Europe
was the central theater and that a war with China made no sense.

Truman and Acheson talked tough to Attlee. They said they
would refuse to negotiate in Korea until the military situation
improved and they were utterly opposed to an effort to reach a general Asian settlement. On the use of the atomic bomb, Truman promised
to consult but declined to put that in writing. Attlee commented later
that "The Americans found it hard to realize that in the eyes of Asia
they had become almost a spearhead of imperialism."

At the same time MacArthur, who was telling the news agencies,
major publications and British as well as American correspondents of
his mordant views, supposedly was leashed—unauthorized military,
public and political statements were banned. Nevertheless he did
what he could to upset the accord with Attlee.

Harold E. Stassen, perennial candidate for the Republican presidential nomination, saw MacArthur in Tokyo as the talks with Attlee
were ending and issued a pro-evacuation statement. He said
MacArthur should be authorized to strike objects of military significance in Korea or China with atom bombs and that air bombardment
and blockade of China should be supplemented "by orders to General
Douglas MacArthur to withdraw land forces from Korea in as orderly
a manner as possible in favor of long-range attacks."

I. F. Stone grasped the situation perfectly, as he often did: "Was
MacArthur, under cover of alarmist statistics and predictions of offensives that failed to occur, withdrawing so rapidly because he hoped for
permission soon to…turn the war into war with China?"[60]

But the same day that Stassen spoke for MacArthur, the news out
of the Attlee-Truman conversations was that soberer views had prevailed. There would be no military evacuation of Korea. This implied
that MacArthur would not receive permission to bomb Manchuria.

On December 24, asked by the Joint Chiefs how he would respond to increased Chinese or Soviet intervention in Korea, MacArthur replied with a list "retardation targets" which would require 26 atom bombs. Four more bombs would be needed to drop on invasion forces and another four for demolishing concentrations of enemy air power, presumably in Manchuria.

In interviews published posthumously, MacArthur advanced a plan he called a "cinch" to win the war in ten days. He would have dropped 30 to 50 atom bombs across the neck of the peninsula, laid down a defensive belt of radioactive cobalt, brought in half a million Chinese Nationalist troops and launched Inchon-like amphibious operations. Cobalt has an active life of 60 to 120 years.

On December 29, MacArthur had much more to say. Responding to a directive from the Joint Chiefs of Staff, he restated now familiar propositions: "Should a policy determination be reached by our government...to recognize the state of war which has been forced upon us by the Chinese authorities and to take retaliatory measures within our capabilities we could: (1) Blockade the coast of China; (2) Destroy through naval gunfire and air bombardment China's industrial capacity to wage war; (3) Secure reinforcements from the Nationalist garrison on Formosa to strengthen our position in Korea...; (4) Release existing restrictions upon the Formosa garrison for diversionary action (possibly leading to counter-invasion) against vulnerable areas of the Chinese Mainland."

In January MacArthur's aides in Tokyo leaked to prominent correspondents that the retreat would continue to the Pusan beachhead and that eventual withdrawal of troops from Korea was a virtual certainty. The panicky Rhee regime carried out mass executions of foes and suspects, resulting in restrained British and American protests.

On January 1, *The New York Times* published a dispatch from Richard J. H. Johnston, noted for his years of closeness to command, that linked evacuation to a wider war. "Korea Exit Is Seen If New War Comes," the headline over it said. Johnston reported that officers were considering shifting some 100,000 South Korean troops to Cheju island, where a Rhee government-in-exile could be located. In fact, hundreds of tons of equipment, supplies, documents and so forth were shipped to the island.

The British press publicized the statements emanating from MacArthur's headquarters and voiced fears that the agreement reached by Attlee and Truman on continuing the ground fighting in Korea was being revised, that a Dunkirk was being planned. London, according to an assessment by Peter Lowe of the University of Manchester, thought that "the Americans might decide to get out of

Korea and concentrate on defeating China, possibly with the use of atomic weapons." Lowe found suspicious what he thought was the excessively "rapid retreat of UN forces in December 1950 and early January 1951."[61]

The British ambassador in Washington, Sir Oliver Franks, raised the evacuation issue and asked if an evacuation would be followed by bombing of Manchuria. On January 11 he was assured that the UN forces "would make every effort to establish a defense position on the peninsula."

A delegation of top Pentagon generals that included also the head of the CIA was ordered to Tokyo to talk to MacArthur and instruct him to end his retreat. General J. Lawton Collins, Army Chief of Staff, told a press conference at Eighth Army Headquarters on January 15 that the UN forces will "certainly stay and fight." The longest retreat in American military history indeed ended.

In a related move, Major General Emmett O'Donnell, an outspoken advocate of bombing China, was relieved of his post as commander of the Air Force's Bomber Command in the Far East. The atom bombing of China was only temporarily not an option. It remained a temptation and a threat until the truce.

General Walker was killed on December 23 when his jeep collided with a ROK truck on an icy highway. He was succeeded as commander of the Eighth Army by General Matthew B. Ridgway, an able officer, fervently anti-Communist but no unquestioning admirer of MacArthur.

As the Chinese and North Koreans again engaged in a third strong offensive (December 30-January 11, 1951), Ridgway found he couldn't rely on the Republic of Korea troops for much: "On New Year's Day I drove out north of Seoul and into a dismaying spectacle. ROK soldiers by truckloads were streaming south, without orders, without arms, without leaders, in full retreat... They had just one aim—to get as far away from the Chinese as possible. They had thrown away their rifles and pistols and had abandoned all artillery, mortars, machine guns, every crew-served weapon."[62]

As observed, the Communist offensive was again a success. It drove into the ROK divisions, forcing five of them to retreat in the eastern and central sectors. Eighth Army units had to fall back to south of the Han River to avoid envelopment. Both Seoul and Inchon were lost. The Sino-Korean forces demolished three ROK regiments and a number of battalions, devastated some American and British units and captured or destroyed substantial quantities of tanks and artillery. But their inferiority in weapons was telling. Frequently again they routed but could not decimate the enemy.

Though repeatedly, even angrily, prodded by Kim Il Sung to ride the "crest of victory" and continue the offensive, Peng Dehuai, painfully aware of the condition of the volunteers, slowed it until directed by Mao to press forward. The battles in two campaigns (December 30, 1950 through February 18, 1951) were fought in snow and bitter cold and the inadequately uniformed and fed volunteers suffered and were exhausted. Some units were at half strength. The very extent of the Chinese advance southward had created a critical logistics problem. The troops could not be properly supplied and reinforced because of the distances.[63]

And the Eighth Army, under its experienced new commander, ended its retreat and underwent strenuous strengthening and morale building in preparation for limited counteroffensives. Better food and warmer clothing, attention to stationary supplies and mail delivery, more MASH medical units, tightening of communications, insistence that troops get off the roads and into the high ground, emphasis on concentrated artillery and air power—there was little that Ridgway didn't think of and act on.[64] To subordinates Ridgway seemed to be everywhere. One said, "Oh, God, he came to every briefing, every morning."

Late in January Ridgway was shocked to be handed a plan, clearly MacArthur's, that envisaged continued retreat in the spring until the old Pusan enclave was reached—"the very lodgment area from which the Inchon victory had set us free," Ridgway noted. He scrawled "rejected" over it.

In March of 1951, as information accumulated about a Chinese military buildup in Manchuria and about an enlarged Soviet bomber presence in the area, MacArthur asked for immediate access to nuclear weapons. The Joint Chiefs thought a crisis necessitating resort to atomic bombs might indeed develop. Truman agreed to transfer control of nine bombs to the military, which placed them in Guam. But the key step of forwarding them to the atomic bomb loading pits at Kadena Air Field in Okinawa was not taken.

Ridgway, attentive to MacArthur's pronouncements, summed up what he called MacArthur's Grand Design this way: "When MacArthur spoke of victory, he did not mean merely victory in Korea. What he envisaged was no less than the global defeat of Communism, dealing Communism a blow from which it would never recover, and which would mark the historical turning back of the Red Tide." He wanted to take Chiang's troops to the mainland to "break the Communist hold." He believed that the "Chinese masses were ready to welcome Chiang back."[65]

MacArthur's repeated public extremisms, violations of silencing orders, brought about his recall and his replacement as Supreme Commander in Tokyo by Ridgway. His fate was sealed by two major provocations. Informed that a formal declaration of United Nations war aims was about to be publicized, MacArthur immediately acted to sabotage it by issuing his own declaration. He followed expressions of contempt for China's military and industrial power by brusquely calling on the Communist commander to discuss a truce with him, suggesting strongly that a negative response would result in war on China. "The enemy therefore must by now be painfully aware," he proclaimed, "that a decision of the United Nations to depart from its tolerant effort to contain the war to the area of Korea through expansion of our military operations to his coastal areas and interior bases would doom Red China to the risk of military collapse."[66]

The final critical provocation was MacArthur's telegram replying to a letter from Joseph W. Martin, Jr., Republican House minority leader, which Martin read to the House on April 5. In it MacArthur called for "maximum counter force" in warring on China. "There is no substitute for victory." He downgraded the strategic importance of Europe and supported utilization of Chinese forces on Taiwan—Formosa to him.

Supportive of MacArthur though he generally was, Truman could not take quietly the general's open challenge to established policies and his bold address to the opposition party in apparent quest of its presidential nomination. He read up on how Lincoln dealt with General George B. McClellan, then made sure of the solid support of both the Pentagon and the State Department and dismissed MacArthur on April 11, bringing down upon himself a deluge of Republican denunciations and abuse, including demands for his impeachment. Truman was screamed at even when he opened the baseball season by throwing out the first ball. But most of the major newspapers and a number of moderate Republicans supported the recall and the Congressional hearings on it had a moderating influence.

Nehru, pressing for peace, commented critically: "Certainly no field commander is going to lay down the policies of the government of India. Political policies are laid down by governments."

The Pentagon supported the recall of MacArthur in part because it wanted a commander in Tokyo who followed instructions and would not be tempted to exceed them to realize a private agenda. The generals understood that the prospect of resorting to nuclear weapons made command reliability imperative.

Blunt rhetorical exchanges tended to conceal the reality that many of those now critical of MacArthur in the State Department,

Pentagon, the White House and Congress were long in collusion with him. They were comfortable with wars on the periphery of China, including the attempted conquest of Korea and defense of French Indo-China and Taiwan. Differences came only when ignominious defeat at the Yalu made a serious issue of war with all of China.

I. F. Stone summarized in a few words the record of MacArthur-Truman collaboration on Korea: "Caution in September might have brought peace. Truman preferred to push ahead across the Parallel. Caution in November might have brought peace. Truman preferred to push ahead into the Yalu border regions. Whenever peace came within talking range a common bond seemed to appear between Truman and Acheson on the one hand and MacArthur and Dulles on the other."[67]

MacArthur was excessively impatient, glory hungry and driven by defeat. He talked of the flag, of duty and honor, often of peace, but vanity and arrogance possessed him, and ignorance of Asian realities undid him.

This is the opinion of General Omar Bradley: "the only possible means left to MacArthur to regain his lost pride... was now to inflict an overwhelming defeat on those Red Chinese generals who had made a fool of him. In order to do this, he was perfectly willing to propel us into an all-out war with Red China and possibly the Soviet Union..."[68]

The Battle for Frozen Chosin

Life photographer David Douglas Duncan saw a marine patiently hacking a breakfast of beans from a frozen tin. The beans were imbedded in ice crystals and more crystals had formed on the man's beard. Thinking of the Christmas issue, Duncan asked, "If I were God and could give you anything you wanted, what would you ask for? The marine hacked away at the beans. "Gimme tomorow," he said.

> *Bless'm all, bless'm all*
> *The Commies, the UN and all*
> *Those slant-eyed Chink soldiers*
> *Struck Hagaru-ri*
> *And now know the meaning of USMC*
> *But we're saying goodby to them all*
> *As home thru the mountains we crawl...*

> —MARINE REWRITE OF WORLD WAR II SONG

X Corps, the separate command in the Northeast, was forced to retreat in the face of assault by nine Chinese divisions and a powerful guerrilla force. But, in contrast to the performance of the Eighth Army, the 1st Marine Division in particular maintained discipline and fought hard as it withdrew from the Chosin Reservoir area, its superior weapons inflicting heavy casualties on the Chinese. In December the entire X Corps was evacuated in good order from Hungnam and taken to South Korea.

The decisive fighting took place in the area of the Chosin Reservoir. It tested two superior, though very different forces. The nine divisions of China's IX Army included veterans of the Japanese war and the civil war and was tactically experienced and ably commanded. But it also included unreliable Chinese Nationalist troops who had surrendered. It was largely equipped with Japanese weapons though they also had American weapons captured in China. It lacked heavy weapons and an air force.

And it had what proved to be an indispensable local ally—guerrillas. The forested swath across northern Korea had been home to guerrillas in the decades of Japanese rule and many a bloody clash and skirmish had kept alive the cause of independence. Remnants of the broken Korean People's Army divisions had retreated purposefully to the northeast and joined experienced guerrillas which quickly demonstrated that captured cities and towns did not bring the surrounding countryside with them.

The 1st Marine Division was the best in the U.S. army and it and units of the 7th Infantry Division were given the task of seizing the mountains and waters of the Chosin area. The marines had a proud heritage of victories at Chateau Thierry, Guadalcanal, Iwo Jima and most recently, Seoul. They were experienced soldiers ready to step forward to victory or death. The command performance was superior. From platoons on up orders made sense and were quickly obeyed.

The two forces had a common enemy: cold that dropped to thirty degrees below. Sherman Pratt described it to Rudy Tomedi: "The cold made us move slow. It made us think slow. Wounded men, men who otherwise might have survived, died because they couldn't be kept warm. Our vehicles wouldn't start. Batteries gave out. The grease on our rifles turned to glue and they wouldn't fire. Our rations would freeze solid. Men would carry cans of food around inside their clothes, under their armpits, trying to thaw them a little so they could be eaten."[69]

And this is a comment on the cold by the Chinese 27th Army: "When the fighters bivouacked in snow-covered ground during combat, their feet, socks and hands were frozen together in one ice-ball; they could not unscrew the caps on the hand grenades; the fuses would not ignite; the hands were not supple; the mortar tubes shrank on account of the cold; 70 percent of the shells failed to detonate; skin from the hands stuck on the shells and mortar tubes."[70]

Repeated hundreds of times in both newspaper accounts and official statements was a comforting explanation for American retreats. The Chinese struck with a "human wave," an overwhelming force that even the good guys could not be expected to withstand. MacArthur's headquarters was not above this explanation of adversity and declared that the 1st Marine Division at Chosin was another victim.

Military statistics defy precise assessment but the reality appears to be that the Chinese force that took on X Corps was outnumbered by it. The three Chinese armies had a total of nine divisions, each of which by Marine intelligence had a strength of about 7,500. That would be a total of 67,500. X Corps numbered over 80,000 early on and 105,000 when it was evacuated in December. But the figure of 105,000 includes ROK units and some others not principally or effectively involved. The Chinese had to face in battle the experienced and well equipped 25,000-strong 1st Marine Division and the 18,000-strong 7th Infantry.

The Chinese attack tactic was remote from human waves. It tried to make sure it had a local superiority when it struck, which it began by sending a succession of small units against a selected point. The first such units might well be wiped out but others kept coming until a breakthrough was achieved. Then a large Chinese force would plunge through the break, its mission to disorganize and dispirit the enemy. Meanwhile another force would make its way to the rear of the enemy, to be in a position to take on a retreat.

Such tactics worked well in the Chinese civil war and in the first battles with ROK divisions allied with the Eighth army, but against the marines in the Northeast the results were often frustrating. The marines constructed strongly fortified outposts in the hilly forested Chosin area and defended them fiercely with a good deal of success. In a five day battle the Chinese did wipe out a regimental combat team consisting of 7th Division units but had less success against the marines.

However the guerrillas were a formidable, elusive presence. Commanded by Kim Chaek, Kim Il Sung's top associate, an estimated 40,000 guerrillas served the Chinese forces as guides and scouts, disrupted rail and road traffic, cut telephone lines, targeted supply dumps, kept close track of UN troop movements, and attacked patrols and rear guards. Their practice was to attack in the small hours and break off engagements at first light.

The guerrilla war was a sequence of brutalities. The guerrillas rarely took prisoners. They killed enemy wounded, killed soldiers in their sleeping bags and in one instance seized a military hospital and killed the patients. The Americans and special ROK anti-guerrilla battalions responded in what had long been the usual way—rounding up and killing guerrillas and suspects, and torching, often by napalm, the villages they came from.

American intelligence reported respectfully on the daily list of vexing incidents. It observed that the guerrillas were skilled in flanking and envelopment and struck frequently at the retreating UN forces. They credited Kim Chaek "with a shrewd ability as an organizer and tactician."[71] Kim died of a heart seizure in February 1952 and was long missed.

Several American officers, including a major who had served in China, urged that captured guerrillas not be executed, arguing that killings would only result in the enmity of the population. They weren't heeded. The common practice, General John B. Coulter observed, was to just turn over captives to the South Koreans, who "take care of them."

The hard pressed marines eventually had no choice but to abandon Chosin and retreat, but they did so in good order, often victorious in local engagements, making good use of air power and artillery and invariably inflicting heavy casualties. In retreating along the main road south to Hamhung, they seized control of the flanking hills to assure the main force safe passage. This is what the U.S. 2nd Division in the west had failed to do with disastrous results.

Excerpts from Shelby Stanton's *America's Tenth Legion* get to the realities:[72]

> "As the Marines started their attack, they were hit by heavy fire from Chinese bunkers hidden in the mountains. These bunkers consisted of logs wired together in double thickness, timbered ceilings, and rock and soil protection several feet deep. They seemed impervious to most artillery fire and air strikes, and could only be silenced by direct rocket hits... enemy machine guns and mortars hidden among the high rocks flared into action whenever the Marines tried to move forward. The Marine attack was stopped at 2:30 p.m."

> "...the onrushing ranks of Chinese were torn apart by Marine machine gunners, riflemen, and mortars, causing frightful carnage. Sections of the Marine front collapsed under this heavy pressure and Chinese infiltrators poured through gaps in the line. The Chinese who accomplished this break through, however, were silhouetted by burning

huts on the battleground and eliminated by Marine direct weapons fire."

"The Marines mustered their forces against Hill 1282 and conducted a frontal assault through a rain of grenades, forcing the Chinese off the military crest in close combat. Machine guns were emplaced and several Chinese counterattacks to regain this part of the hill were defeated. Fighting raged across Hill 1240 during the day, but the Chinese held on to the summit. The snowy peaks and rock slopes of North Ridge were covered with smashed equipment, wounded troops immobilized by the freezing conditions, and scores of bodies piled up around boulders and gullies."

General Edward (Ned) Almond, MacArthur's Chief of Staff and commander of the X Corps, had several nicknames. One was Ned the Anointed because he was MacArthur's pal, and one was Ned the Dread because of his brusque manner and arbitrary actions. Early during the so-called Home by Christmas offensive, he addressed members of a 7th Infantry battalion that soon was to be nearly wiped out. "The enemy who is delaying you for the moment is no more than remnants of the Chinese divisions fleeing north," he said. "We're still attacking and we're going all the way to the Yalu. Don't let a bunch of Chinese laundry men stop you."

He presented three medals, Silver Stars. When he left, the commanding officer, Lt. Col. Don C. Faith, tore his off his parka and threw it into the snow.[73]

Several days later, when the retreat had begun, Almond said "We're having a glut of Chinamen." He said he hoped to have a chance "to give these yellow bastards what they deserve."[74] By then Faith had been killed and his command decimated.

Not all in X Corps dismissed the Chinese as "yellow bastards." This is what Lt. Col. Roy E. Appleman observed about their performance: "Looking to the other side of the hill, as Wellington was wont to do, one cannot withhold some admiration, and humanitarian sympathy, for the Chinese peasants who made such great effort and sacrifice in trying to carry out their orders. One must say of them that Sung's IX Army Group did some spectacular things. It fought without air support, it had no tanks or artillery and almost no heavy mortars, it had poor and almost nonexistent ammunition after the first day or two of battle and no food or ammunition resupply once it crossed the Yalu River...and it possessed no adequate footgear for feet or mittens for hands of its soldiers in an arctic clime…

"In fact, the operations were a mismatch of a fine modern, mechanized body of soldiery against a peasant army of light infantry—but one that was highly mobile and expert at night fighting. The best weapons the Chinese possessed were the American Thompson sub-machine guns, 81-mm mortars, grenades, and rifles they had captured from Chiang Kai-shek's armies...Yet they did drive the X Corps completely out of northeast Korea and occupied and held henceforth that part of the country. No American troops ever returned there."[75]

The serious shortcoming in Appleman's summary was his failure to observe the important contribution of guerrillas to the U.S. abandonment of Chosin and retreat.

The marines lost 4,418 battle casualties, X Corps as a whole 11,500. The Chinese lost far more heavily. Both sides lost many to hypothermia and frostbite.

The Failed Chinese Offensives

The past campaigns have shown that our enveloping, outflanking and penetrating operations at both campaign and battle levels have encountered such great difficulties that we were prevented from achieving the goals of completely annihilating several U.S. divisions or even a whole U.S. division or regiment.

—MAO TO PENG DEHUAI, MAY 26, 1951

This was the state of the Chinese volunteers as summed up by Peng Dehuai following the third offensive in the winter of 1951: "By now the Chinese People's Volunteers had fought three major campigns… They had neither an air force nor sufficient antiaircraft guns to protect them from enemy bombers. Bombed by aircraft and shelled by long-range guns day and night, our troops could not move about in daytime. And they had not had a single day's good rest in three months."[76]

Peng agreed with misgivings to continued offense, which Mao as well as Kim Il Sung eagerly wanted, but kept pointing out supply shortages and the need of the troops for a period of rest and recuperation. He seemed to suggest that the Chinese were faring badly in a war of attrition. Mao remained optimistic, instructing Peng on February 20 to "win a quick war if you can, if you can't, win a slow one." As a result of Mao's persistent optimism, Zhou Enlai rejected a number of overtures by America's allies that might have led to an earlier truce. But the fourth offensive, which began on January 27th and slowed in mid-March, was a failure. Seoul again had to be evacuated on March 14 and the Sino-Korean forces were driven north of the 38th parallel.

Large Chinese forces were being assembled in Manchuria and transferred in stages to Korea. When the weather warmed in the spring, Mao pressed Peng to act. On the 22 of April some 250,000 Chinese troops plus three North Korean divisions launched a massive offensive, mainly directed at Seoul. The ROK 6th Division collapsed, the British Gloucester Battalion was virtually annihilated in the course of stubborn resistance—all but five officers and 41 Other Ranks were killed or captured.[77]

The Communists gained some territory but were halted after six days. They incurred enormous casualties and were compelled to call off a planned assault on Seoul. A stream of intelligence reports persuaded the Chinese that the U.S. was preparing another amphibious landing to the north and Peng worried that the losses suffered by the volunteers would invite the Americans to proceed with it.

On May 10, a force of 21 Chinese and nine North Korean divisions advanced again, this time in the east. Once again an envelopment succeeded and they nearly destroyed the two-division ROK III Corps. This is part of the account of General Paik Sun Yup, then in command of the adjacent ROK I Corps: "Blowing flutes and pounding gongs, Chinese units crossed the upper course of the Soyang River southwest of Inje on the morning of May 16 1951, and hurtled like a battering ram into Namjon, a hamlet that marked the boundary between the ROK 7th and 9th divisions and between the U.S. X corps and ROK III Corps. The Chinese broke through Brigadier General Kim Hyong Il's 7th Division at a stroke and pushed southeast during the night to occupy Omachi Pass."[78]

ROK III disintegrated without a fight. Personnel discarded both crew-served and personal weapons. Officers stripped off rank insignia. All fled south and into the hills, where some died of exposure to the cold and lack of food.

But the follow-up was very different from those resulting from some earlier breakthroughs. The Eighth Army and ROK I Corps were stronger, in well chosen positions and well commanded, and benefited from Chinese tactical errors. They turned back the offensive, launched a powerful counterattack and again inflicted huge casualties. The routes the Chinese had to take were brought under prepared artillery barrages, their sequence of bayonet charges cut down. Air support wiped out groups of attackers with napalm. Large Chinese units surrendered. The fighting subsided on May 21st. Peng Dehuai reported that the casualties in the spring campaign "were the highest suffered by our forces in the War to Resist U.S. Aggression and Aid Korea."

A Chinese sixth offensive was contemplated for the fall but thought of it was abandoned when intelligence reported the strength of the UN positions. The strategy of massive offensives was then abandoned.

The Chinese dug in defensively, were converted to stalemate and diplomatically worked for a truce. In June, Mao revealed the flexibility he had extolled in his 1938 essay, "On Protracted War," and put the change in a directive, ordering Chinese forces to go over to an "active defense." Similarly he ordered that the enemy be destroyed in small bites. To make plain what he meant by small bites he told commanders they should think of the well-known Hunan candy called *niupitang*, so big and sticky that it had to be cut up and eaten bit by bit. He agreed to the truce negotiations which began on July 10 at Kaesong. Peng, who as a Hunanese knew all about sticky candy, told a gathering of all high-ranking commanders that the Volunteers "must determinedly adhere to the policy of protracted war."[79]

An undramatic but central success was to effect the transition to defense. The Chinese countered the American superiority in killer weapons by digging in. Their mountain positions became a maze of tunnels and camouflaged entrenchments. By Chinese count, 776 miles of tunnels and 3,427 miles of trenches involving the shifting of 78 million cubic yards of rock and earth were dug along the front—which was called an "underground Great Wall." Underground storage granaries held several months' food supplies. A succession of linked defense lines extended 15 to 25 miles to the rear, in effect virtually negating the possibility of a major defeat.

The five Chinese armies deployed were supplied with heavier Soviet artillery and large quantities of supplies of all sorts. Chinese basic weaknesses in logistics, the air war and antiaircraft fire were gradually overcome to a considerable extent. A directive titled *The Protracted War in Korea* was distributed to all commands. The shift to protracted war permitted the rotation of troops and withdrawal of substantial numbers to Manchuria for extended training.

The discussions with Stalin early in the war resulted in some warranted Chinese pessimism regarding the extent of Soviet military aid that could be expected. But the amount received was substantial. Over the war years the Soviet Union provided the Chinese with enough arms for 64 infantry divisions and 22 air divisions. The first air divisions arrived early in the war, in October-December of 1950. Early deliveries were of the antiquated MIG-9s but Stalin later directed that the advanced MIG-15s be substituted. Up to 90 percent of Chinese munitions were Soviet.[80]

But the Soviet Union withheld its heaviest tanks, its newest howitzers and heaviest artillery. And too much of what it did send, World War II leftovers, was old and shoddy. China sent protesting missions to Moscow but marathon negotiating sessions brought only limited improvements. Chinese negotiators speculated that two Soviet fears— fear of getting into a war with U.S. and fear that China might get too strong—were affecting the military aid package.

The result of the Korean war experience on Chinese military thinking was to strengthen the argument for armament moderniza- tion. The ideology of people's war long dominated the rhetoric but weapons were in the back of the minds of the generals.

When in June and July of 1953, on the eve of the truce, the Chinese forces did undertake limited offensives, they had been strengthened by two armored divisions and a number of rocket-gun regiments, how- itzer battalions, more heavy artillery and some supporting aircraft. They put much of it to good use. In drives calculated to expose the frailty of the ROK divisions, which Syngman Rhee was threatening to send on an independent march north, they again targeted ROK divi- sions with the usual results. ROK General Paik Sun Yup wrote, "The Chinese pushed through ROK Army units all along the twenty-one miles of front. The tactical surprise, the darkness, and the overwhelm- ing enemy numbers worked the usual Chinese magic."[81]

By then Peng Dehuai had assembled a massive force with which he hoped to undertake a major offensive. To his dismay, the strong forces on both sides favoring a truce prevailed.[82]

The Bloody Years of Stalemate

The United States has broken the second rule of war.
That is, don't go fighting with your land army on the
mainland of Asia. Rule number one is don't march on
Moscow. I developed these two rules myself.

—Viscount Montgomery of Alamain

By mid-April 1951 the Joint Chiefs of Staff and the State Department were for the most part inclined to agree on a moderated war policy: the aim would be merely restoration of the prewar division of the penin- sula and the task of the U.S. forces therefore would be to inflict such heavy enemy casualties that the Communists would agree to that.

General Ridgway, MacArthur's successor, and Secretary of State Acheson favored a limited war effort and that was a powerful combi- nation. General James Van Fleet, who became commander of the Eighth Army, persisted in believing that victory was still possible, and had to be held in check by Ridgway in Tokyo. General Mark Clark, Ridgway's successor, was a MacArthur think-alike who pressed for substantial troop reinforcements and great quantities of equipment with which to launch a drive to the Yalu, but these were denied him by both the Truman and Eisenhower administrations. The start of truce talks in July 1951 presumed moderation.

This was the strategic situation as understood by 1st Cavalry Division officers at the time: "After the beginning of truce negotiations in July 1951, the mission of Allied ground forces was changed from initiating offensive operations to one of maintaining an active defense of the MLR (Main Line of Resistance) across Korea. The basic strategy became one of containment and prevention of any further enemy gains south of the 38th Parallel. It involved attempting to inflict maximum losses on the enemy while attempting to minimize those of the UN. Militarily, these restrictions removed the possibility of winning a decisive victory. For the next two years, fighting seesawed back and forth across the parallel."[83] For some the reality was put in a few words: "We die for a tie."

The seesawed battle for Heartbreak Ridge sealed in blood the lesson of stalemate. Heartbreak Ridge was the collective name given three north-south ridges that American troops sought to take from North Koreans in mid-September 1951.

These are excerpts from the account of the battle by the North Korean commander, General Choi Hyun:

> "Height 1,211 (Heartbreak Ridge), once clad with a thousand-years-old virgin forest, was now swathed in flames like an active volcano; boulders were pounded into fragments, the whole mountain was ankle-deep in rock dust." Tunneling was the only way to keep alive and fight back. "But there were no drills, sledge hammers or wheelbarrows...so the troops melted down the enemy's dud shells for sledge hammers and drills, and wheelbarrows were made from downed planes.... At first the artillery men built tunnels for their batteries, then the infantrymen followed suit. They built solid comfortable living quarters in the tunnels they carved out of the rock. When they had no more oil for their guns, they caught squirrels and badgers for oil; they repaired their rifles from enemy cartridge clips picked up on the battlefield. Ridgeway's plan of pushing the front line up to Wonsan at one stroke by taking Height 1,211 remained on his operational maps only."[84]

At the war museum in Pyongyang and in the English-language publications there the battle for Height 1,211 is celebrated as a glorious victory. Visitors to the museum gather round a skillfully executed model of the terrain and hear the narrative of the guide. The loss of the peaks to the American-French forces in October is not mentioned.

Ridgway wrote that fighting on Bloody Ridge and Heartbreak Ridge (August-October 1951) was the bloodiest and most strenuous, continuing: "The enemy worked with Oriental doggedness to fortify himself in the hills, so that he could pull out of his forward positions under air and artillery attack and find shelter on the reverse side of the hill, where it was difficult to zero in on him with air strikes and heavy howitzers. He might build tunnels as much as a thousand yards long to enable him to take quick shelter from bombardment, yet move forward to meet an attack on the ground. The forward ends of these tunnels were usually camouflaged with great skill and care, and it took sharp observation to spot them. Once spotted, however, they could be knocked out by direct hits..."[85]

So much artillery was used that it resulted in an ammunition shortage throughout the Eighth Army. The 15th Field Artillery Battalion set a record by firing 14,425 rounds in 24 hours.

The 2d Division historian thus described the fighting for Bloody and Heartbreak Ridges: "Sweating, heart-pounding, heavy-footed soldiers dragged their throbbing legs up those tortured, vertical hills. Those who succeeded in grasping their way close to the bunkers were greeted by the crump and shower of black smoke, dirt and sharp steel as grenades were tossed down on them. Dirty, unshaven, miserable, they backed down, tried again, circled, climbed, slid, suffered, ran, rolled, crouched and grabbed upward only to meet again the murderous fire, the blast of mortar and whine of bullets...."[86]

In mid-October an assault called Operation Touchdown by the 2d Division and its French battalion and some other units did seize Heartbreak Ridge but at a cost of so many casualties that it argued against further such offensives. The 2d Division and its associated units suffered over 3,700 casualties, the North Koreans certainly very many more. The territorial gains were insignificant. A sag in the UN line was straightened, a ridge was gained, another was just ahead.

A comprehensive military account of the ridge battles observed that "The North Koreans at Bloody and Heartbreak Ridges had fought with determination and courage throughout the battles until attrition and superior strength had forced them to yield their real estate."[87]

Ridgway was a zealous anti-Communist but his grasp of the realities made him a somewhat reluctant convert to stalemate. He wrote after the war that the Eighth Army could have pushed to the Yalu in 1951 if ordered to do so, but "the price for such a drive would have been far too high for what we would have gained, however. We would have lost heavily in dead and wounded—my estimate at the time was 100,000—fighting against stern resistance across the rugged northern face of the country, and our prize then many square miles of inhospitable real estate, much of it a-swarm with guerrillas for years to come. The enemy would have shortened his supply lines as we lengthened ours, and he would have faced us finally in great strength behind the broad Yalu and Tumen Rivers."[88]

Threats beyond the Korean battlefield, among them the perceived need of strong forces in Europe, strengthened the argument of those for whom there had to be a substitute for a Korean victory. The European factor importantly influenced Britain and other allies to acceptance of stalemate and support of a negotiated settlement.

Such battles for heights as Pork Chop Hill and Heartbreak Ridge brought heavy casualties but came to be pointless exceptions. Some in the American command and in Washington clamored for offensives in Korea and war with China, but to a considerable extent the two sides understood and accepted the overall stalemate. They both stated or plainly inferred this understanding in public declarations—the MacArthur hearings in the Senate for example—and on the battlefield they signalled it by what they did and did not do. To D. Clayton James, "the most remarkable phenomenon of the Korean conflict was inexplicable communication, neither oral nor written, between implacably hostile camps who signaled restraint to each other. Without a single word of formal agreement they set up an intricate system of limitations amid the fighting of 1950-1953..."[89]

The UN forces gained and held a generally stable 120-mile long line somewhat above the 38th parallel in the east, slightly below it in the far west. Just north of them the reinforced Chinese held strong entrenched positions. North Korean divisions, which MacArthur earlier had declared were virtually destroyed, held the east section of the cross-peninsula line, their strength a minimum of 140,000, the maximum probably closer to 200,000.

The two sides were evenly matched in numbers in July 1951 when truce talks began—one of a number of estimates is that each had about 550,000 men. They had offsetting strengths and weaknesses which were the ingredients of stalemate. Geography well served the UN forces in most respects. The narrowness of the mid-peninsula compressed targets for American air power and artillery and severely limited the Chinese ability to fight a war of maneuver. To survive Chinese troops were forced into an often deadly scramble for cover, as described by a talkative Chinese prisoner:[90]

> PRISONER: "…we had to march only at night."
> Interviewer: "What enemy weapons did the men in your unit talk about the most?"

PRISONER: "The artillery, and the next was the airplane. The artillery was frightening because of its rapidity. Most frightening of what airplanes did was strafing."

INTERVIEWER: "How much of the march was on foot? How much in vehicles of any sort?"

PRISONER: "We walked all the way down. We could never utilize any vehicle. Only the transportation unit could use the vehicles… "

INTERVIEWER: "While traveling on the road, what measures did your unit take to avoid being seen and being surprised by enemy airplanes?"

PRISONER: "When it snowed, we covered white cloths over us. If one had no white cloth, he wore the uniform inside out because the inside of the uniform was white. Even under the moonlight there was less possibility to be found by covering white cloths over us. When it wasn't snowing, we camouflaged with twigs and grass. For the equipment, artillery, machine guns etc., it was the same… "

INTERVIEWER: "How much time did you have between the warning and the time the airplane appeared?"

PRISONER: "Usually one or two minutes… The way of alert was just blowing the trumpet two or three times regardless of the kind of airplane."

The 5,000 miles of coastline invited naval interdiction and such amphibious assaults as those realized at Inchon and Wonsan. American naval ships—two task forces had a total of 150 warships, including some from the Allies—stood off the coast and provided near UN forces with gunfire that served as artillery. Their carrier aircraft helped to flatten cities, towns and villages. The numerous small offshore islands, over 3,000 of them off the west coast, were for the most part under U.S. control, havens for pilots in trouble and bases for small raids on the mainland.

In 1952, particularly after Eisenhower was elected president, China expected a major American offensive, taking seriously Eisenhower's militant campaign rhetoric (he pledged to lead a global crusade against Communism) and keeping in mind that he had commanded the Normandy assault. Of the various possibilities Mao was convinced that another Inchon-type amphibious landing on the west coast was most to be feared. China prepared for that, training its troops by relevant exercises and constructing new fortifications. Peng Dehuai sought to meet the threat by deploying an army to the immediate rear at both coasts.

The American offer that led to Little Switch of injured and ill prisoners in April 1959 and a number of similar conciliations reduced Chinese expectations of an enemy offensive. And some in the American command seemed to understand that the June-July 1953 Chinese drives were intended to discredit Syngman Rhee's boastful threat to ignore a truce and fight on with the ROK divisions. China verified its limited intent by returning gains south of the 38th parallel to UN control. It kept some 75 square miles, eliminating an eastern bulge in the line that included Heartbreak Ridge.

The northern Koreans usually were capable, well-commanded troops. Ridgway wrote of them, "We had never…imagined that the NKPA was a force so well-trained, so superbly disciplined, so battle-ready."[91] The ROK troops tended to break and run though individual units were effectively commanded and fought well. By the end of the first year the ROK had lost on the battlefield enough arms and supplies to equip 10 divisions.

Technology was an American asset. The UN forces had the most and superior weapons and transport, though the advantage diminished when quantities of Soviet arms strengthened the Communist armies. The Communists had to counter their adversary's superiority in weaponry by extensive digging. Also Chinese firepower was increased by additional artillery and supply was improved by the substitution of some 7,000 trucks for most of the human carriers. In April of 1953 the Communists fired 51,690 artillery rounds. The figure almost doubled to 99,340 rounds in May and in June, the climactic period of the anti-ROK offensive, the number jumped to 329,130 rounds.

Ridgway, arriving to take command in December of 1950, looked down on Korea from his plane and commented: "The sight of this terrain was of little comfort to a soldier commanding a mechanized army. The granite peaks rose to 6,000 feet, the ridges were knife-edged, the slopes steep, and the narrow valleys twisted and turned like snakes. The roads were trails, and the lower hills were covered with scrub oaks and stunted pines, fine cover for a single soldier who knew how to conceal himself. It was guerrilla country, an ideal battleground for the walking Chinese rifleman, but a miserable place for our road-bound troops who rode on wheels."[92]

The hills and mountains—about 80 percent of Korean topography—were the key battleground and in 1950 only the Communists exploited it. The U.S. forces tended to stick to the roads and by doing so invited defeat. Urged by officers to get off the roads, they acted as if a basic right was being infringed. But later commanded by Generals Ridgway and Van Fleet they were turned into much more effective high rise fighters. Similarly Allied units learned to construct all-around perimeter defenses to frustrate attacks in the rear by infiltrated forces.

This is a very early Chinese estimate of American army strengths and weaknesses published by the 66th Army Headquarters on November 20, 1950: "...the U.S. Army relies for its main power on the shock effect of coordinated armor and artillery...and their air-to-ground capability is exceptional. But their infantry is weak. Their men are afraid to die, and will neither press home a bold attack nor defend to the death... Their habit is to be active only in the daylight hours. They are very weak at attacking or approaching an enemy at night and at hand to hand combat...without the use of their mortars they become completely lost...dazed and completely demoralized... If their source of supply is cut, their fighting spirit suffers, and if you interdict their rear, they withdraw on their own."[93]

Mao himself made a somewhat similar eight-point assessment based on the first battle reports. Point One was: "The enemy's combat effectiveness is low. His assaults and counterattacks must always be accompanied by firepower support because he fears close combat..."[94]

General Ridgway initially found reason to reach some similar conclusions but his vigorous efforts to strengthen morale and combat performance soon invalidated the early Chinese derogations.

Late in 1952 the U.S. 2d Division, much battered by the Chinese, publicized an eight-point appraisal of their performance, stressing their good points this way: "The Chinese soldier is not a superman. He is well and courageously led at the small unit level and the results of actions at this level offer definite proof that he is thoroughly disciplined. His industry is shown by his thorough fortifications. His conduct of the defense is accomplished in spite of UN air superiority, UN liaison aircraft and inferior communications equipment. He is operating on a shoestring basis as is evidenced by the hodge-podge of equipment piled up on the battlefield after every encounter."[95]

The Chinese and North Korean soldiers had packets of millet or other food strapped to their bodies. Corespondents observed during the retreat of the UN forces in 1950 that the wayside was strewn with coca cola bottles, jam, candy and other goodies as well as C rations and cigarette packages. The UN fighter had a supply backup of eight or nine persons; the Communist fighter early on had one, a porter who brought food and ammunition over the mountains.

Tom Clawson, who served in Baker Company, 5th Cavalry Regiment, 1st Cavalry Division, recollected what it was like during the stalemate years: "The Chinese would try to take a position, we'd try to hold them off. Meanwhile the MLR (Main Line of Resistance) stayed pretty much where it was.

"Mail was brought up almost every day. That's probably what we looked forward to the most. We even got hot meals once in a while, in thermal containers. Insulated green containers about three feet long and a foot wide. They'd fix the meals in a field kitchen, miles in back of the lines, and put the food in those containers and get it up to us, maybe not hot, but at least warm. Mostly though we ate cold C rations.

"I don't know what the rats ate. There were rats in all the bunkers and trenches, and I don't know what they all found to eat."[96]

General Clark, denied troops and supplies to march north in force, turned to an unwarranted confidence that massive bombings would force the Communists to knuckle under. American air power remorselessly flattened North Korea and forced its surviving population to live in caves and underground shelters but the critical failure of Operation Strangle proved that it could not halt the flow of supplies to the Communist armies.

The Chinese army was the most disciplined and correct in a brutal war. The U.S. came close to admitting it in official observations that atrocities declined after its intervention. General Ridgway made evident that he was impressed by the fact that towns recaptured from the Chinese had escaped vandalism, though he was not therefore deterred from requesting the napalming of villages in the way of the Eighth Army.

Atrocities were perpetuated by both sides. Contrary to the easy assumptions of American scholars and commentators, the U.S.-South Korean record is the worst. That followed from the fact that the north had popular support in the south and waged guerrilla war in both north and south. Guerrillas are fish swimming in the water of the people, as the Chinese say, and their suppression requires the draining of the water. Both the Rhee regime and the United States emulated the "Kill All, Burn All, Loot All" suppression tactics of the Japanese in China. They slaughtered villagers and made torture routine practice.

The Americans were guilty of an atrocity of their own—large-scale use in the countryside and elsewhere of the relatively new weapon of napalm.

In an article in *The Compass* in December, 1951, I argued that "The Korean war is a study in the military consequences of counterrevolutionary politics. The basic fact that since 1945 the Korean left has been politically stronger than the Korean right has given rise to harsh military imperatives, forcing the U.S. to use weapons and tactics which Americans once regarded as beyond the pale of 'civilized war.'"[97]

I cited various instances including this one. "I figured if we had to kill 10 civilians to kill one soldier who might later shoot at us, we were justified," Ensign David Tatum remarked after returning from a strafing mission, *Time* magazine reported in January, 1951.

Another: A *New York Times* caption, November 13, 1951: "An airborne Marine demolition crew spraying a native hut with gasoline preparatory to setting it afire with a phosphorous grenade during drive on guerrillas. The movement was called 'Operation Rabbit Hunt.'"

And one more: In response to the deaths of five GIs whose advance patrol had been ambushed, U.S. tanks, planes and artillery today obliterated the village of Tuom-ri, N. Harry Smith reported in *The Compass* November 9, 1950.

On January 17, 1951, the United Press reported the razing of the South Korean city of Wonju by the U.S. 2d Division: "Before the retreat, every house in Wonju was set afire, every bridge demolished, every morsel of food destroyed. Patrols were sent into the countryside to set fire to the huts and haystacks... Then the artillery and aviation entered the picture." The London *Times* also reported on activities of the 2d Division in the Wonju area. Twenty-two villages and 300 haystacks were burned, it declared on January 15th.

On both sides the war was especially savage. Because it was a war between most of the people and technology, between the lightly armed and the heavily armed, most of the killing and most of the destruction was done by the U.S. and its allies. On February 21 a *New York Times* correspondent noted that "when the Koreans saw that the Communists had left their homes and schools standing in retreat while the United Nations troops, fighting with much more destructive tools, left only blackened spots where towns once stood, the Communists even in retreat chalked up moral victories."[98]

On September 10, 1950 Secretary of State Acheson told a television audience that, "I believe with modern weapons and ingenuity we can do again what was done for so many centuries at the time of the Roman Empire. It doesn't make any difference that you are outnumbered. It depends on the strength of your organization, the superiority of your weapons. You can hold back all sorts of hordes if you have that."

Acheson's reference to the Roman Empire recalls Tacitus' comment on a Roman general who campaigned in Scotland: "He made a desert and called it peace."

Years later General Willoughby reacted scornfully to all the fuss being made of the Mylai massacre in Vietnam. "In Korea we had Mylais all the time," he said.

The Air War

I do not like this napalm bombing at all… Napalm in the war was devised by us and used by fighting men in action… No one ever thought of splashing it all over the civilian population. I will take no share in the responsibility for this.

—WINSTON CHURCHILL

Three bombers "whipped down to the valley, whirled around and came back again… They knew what they were doing. They knew they were destroying private houses in a helpless village…and people in those houses if they were not quick enough.

"The story of air warfare of this sort has been told and retold… It is not an accidental 'atrocity'… It is an attested, studied, boasted method of attack. These are the gangsters of the air..."

Thus did *The New York Times* comment on a Nazi air raid in Norway. The date was May 10, 1940, still a time of some innocence, a time when war was not supposed to be entirely total and portions of mom's apple pie awaited victorious survivors.

The U.S. Air Force brought to its Korea tasks its recent achievement in bombing Japanese civilians. Its outstanding successes were the incinerations of Hiroshima and Nagasaki, but there was much more. Under the command of General Curtis LeMay, hundreds of thousands of civilians were killed in raids on 80 Japanese cities. Seventeen square miles of central Tokyo were burned out and the canals were brought to boiling. Napalm was the weapon of choice.

But in Korea the Air Force was assigned to ground attack in support of infantry as well as dropping bombs from on high. That led to costly errors until pilots gained experience. According to a candid report cited by Callum MacDonald, "American pilots attacked a column of thirty ROK trucks, killing two hundred South Korean troops. An American officer working with an ROK unit said he was attacked by 'friendly' aircraft five times in one day," hitting ammo dumps, an airstrip, trains, motor columns and a ROK headquarters. About half of the correspondents killed in the war (11 or 12) were killed by the U.S. Air Force.[99]

According to Robert Jackson, when the Chinese got into the war, "…the kid gloves were off; there was to be no attempt at ultra-precise bombing to avoid high civilian casualties. The B-29s were to carry full loads of incendiaries and their task was to burn the selected cities from end to end."[100]

The U.S. had a formidable air armada in the area of Japan at the outset of the 1950 war. It included 375 F80 jet fighters, 30 F82 twin Mustang fighters, 32 B-26 light bombers and 30 B29 superfortresses—all obsolescent but still able to de-urbanize Korea in a matter of months. General Emmett (Rosie) O'Donnell, who commanded the devastating raid on Tokyo and was then head of the Bomber Command in Asia, testified at the MacArthur hearings that by the time the war was three months old "almost all the Korean peninsula" was "just a terrible mess." "Everything is destroyed. There is nothing standing worthy of the name. Just before the Chinese came in we were grounded. There were no more targets in Korea." Senator Russell, in the chair, told O'Donnell that "I think you have demonstrated soldierly qualities that endeared you to the American people."[101]

Actually there was a near infinity of additional targets which occupied the air war until the truce as the overall purpose came to include destruction of villages and decimation of the civilian population.

The authoritative British military publication *Brassey's Annual* had this to say about the devastation of the south in its 1951 edition: "The war was fought without regard for the South Koreans, and their unfortunate country was regarded as an arena rather than a country to be liberated. As a consequence, fighting was quite ruthless, and it is no exaggeration to state that South Korea no longer exists as a country. Its towns have been destroyed, much of its means of livelihood eradicated, and its people reduced to a sullen mass depending upon charity..."[102]

MacArthur initiated discussions of the possible use of nuclear bombs in the second week of the 1950 war; the Joint Chiefs of Staff observed that 10 to 20 such bombs could be spared but were then opposed to dropping any. But the possibility was raised again and again in real or potentially critical situations—even during the final phase of the truce negotiations in 1953.

Serious consideration of resort to them followed the Chinese intervention and the flight south of the UN forces. As observed, President Truman told the press that use of the bomb was "under active consideration" as indeed it was. His remarks caused jitters in London and other allied capitals and Attlee hurried to Washington. The British prime minister was given only oral assurance that the bomb would not be used in Korea. In fact, as observed, steps to create a real nuclear bomb capability were being taken.[103] The hydrogen bomb was ready for testing shortly after Eisenhower's election in November 1952.

In December of 1950 MacArthur asked for commander's discretion to use nuclear bombs, requesting 34 of them. After his death it was revealed that he proposed spreading a belt of radioactive cobalt across the neck of Manchuria. As noted, Congressman Albert Gore a few months earlier publicly proposed a radiation belt across the Korean peninsula. General Ridgway, succeeding MacArthur, asked for 38 atomic bombs but was refused. Ridgway also raised the question of using chemical weapons.

Perhaps the U.S. came closest to dropping nuclear bombs in April 1951. The Chinese were massing troops in preparation for their spring offensives and the Soviet Union was countering American threats to take the war to China by stationing 200 bombers in Manchuria. Soviet MIG pilots were covertly involved in the air war over northern Korea. President Truman approved the Pentagon's request for the transfer of nine nuclear capsules—that would make nine bombs operational—to military custody, specifically the Ninth Bomb Group in Guam. The bomb loading pits in Okinawa were then in readiness but the Ninth Bomb Group was not transferred from Guam.[104]

In the fall of 1951, in what was called Operation Hudson Harbor, raids with dummy atomic bombs were carried out on northern Korea by lone B-29s from Okinawa to determine if the real thing could be effective. The conclusion was that their practicality was limited on the peninsula because identification of masses of enemy troops was difficult and rare.

Nevertheless, use of the bomb on the Korean battlefield and especially in China continued to be an option. Fighter-bombers were given delivery capability and accelerated efforts were made to make atomic bombs in the form of artillery shells.

Documentation is incomplete but the reasons why the bomb was not dropped include stabilization of the ground war, the failure of China to engage in escalation, the strong opposition of Britain and other major allies, and in particular the presence in Manchuria of the fleet of 200 Soviet bombers. President Eisenhower's role was crucial but somewhat ambiguous. He said privately he just could not drop the bomb—that to do so again would alienate Asians—but publicly threatened to use it if the Communists kept rejecting truce proposals. See below, *Armistice and Aftermath*, for more on this.

Korea was hardly spared. The flattening of it was realized by high explosive and the favorite newer weapon, napalm. After the truce the U.S. embassy in Seoul was able to conclude that northern industry was beyond repair and would have to be constructed anew. In 1953 power production was 26 percent of the prewar figure, fuel 11 percent, chemicals 22 percent, metallurgy 10 percent.

After the Chinese entered the war in October-November of 1950 MacArthur ordered that a huge area north of the retreating UN line— several thousand square miles—be bombed into waste land, destroying from the air every "installation, factory, city, and village."

General Ridgway, succeeding MacArthur, ordered that Pyong-yang, the capital, be burned to the ground by incendiary bombs. Also dropped on the northern capital were delayed-fuse demolition bombs, calculated to blow up when people are out rescuing the injured and putting out napalm fires. By northern count, over 400,000 bombs, high explosive and napalm, were dropped on the city, converting it to a field of rubble and building fragments.[105]

General Edward M. Almond, X Corps, called for the napalming of the "huts and villages" to which guerrillas retire. General Barr flew over Tanyang and found that "Smoke from burning villages and huts has filled valleys…with smoke three thousand feet deep and blinded all my observations…"

General William Dean, traveling north toward the Yalu while a prisoner, was astonished by the pulverized city of Huichon. "The city I'd seen before—two-storied buildings, a prominent main street—wasn't there any more. If it hadn't been for the river crossing I would not have believed this could be the same place. What few people remained lived in dugouts and what had been a city was snow-covered fields."[106]

Wilfred Burchett, traveling south from the Manchuria-Korea border en route to covering the start of the truce negotiations, found that "Roadside villages which had existed even within a few miles of the Yalu were now nonexistent. There were shells of houses and empty, black patches where houses had been. Wisps of smoke issued from holes where people were living, as our truck headed underground to the dusk toward Pyongyang."[107]

Bombings aimed at civilians as well as military targets failed both to impair the Communist defense and break the civilian morale. Indeed the population seems to have been enraged. General Dean concluded that "The civil population became so inflamed that a downed airman had no chance of getting away from his wrecked plane or parachute."[108]

A particular failure was Operation Strangle, begun in June 1951, a prolonged effort by the U.S. Air Force to destroy rail and road transportation so that front-line Sino-Korean forces could not be supplied. Pilots had a theme song—"We've been working on the railroads." But the Communists took the joy out of it, responding by organizing swift repair of bridges and by placing many more heavy antiaircraft artillery around likely targets. By February 1952 North Korea had in place 398 such guns as well as some 1,000 automatic weapons. The Air Force was embarrassed by the negative results of its strangulation effort. A sardonic American report said that "we are exchanging planes for dead coolies." During Operation Strangle the Communists downed 343 planes and damaged 290.

General Dean eye witnessed the failure. Traveling early in 1953, he saw piles of bridge sections waiting to be placed, two bridges thrown across streams where one bridge was vulnerable, railroads that had been smashed being swiftly repaired, villages moved to canyons or sites difficult to bomb. Though gladdened by the sight of the damage, he observed that, "These people had been hurt by bombing, and were still being hurt by it, but it looked to me as if their countermeasures were improving faster than our measures of destruction."[109]

Hanson Baldwin reached the same conclusion. He wrote in *The New York Times* of November 29, 1951 that "There is good reason to believe that the enemy is as strong, if not stronger, than he was when the interdiction and isolation campaign started."

In late June 1952, the Suiho hydroelectric plant on the Yalu was severely damaged by naval aircraft, causing a blackout in the area, a production decline in Manchuria and protests in Britain. Other electricity generating plants were bombed and wholly destroyed, depriving the north of nearly all electricity until the end of the war.

In a calculated effort to destroy civilian as well as military food supplies, over two weeks beginning May 13, 1953 Thunder jets and B-29s bombed five North Korean irrigation dams, resulting initially in massive flooding of rice growing areas—the arduous work of transplanting seedlings had just been completed. Many villages were drowned. Pyongyang, some 27 miles to the south, was flooded. The official U.S. military history describes what happened when F-84s bombed the irrigation dam at Tokchon which had a three square mile lake behind it. "Flood waters poured forth and left a trail of havoc… Buildings, crops, and irrigation canals were all swept away in the devastating torrent."[110]

A comparable Nazi destruction of Dutch agriculture by dike demolition in 1944 was listed as one of the Nuremberg war crimes.

Driving north from Pyongyang in 1997, I saw a number of neat villages that I presumed had replaced those drowned by the dam bombings. Orderly rows of one-story houses, whitewashed walls, tile roofs, doors and window frames painted a light blue.

The Chinese and Koreans quickly discovered that reduction of the water level behind the dams reduced the damage inflicted. Of the five dams attacked (out of 20) only two suffered catastrophic damage. MacDonald observed that "The ingenuity of FEAF (Far Eastern Air Force) in devising new methods of knocking out enemy targets was outmatched by the Communists' ingenuity in patching them up."[111]

In pursuing weapons development, the Pentagon was always on the lookout for new weapons that would be as destructive as nuclear bombs without acquiring their opprobrium. A major success was napalm, invented near the end of World War II by a Harvard professor who was under the illusion that it would only be used on military personnel. Called jellied gasoline early on, napalm is a combination of naphthenic and palmitic acids, ignited by phosphorous to make it a slow, lasting burn. The word napalm is an acronym derived from the two acids.

Used in Korea, south as well as north, in lieu of nuclear weapons, napalm killed painfully hundreds of thousands of people. Planes flew low down city and town streets killing clusters and targeted peasants in the fields. More than two million northern civilians died, reducing the population by 20 percent. In World War II overall 40 percent of casualties were civilian, in Korea 70 percent. By the end of the war, by which time 33,000 tons of napalm had been dropped, most of the survivors were living in caves or underground shelters.

Napalm was first used in the third day of the 1950 war and quickly became the ingredient of most of the bombs. During the first five months the Air Force was supplied with nearly two million pounds of napalm powder, enough to make 100,000 napalm bombs. On October 15, 1950 the *New York Herald Tribune* informed the public in a comprehensive article headed "Napalm, The No. 1 Weapon in Korea."

Soon the use of napalm was a celebrated weapon in military journals. An article titled "Napalm Jelly Bombs Prove a Blazing Success in Korea" (*All Hands*, April 1951) reported that napalm bombs burn at a temperature of 3,000 degrees for 30 seconds, setting fires after that. They not only torch victims but kill others simply by consuming large quantities of oxygen.

Lieutenant Earle J. Townsend's article, "They Don't Like 'Hell Bombs'" (*Armed Forces Chemical Journal*, January 1951), meaning the enemy didn't, reported that "When a napalm bomb hits the ground, its flaming liquid spreads over a pear-shaped area about 30 yards wide and 90 yards long...it sets aflame everything it touches and all that is nearby." The number of "hell bombs" dropped rose to "astronomical figures" and pilots soon were complaining about the scarcity of targets.

I. F. Stone quoted communiqués reporting "excellent" results from the bombing of villages and noted that "There were some passages about these raids on villages which reflected, not the pity which human feeling called for, but a kind of gay moral imbecility, utterly devoid of imagination—as if the fliers were playing on a bowling alley, with villages for pins."[112]

Robert P. Martin reported from Tokyo in January, 1951 that American "war techniques" in Korea had made a far from favorable impression on European observers. He quoted the recollection of an appalled Englishman: "There were two or three snipers in a village. A combat team could have wiped them out with very little trouble. But… pilots leveled the village with napalm."

John Ford's 1951 film, *This Is Korea!*, has extensive footage on napalm, part of it staged. Over a scene with a flame-thrower, commentator John Wayne says "Burn'em out, cook'em, fry'em."

George Barrett, a front-line corespondent of *The New York Times*, described what he called "a macabre tribute to the totality of modern war" in the February 9, 1951 issue:

"A napalm raid hit the village three or four days ago when the Chinese were holding up the advance, and nowhere in the village have they buried the dead because there is nobody left to do so. This correspondent came across one old woman, the only one who seemed to be left alive, dazedly hanging up some clothes in a blackened courtyard filled with the bodies of four members of her family.

"The inhabitants throughout the village and in the fields were caught and killed and kept the exact postures they had held when the napalm struck—a man about to get on his bicycle, fifty boys and girls playing in an orphanage, a housewife strangely unmarked, holding in her hand a page torn from a Sears-Roebuck catalogue… There must be almost two hundred dead in the tiny hamlet."

This is a soldier's account of a mistaken drop of napalm on about a dozen American GIs by a Marine Corsair in northeast Korea: "Men all around me were burned. They lay rolling in the snow. Men I knew, marched and fought with begged me to shoot them...I couldn't. It was terrible. Where the napalm had burned the skin to a crisp, it would be peeled back from the face, arms, legs…like fried potato chips."[113]

In the last years of the war great numbers of northern civilians lived in caves or underground communities. Government offices, factories, hospitals, schools and repair shops as well as living quarters were in bunkers deep underground.

Supplied with hundreds of Soviet swept-wing MIG-15 fighters and instructors, China built up an air force based in Manchuria. The main victims were the aged B-29 bombers. On October 23, 1951 MIGs downed three B-29s and damaged five while three of them were lost. But by early fall of 1952 the U.S. Air Force was re-equipped with F-86 Sabre jets which, flown by superior pilots, restored American air supremacy in combat with MIGs. Hot pursuit into Manchuria helped. Ten MIGs were downed for every Sabre lost—792 MIGs down, 78 Sabres.[114]

Overall the U.S. Air Force lost 1466 aircraft. The Navy, Marines and allies lost an additional 420 planes. Most of the losses were from ground fire and accidents.[115] But the Chinese air force put a stop to nearly all precision daylight bombing, accomplishing what the Luftwaffe had failed to do. By the end of the war B-29 losses were mounting as a result of increased flak and searchlights.

More bombs were dropped on Korea than in the Pacific theater in World War II—635,000 tons compared to 503,000 tons.

LeMay went on to do all he could to realize a first nuclear strike on the Soviet Union and for years advocated "nuking the Chinks." At the time of the Soviet missiles in Cuba, Le May said that "the leg of the bear is in a trap and we should demolish it up to and including the testicles." In retirement, frustrated by peace, he was the candidate for vice president on the far right George Wallace ticket.

The section on Air Warfare in the Encyclopedia Britannica's account of the Korean War (1973 edition) is silent on the relentless bombing of North Korean cities and towns, power plants and dams and it describes the failed Operation Strangle as a success. It states accurately that UN pilots were "never permitted" to engage in "hot pursuit" into Manchuria but fails to acknowledge that they did so routinely without permission. The word napalm was not in the encyclopedia's vocabulary.

I concluded in an article on the air war in the *New York Daily Compass* of December 18, 1951, that "the fundamental lesson of the Korean war is that strategic bombing is not quickly or easily decisive even when there is no direct defense against it."

Biological Warfare

Available documents do not reveal whether anyone knows even the names of the Chinese, Russians, 'half-breeds,' and Americans whose lives were prematurely ended by massive doses of plague, typhus, dysentery, gas gangrene, hemorrhagic fever, typhoid, cholera, anthrax, tularemia, smallpox, tsutusgamushi and glanders, or by such grotesqueries as being pumped full of horse blood or having their livers destroyed by prolonged exposure to X-rays, or those subjected to vivisection.

— JOHN W. POWELL ON JAPANESE BIOLOGICAL WARFARE

In February and March of 1952, during the truce negotiations, North Korea and China accused the U.S. of resorting to biological warfare in Korea and Manchuria, exacerbating the negotiations and causing an international furor.

The U.S. was alleged to have dropped disease-ridden flies, fleas, spiders, other insects and feathers, a charge supported by an international commission of prominent scientists, all but one Westerners, and by the confessions of 25 captured airmen and other prisoners.

The U.S. and its allies denied the accusation as a total fabrication. Not a single released prisoner repeated his confession, but this is not as conclusive as it might seem for all were subjected to the heaviest pressure by the Army. Retractions were demanded by officers of a military court on the ocean voyage home, and later on U.S. Attorney General Herbert Brownell went on record as stating that American prisoners of war "who collaborated with their Communist captors in Korea may face charges of treason."

The highest ranking officer who confessed as a prisoner and retracted when freed was Air Force Colonel Walker Mahurin, a World War II ace. Stephen Endicott of York University, Ontario, closely examined the retraction, finding it characterized by rhetorical distractions and, more important, by misstatements regarding his background. Mahurin repeatedly disclaimed any pre-Korea connection with biological warfare but acknowledged during questioning by his captors that he had been provoked into reporting a visit to the biological warfare center at Fort Detrick. He replied evasively when questioned several times about it back home. Just before the 1950 war began, he had served in the Pentagon under Air Secretary Thomas Finletter, an advocate of readiness to engage in biological warfare. Sent to Korea, he had reportedly taken part in briefings about biological warfare and dealt with F-86 fighter wing adjustments that conceivably could have prepared them for carrying biological bombs. In his denying statement he had stressed that insects could hardly survive the 50 below zero cold of flights at high altitudes, but in his earlier confession he had said that germ flights flew low.

Endicott concluded that the documents "contain so many contradictory statements as to make part of the record untrustworthy... Perhaps inadvertently, Mahurin's autobiography (and the other material which he provided after returning to America) tends to confirm the truth of his original confession."[116]

The charge that the U.S. waged germ warfare remains unproved. But as made evident in detail by John W. Powell in the Bulletin of Concerned Asian Scholars (October-December 1980), linked to this uncertainty are two certainties. The first is that the Japanese undertook major biological warfare research and experimentally engaged in such warfare in China, Siberia and southeast Asia. The second is that the U.S. gained exclusive possession of Japan's biological warfare data in exchange for a pledge that the leading Japanese involved would not be tried for war crimes. The Japanese research files and slides were transferred to Camp Detrick, later Fort Detrick, near Frederick in Maryland.[117]

Japan's principal biological warfare operation, Unit 731, was located near Harbin in what was then Manchukuo. It had a staff of 3,000, of whom 10 percent were leading pathologists and bacteriologists. It killed some 3,000 prisoners in experiments. The victims, called maruta (blocks of wood), were infected with doses of plague, typhus, gangrene, typhoid, smallpox and other diseases. The arms of some prisoners were frozen and then thawed in experiments which resulted in rotting flesh and protruding bones. Livers of prisoners were destroyed by repeated x-ray exposure. The blood of prisoners was drained and horse blood pumped into them. Surgical vivisections were performed and entrails cut out. Eyeballs were forced out by tremendous pressure on the heads. Bodies were reduced to a fifth of their weight by dehydration. The Japanese killed infected prisoners and then performed autopsies on them sequentially so they could measure the progress of the disease.

The Unit 731 staff member in charge of printing testified that "Sometimes there was no anesthetic. They screamed and screamed, but we didn't regard the maruta as human beings. They were lumps of meat on a chopping block."[118]

Both the Chinese (Kuomintang) government and the Soviet Union offered evidence of Japanese biological warfare criminality. China reported that Japan had tested germ warfare in eleven cities, four in Zhejiang, two each in Hebei and Henan and one each in Shanxi, Hunan and Shandong. One target was the hamlet of Congshan in Zhejiang Province. This is from an account of the Congshan experience in *The New York Times* of February 4, 1997:

> "At its peak that terrible November, the plague here was killing 20 Chinese a day, all of them civilians. Their screams sundered the night from behind shuttered windows and bolted doors, and some of the most delirious victims ran or crawled down the narrow alleys to gulp putrid water from open sewers in vain attempts to vanquish the septic fire that was consuming them."

A sub-unit of 731 in Nanjing handled most operations in China. Named the Tama Detachment, it developed into a large independent organization with 12 branches, 1,500 personnel, and equipment for growing bacteria. It too performed experiments on prisoners. China sent a report on Tama to the International Military Tribunal in Tokyo and asked that it be added to the war crimes charges against Japan.

The U.S. successfully opposed this as it opposed all attempts to punish Japanese for biological warfare.

Late in 1996 Japan at last agreed to help in taking steps toward cleaning up what remains of bacteriological arsenals abandoned by its forces in China in 1945.

Russian forces in Manchuria captured Japanese who had been part of Unit 731 and found 12 of them guilty in a trial in Khabarovosk in 1949. But the U.S. dismissed the Soviet trial findings as propaganda and also dismissed, without publicity, a Soviet proposal, supported by China, that an international court place on trial others in the leadership of Japan's germ warfare criminality.

One of the many contributions of a 527-page British book, *Unit 731*, by Peter Williams and David Wallace, is that it corrects the hostile verdict on the Khabarovsk trial: "The trial at Khabarovsk has for thirty-five years been dismissed in the West as an exercise in propaganda. Yet the evidence recorded there was, we now know, accurate in most details. The fact that it was ignored, obscured by a fog of Cold War bitterness and laid to rest because it suited the Allies to do so, is one of the scandals of the Second World War. The interests of justice were not served."[119]

John W. Powell, editor of the *China Monthly Review* and earlier the *China Weekly Review*, Shanghai, supported the germ warfare accusation in print and for that, and other departures from establishment truth, upon his return from China found himself assaulted by the judicial system. An appearance before the Senate Internal Security Subcommittee along with his wife Sylvia and Julian Schuman, associate editors of the Review, was just an introductory torment. Again with his wife and Schuman, he was placed on trial twice in San Francisco, charged first with sedition, then with treason.

The essence of the defense was that the biological warfare reports in the *Review* were the truth and that this could be established by the contents of Pentagon documents and by the testimony of Chinese and Korean witnesses. The government, for reasons suggesting its culpability, was determined to avoid any probe of biological warfare at the trial and this pressured Attorney General Robert Kennedy regretfully to end the second trial, by which time the defendants had lost their jobs and were financially and emotionally drained.[120]

Powell initiated and pursued an investigation into Japan's germ warfare effort and the American cover-up. When the U.S. denied involvement, it also claimed falsely that Japan's actions were unproven. But the evidence of Japan's germ warfare pioneering mounted as a number of Japanese spoke out and as Powell and others dug deeper. A Japanese documentary film in 1976 made U.S. deceit no longer possible.

Nevertheless, many Unit 731 veterans not only escaped punishment but enjoyed successful careers in civilian life. The doctor who pumped horse blood into prisoners became president of a prosperous blood bank company. A colleague who directed the freezing experiments was employed by the giant Tokyo Fishery Company as a "freezing consultant." Nine became medical school professors and four became hospital directors. Lieutenant General Shiro Ishii, principal biological warfare innovator and in command, died at 67 in 1959. Near his death bed, he was baptized into the Roman Catholic Church, perhaps feeling some remorse for his decades of evil deeds.

The charge that the U.S. was indeed guilty of germ warfare can hardly be dismissed on the ground that Americans would never consider such criminality. That persuaded great numbers at the time, but since then evidence of ongoing American development of bacteriological warfare capabilities and the actual use of chemical weapons in Vietnam have come to light. Several American military high-ups, including General Charles E. Loucks of the Army Chemical Corps, on January 22, 1951, made statements unequivocally giving their support to resorting to germ warfare.

The Chinese and Koreans sought to make evident U.S. interest in biological warfare by citing revealing articles in *The Journal of Immunology, Science News Letter, Look, Science Digest* and *Discovery* magazine. Cited also were Canadian press reports in the summer of 1949 that American experiments on Eskimos resulted in an epidemic of bubonic plaque among them.

The International Scientific Commission for the Facts Concerning Bacterial Warfare in China and Korea, formed on March 29, 1952, in Oslo by the World Peace Council, conducted a two-month investigation. Its findings were based on a rigorous methodology developed to take into account the characteristics of relevant data submitted to it, painstaking interrogation of Chinese and Korean witnesses, scientific testing of material evidence, careful checking of specimens collected by Chinese scientists, and elaborate statistical calculations. Four of the scientists were renowned scholars at leading universities, two were directors of laboratories and another was the most distinguished scientist Dr. Joseph Needham of the University of Cambridge, now deceased. Years later Needham said that he remained "97 percent convinced" that the germ war charges were true. A professor from the USSR Academy of Medicine was the sole non-Westerner.

The ISC report, released on August 31,1952, was dismissed and vilified in the U.S. and Britain, but now, according to *Unit 731*, written by Williams and Wallace, is "generally accepted today as being of high quality."

Unit 731 is important not only for corrections and informative contents but for what it had to eliminate in order to get the book published in the U.S. by the Free Press, Macmillan, 1989. It was obliged to withhold a 70-page chapter on the Korean war. Pressure was put on it to do that because the chapter, Chapter 17, assembled detailed evidence of American guilt. The authors subjected this evidence to critical analysis and pointed to "merits and demerits," but the merits were the most persuasive. Four episodes pointing to American guilt follow:[121]

> • The commission was told that of a swarm of voles (small rodents) fell from the sky on several villages in Kan-Nan district, northeast China on April 4, 1952, following the flight overhead of an American F-82 night fighter. A total of 717 rodents, many evidently sick, were found. Villagers, frightened, buried most of them deep but plague bacilli was found on the few who weren't. A telling detail was that all of the voles were adults. Kan-Nan had never known plague in its history. Unit 731 had specifically devised means of landing rats from planes. The commission concluded that "there remains no doubt that a large number of voles suffering from plague were delivered to the district of Kan-Nan during the night of 4-5 April, 1952 by the aircraft which the villagers heard.. This was identified as an American F-82 double-fuselage night-fighter."

> • Near Pyongyang in Korea the commission was told of this episode: "Early in the morning after a night (16 May) during which a plane had been heard circling round for an hour or more as if its pilot was trying to find something, a country girl picking herbs on a hill side found a straw package containing a certain type of clam. She took some of the clams home and she and her husband made a meal of them raw. On the evening of the same day both fell suddenly ill, and by the evening of the following day both were dead. Medical evidence showed that the cause of death was cholera. Further packages of clams were found on the hillside by the local Home Guard, and bacteriological examinations by the Korean and Chinese specialists proved that the clams were heavily infected with the cholera vibrio." Cholera had never been endemic in Korea.

> • A group of incidents in Liaotung and Liaoshi, Northeast China, involved beetles, house flies and feathers contaminated with anthrax. They were discovered after American flights from south of the Yalu. Five people, including four who hunted for the insects, died of respiratory anthrax and haemorrhagic anthrax, exceedingly rare diseases in the area.

• A platoon sergeant with the British Middlesex Regiment related this experience: Retreating from the Chinese offensive, his unit came to a small village south of Kunari. "As we were walking through the village I saw other chaps in fatigues who were very busy. It looked as if they had just got into the village. First I saw three or four of them with handfuls of feathers going into houses. They looked like fowl feathers. Then I saw them taking the feathers out of containers and going into houses. They were running in and spreading them. They were holding the feathers at a distance from their bodies, not in the normal way. I wouldn't have noticed the feathers otherwise. These other men... were also wearing masks over their faces." Just over a week later the sergeant and his buddies were given additional injections.

Unit 731 also examined allegations that a landing craft converted into a floating laboratory and commanded by Brigadier General Crawford Sams was involved in bacteriological activities in Korea. According to John Powell, the U.S. had sent the vessel commanded by Sams "to the east coast of Korea, which, although masquerading as an epidemic control ship, was actually loaded with bacteriological installations and was used for testing germ weapons on North Korean and Chinese prisoners."[122]

Sams had served MacArthur as chief of the Public Health and Welfare Section. During this same period he had links with former members of Unit 731, including Ishii, and the 406 Corps, a vaccine producing agency that reportedly was America's germ warfare base in Japan. *Newsweek* reported on April 9, 1951 that "landing parties have been grabbing off numbers of Chinese Reds from the tiny islands of the harbor and taking them back to the ship, where they are tested for symptoms of the dread bubonic plague." A month later the *New York Herald Tribune* reported that Sams had been awarded the Distinguished Service Cross. Sams' activities in Korea were classified information. See The Prisoner Guinea Pigs, below.

A number of other Westerners testified that the U.S. indeed had introduced bacteriological warfare in Korea. In December of 1951, two U.S. officials who insisted on anonymity reported that several former Unit 731 leaders and a freighter of bacteriological supplies, "all the necessary equipment," had been sent to Korea.[123] Wilfred Burchett, *Ce Soir* correspondent, happened upon water thickly covered with two varieties of non-aquatic insects near the Yalu and was told by schoolboys they had seen "silvery globes" coming down and found masses of insects where they landed.[124]

In Canada James Endicott, peace activist and former China missionary, supported the germ warfare accusation after his own investigation in China and Korea. Denunciations and vilifications followed. His papers were seized at the airport, he was rebuked by his church, and he was tailed everywhere by the Canadian Mounted Police. But a gathering of 10,000 organized by the Canadian Peace Congress gave him a standing ovation.[125]

Whatever the truth, China certainly believed that germ warfare was being conducted. It carried out inoculations, insect elimination, and protective clothing campaigns involving many thousands of people and at great cost. In two weeks in March of 1952 some 129 teams consisting of more than 20,000 people established 66 quarantine stations along seaports, borders and transportation routes. In the Northeast nearly five million people were inoculated against plague. Anti-bacteriological warfare research centers were opened in Shenyang, Beijing, Tianjin and Qingdao. The effort was coordinated by a central commission headed by Zhou Enlai. Guo Moruo and General Nie Rongzhen were deputy directors.[126]

In later years what appears to be corroborative evidence has persuaded some in the U.S. and elsewhere that the germ warfare accusation may well have been true. An editor of the *Stanford Law Review*, Paul Cassells, wrote that "There is mounting evidence that the Chinese allegations were true." Nobel Prize Winner Professor George Wald of the Harvard Biological Laboratories has stated: "As for the allegation that the U.S. used germ warfare in the Korean War, I can only say with dismay and some shame that what I dismissed as incredible then seems altogether credible now."

Scientists who did not believe the germ war charges were nevertheless uneasy. As I reported in the *New York Compass* on May 9, 1952, the Federation of American Scientists said in a statement that "The question raised in the world's mind is not so much whether we did use BW (biological warfare) in Korea, but whether we are in fact prepared and willing to use it in the future." It amplified: "The question is being given point by U.S. official statements that we are developing BW weapons and recent reports that the Defense Department is seeking funds for expansion of the BW program, possibly including mass production of actual BW agents."

On August 20, Hanson Baldwin reported in *The New York Times*: "Steady and methodical advances in the synthetic manufacture of wholesale quantities of biological weapons for use against man, beast or crops have been made since the war… However, the problem of distribution through the air has not been solved completely… Development is continuing, and in some applications BW is a practical weapon now—we were about to use biological agents against Japanese rice crops when World War II ended."

But as the 1960s ended the U.S. joined many other nations in renouncing use of biological weapons. On November 25, 1969, President Nixon declared: "Biological weapons have massive unpredictable and potentially uncontrollable consequences. They may produce global epidemics and impair the health of future generations. I have decided therefore that the U.S. shall renounce the use of lethal biological agents and weapons, and all other methods of biological warfare." He ordered existing stocks destroyed.

In April of 1972 the U.S. and the Soviet Union signed pledges never to develop, produce or stockpile any biological weapons. Altogether more than 80 nations signed the Biological Weapons Convention.

But within hours of the Nixon declaration it was qualified. The U.S. would continue research in defensive biological warfare. It did so, even developing new infectious strains so that it could learn how to defend against them. Contrary to an early White House promise, its work was classified and secret.

Like the CIA, it minimized the extent of its effort by contracting out specific projects. In 1977 it was revealed in the Senate that 277 outside contractors (one of them the Smithsonian) had worked on 740 biological warfare research projects. Some tasks were exported to Britain.

The Army's Dugway Proving Grounds in Utah became the defensive biological warfare center. Some 240 civilian and 190 military personnel were transferred there from Fort Detrick. But a section of Fort Detrick was turned over to a "bio-defensive" research program. The CIA itself undertook separate biological warfare activity as part of its overall dirty tricks preparations. It maintained and kept ready for use small supplies of toxins and bacterial agents and developed its own sophisticated delivery systems, initiating such efforts in 1952 if not earlier. In early 1970, following President Nixon's ordered destruction of biological agents, the CIA conducted an inventory of stocks held "in support of operational plans." It disobeyed the destruction order, storing some supplies in Fort Detrick and transferring others to outside organizations. It is credited with introducing a swine virus into Cuba in 1971.

In 1959 an involved Navy captain estimated that 33,000 scientists' years and nearly half a billion dollars had been spent on biological warfare research.[127]

Prisoners in the Chinese Camps

> *All that we know who lie in gaol*
> *Is that the wall is strong,*
> *And that every day is like a year,*
> *A year whose days are long.*
>
> — OSCAR WILDE

North Korean troops frequently killed prisoners in violation of high-level orders, several of which were captured by the U.S. Eighth Cavalry Regiment on September 6 of 1950. An order of the North Korean advanced headquarters dated July 28 forbade "the unnecessary killing of enemy personnel when they could be taken prisoners of war... Those who surrender will be taken as prisoners of war, and all efforts will be made to destroy the enemy in thought and politically."

A North Korean 2d Division order dated August 26 said that "Some of us are still slaughtering enemy troops that come to surrender. Therefore, the responsibility of teaching the soldiers to take prisoners of war and to treat them kindly rests on the Political Section of each unit."[128] For all such exhortations, several groups of 30 to 40 surrendered Americans were killed by bullets to the back of the head. Most of these killings seem to have occurred when the captives were likely to be freed by a U.S. attack or after the Inchon landing made taking prisoners north difficult.

The treatment of prisoners was worst after Inchon and the retreat of North Korean units. They got little and poor food and, thinly clothed, some collapsed and died during long, cold forced marches to collection points—the North Koreans made no effort to organize real prisoner of war camps. Of the 7,140 American prisoners, 2,701 died in captivity—the large majority, perhaps 90 percent, in the first year.

The guards were panicky, vengeful and often brutal, though some intervened to protect prisoners from angry civilians. Victorious NKPA units sometime celebrated by freeing small numbers of prisoners. During this early chaotic period the plight of the prisoners was often no worse than that of the northern soldiers and people. An unknown number of prisoners were killed along with North Korean civilians when U.S. planes bombed and strafed villages in the area immediately south of the Yalu.

Among the early prisoners was Philip Deane, correspondent of the *British Observer*, captured in July near Pusan. He watched a security officer and other guards kill fallen prisoners. Following the fall of

Pyongyang, the capital, about 100 American prisoners being held in a train hidden in a tunnel were taken off the train and executed.

The Chinese policy, developed during wars against the Japanese and Nationalists for reasons of self-interest, was to treat prisoners decently and work to convert them. This background of experience may have led to the decision in 1951 to place all foreign prisoners in Chinese camps.

For Howard Adams, a prisoner I interviewed years later, capture during the U.S. retreat from the Yalu came this way: "He jumped in a ditch, drawing fire. Safe for the moment, he dug a hole in the deep snow and buried the secret communications equipment in his charge. He put code books and secret papers inside his shirt. He was crawling away through the snow when Chinese jumped out in front of him and he was a prisoner. Several other GIs were taken at the same time. 'I was sure I would die and tried to prepare myself for it. I only dared hope that napalm wouldn't get me,' he said. But hours later Chinese brought him rice and captured jam and a young soldier gave him an overcoat. 'I stopped thinking of death.'

"With hundreds of other prisoners he was marched north to a mining camp, a layover or collecting point for prisoners destined for camps further north. The captives called it the bean camp because of the steady diet of soybeans and millet cakes. 'Later I spent a year in a village near Pyongyang, the northern capital, and got to swim in a river, read what they gave us. I read the *History of the Communist Party of the Soviet Union.*'

"The prisoners' hopes soared when the peace talks began. 'We thought we'd be free soon. The Chinese thought so too at one point and gave us a feast, but the talks dragged on and on as the U.S. side made ridiculous demands regarding prisoners and other issues.'

"Adams is still indignant over the treatment of Chinese prisoners, who were subjected to heavy pressures to defect. Many Chinese families still do not know what happened to their sons."[129]

The Chinese were unprepared for the exceptionally cold winter of 1950-1951. Their troops suffered from it severely and many prisoners died from insufficient food and exposure. Warmer weather brought improvements and amenities.

A serious postwar study in the U.S. indicated that some prisoners died of what came to be called "giveupitis"—loss of a will to live shown by refusing to eat. The Chinese included rather scarce soybeans in the diet but some prisoners pushed them aside, thus depriving themselves of an important source of protein. The caloric level in the camps sometimes rose to 2,400, higher than much Asian diet.

This is an account of the routine at a camp at Kanggye as told later to an interviewing officer, Major James MacDonald, by a just-freed prisoner:

"Prisoners rose at 7 a.m. and either took a short walk or performed light calisthenics. They washed their faces and
hands, and at 8 a.m. representatives from each squad drew
the appropriate number of rations from the kitchen. Food
was cooked by the Chinese and the diet was essentially the
same as that provided the Communist soldiers consisting of
singular items such as sorghum seed, bean curd, soya bean
flour, or cracked corn and on certain special occasions such
as Christmas or Lunar New Year, the prisoners received
small portions of rice, boiled fatty pork, candy and
peanuts."[130]

Perhaps treatment in some camps was harsher than in others.
Nick Tosques, a drafted GI, was a prisoner for two and a half years in
one of the smaller camps, Camp Number One at Changsong, and he
took away with him unpleasant memories.

Camp Number One turned out to be just a collection of old
Korean huts and a few wooden buildings. There was no
fence... The first thing they did was to break us up into
small groups. Ten men were put in each little room... The
rooms were about the size of a small closet. You couldn't
move without touching somebody. They took our clothes
and gave us thin blue uniforms. We were all filthy, nobody
had had a bath for two months, but we were not allowed to
bathe. Everybody had body lice... Right away the interro-
gations started. They interrogated us every day, and also at
night.... You never knew when they were coming for you.
And when I couldn't answer, whap, I'd get hit with a rubber
hose on the back of the neck. Pretty soon I was telling them
anything, just to keep from getting hit."[131]

The very different accounts of conditions at the Kanggye and
Changsong camps perhaps reflect the two-part China policy. The general policy, that carried out with some success in China's civil war, was
to try to establish friendly ties with prisoners by fair treatment, by
sports programs and entertainment and by various forms of persistent
indoctrination. Camp Number 5, at Pyuktong, near the Yalu, was the
largest and best of the camps. Olympic-like games in which over 500
prisoners from all the camps competed were held in the Pyuktong
camp in November 1952 and were a well-publicized high point.

The second policy was to do whatever was necessary to extract
militarily useful information from carefully selected prisoners.
Examining the prisoner records, Chinese involved in intelligence
selected prisoners who appeared to be their enemy counterparts, those
in intelligence, and subjected a relatively small number to close ques-

tioning and persistent abuse if they didn't cooperate. Often kept in solitary confinement, deprived of food and sleep, forced to stand for long stretches, even all night, shouted at hour after hour by teams of questioners, sometimes cuffed or struck, denied medical attention, the time came when those ready to admit to anything were identified and handed pens.

Pilot prisoners were the main target when the germ warfare charge arose. As observed, whether or not the U.S. was engaged in biological warfare, the Chinese at the very top were convinced of it. Certain therefore that the pilots must know the answers very well, the questioners had no qualms about methods used to loosen tongues.

On April 12, 1952 the Department of Defense in Washington released an eight-page appraisal of Communist Indoctrination and Exploitation of American and Other United Nations Prisoners. While of course generally an expose, it included some relatively favorable comment. "Many Americans now held captive have received much better treatment than normally is expected from Communist nations—and this will undoubtedly continue to be the case so long as it serves Communist purposes.

"According to the Communists themselves and the messages they permit prisoners to send, prison food while far below American standards is better than that available to North Korean civilians in neighboring towns. Barracks, while crowded and far from luxurious, are livable. Work, while it is hard, is not incessant. Clothing, though crude, is issued to the captives to give them some protection against the elements. Time is set aside for rest and recreation. The treatment is designed to create an atmosphere in which prisoners will be more susceptible to indoctrination."

Books available to the prisoners included *Uncle Tom's Cabin, War and Peace*, Lenin's *One Step Forward, Two Steps Back*, William Z. Foster's *Outline History of the Americas*, a number of books by Steinbeck and Dickens. The last page of Daphne Du Maurier's *Rebecca* was torn out because of an anti-Communist slur, frustrating readers.

In November of 1951, at a time when many GIs were fretting about the long delay in reaching a truce agreement at Panmunjom, the Judge Advocate of the Eighth Army Colonel James M. Hanley, made banner headlines in the U.S. with the charge that some 5,500 American prisoners had been murdered by the Communists—many times the estimate of 400 such victims publicized months earlier by MacArthur. Hanley broke the story while Ridgway was duck hunting. Ridgway allowed himself to regret the "coordination" of the charge but suggested that perhaps "in his inscrutable way" God had chosen this way "to bring home to our people and to the conscience of the world" the character of the enemy in Korea."

I. F. Stone devoted two feisty chapters to demolishing what he called "statistical slapstick," but of course many more read an editorial in *The New York Times* alleging that the Communists "butchered prisoners in cold blood" or were shocked by a gory Associated Press claim that "Reds Butchered More Americans Than Fell in '76." As Stone observed, this atrocity story—a "stink bomb" he called it—faded out of the headlines and dispatches within two weeks.[132]

At a later peak of American allegations that a great number of prisoners had died and that the treatment of those remaining was abusive, a prisoner who was an Associated Press photographer, Frank "Pappy" Noel, was allowed to go from camp to camp taking photos which AP distributed widely. Of course they showed apparently decently fed, smiling prisoners engaged in sports. The names were good news to many a family.

The Communist record is thought by some close observers to be somewhat better than that of the U.S. According to Field Marshall Lord Carver, Britain's former Chief of the Defence Staff, "The UN prisoners in Chinese hands, though subject to 'reeducation' processes of varying intensity…were better off in every way than any held by the Americans, whether the latter's compounds were dominated by the Communists or by the Korean or Chinese Nationalists."

Meyer and Biderman argue in Mass Behavior that the use of force in the Communist camps was "purposive and minimal in contrast to the vengeful brutality of the anti-Communist leaders."

General Dean was harshly treated, though never tortured during the first stages of his captivity. About to be repatriated, he had hard thoughts about those who had abused him. "But mostly I thought about the guards, those sergeants who would hold a blanket for hours around the shoulders of a chilling man or laugh when they saw a dog tortured to death; gorge themselves one week and share with you their last bowls of rice the next; steal from one another and give away their precious pens and buttons; enforce the most rigorous regulations and walk ten miles through the bitter cold for a letter because they knew you wanted it."

Dean also thought "of a couple of men who risked their lives for me and probably saved mine…" He said his "most important discovery" was that his guards "really believed they were following a route toward a better life for themselves and their children."[133]

A number of Americans captured during the Korean war were taken to the Soviet Union for intelligence purposes. In 1994, perhaps earlier, a Russian-American commission on prisoners of war was formed and despite bureaucratic entanglements, both American and Russian, collected evidence of this. About 30 F-86 pilots and crewmen captured in Korea were transferred to the Soviet Union in an aircraft industry intelligence operation. A former worker in a forced labor gold mine said he witnessed the death of a Marine sergeant from Queens, Philip V. Mandra, reported missing in action in Korea in 1952. A former camp guard recalled hearing of an American prisoner from the Korean war being held under maximum security in 1983.[134]

For the American prisoners released by Big Switch in August-September 1953 the joy of freedom was lessened by the stern, censorial welcome. They were forbidden to speak freely of their prison camp experiences even when at home and they had to sign statements that they understood the censorship rules. They were questioned exhaustively and lectured by counterintelligence personnel while in rest camps in Korea, in troopships on the way home and at hospitals.

To speak favorably about the camps was to be classified as pro-Red and some who failed to change their mind were incarcerated in the army's mental institution at Valley Forge.

The first prisoners interviewed by American reporters generally had favorable things to say about their experiences and the first stories home reflected that. Pressure on the media to stop that and focus on atrocities followed. United Press in New York sent an urgent message to the Tokyo office: "Need only limited coverage of returning POWs except for tales of atrocities and sensations. Payette."[135]

Time magazine's correspondent soon reported that "Somehow a headline hunting competition for 'atrocity' stories had started. Most of the voluminous file of atrocity stories last week was highly exaggerated, and the total impression was entirely false. Under press interrogation at Munsan, prisoners talked of cruelty only when pressed by leading, insistent questions. Most of the prisoners said they had not seen their comrades murdered or subjected to deliberate cruelty. And when successive prisoners talked of deaths in the prison camps, some newsmen piled statistic on statistic of 'atrocity deaths' without checking on how much they overlapped."[136]

An Associated Press cable by Bill Barnard noted that in a sense some prisoners "are still captives"—"they are held incommunicable in U.S. Army hospitals."

Keyes Beech wrote in the *San Francisco Chronicle* on August 11: "This is a fear-ridden atmosphere in which American POWs are being processed and being shipped back to the U.S.... All interviews with repatriates are conducted in the presence of a sensor and a Counter-Intelligence Corps agent. Unless the repatriate is an exceptional man, this is, to say the least, an inhibiting influence.... Often during the course of the interviews, ex-prisoners have turned to the counterintelligence men for consent before answering questions."

Korean and Chinese Prisoners

The prisoners are the happiest Koreans in Korea. They are clean and well-fed for the first time.

—MacArthur to Truman at Wake Island

Koje Island is a living hell. The shores of this island are no longer washed by sea water, but by our tears and blood. There is no breath of fresh air here, the pungent stench of blood fills our nostrils in every corner of the island.

—Smuggled letter signed by inmates, 1952

The American armed forces did not invariably make prisoners of Communists who surrendered. Max Hastings found in interviewing American officers and men for his book on the Korean war that many "admitted knowledge of, or participation in, the shooting of Communist prisoners when it was inconvenient to keep them alive. It is fair to suggest that many UN soldiers did not regard North Korean soldiers as fellow combatants, entitled to humane treatment, but as near animals, to be treated as such."[137]

And in negotiating a truce, the United States subjected many of those it did make prisoners to gross maltreatment. It did so in two ways. By coercion that included deprivation of food and fatal beatings it induced many to refuse to be repatriated following the armistice being negotiated. And it treated a number of wounded prisoners as guinea pigs, subjected to experimental medical treatment and practice surgery. See below, *The Prisoner Guinea Pigs.*

The repatriation issue was placed on the table at Panmunjom in January 1952 and stalled the talks for a year and a half.

The U.S. decided not to respect Article 118 of the Geneva Convention, which states that all prisoners were to be repatriated when hostilities ended. It had a substantial argument. The war involved two Chinas as well as two Koreas and evident clashes in ideology. The People's Liberation Army included thousands who has served in the Kuomintang forces. Similarly captured South Korean soldiers were enrolled in the northern army. So some prisoners certainly had reason to dislike or fear repatriation.

In early April, the American command estimated that 116,000 prisoners would be repatriated, indicating that only a modest number of prisoners would refuse to return home. The Communists then seemed to be going along with screening. But two weeks later the Americans produced a shrunken figure—about 70,000. The Communists were stunned and disbelieving. On April 26 the *New York Times* reported that a quick solution to the prisoner of war issue had been upset.

Reduced estimates reflected the results of the savage coercion in the compounds. President Truman and an increasing number of others in leadership had come to envisage a substitute for the victory the U.S. had failed to get on the battlefield—a propaganda triumph in line with the rollback doctrine that was prevailing over mere containment. An impressive number of prisoners were to refuse adamantly and publicly to go home to the Communist evils awaiting them.

To do the brunt of the dirty work in selected compounds (there were 32 of them on Koje, all overcrowded) the U.S. secured some 75 persuaders from Taiwan, most of them from Chiang Kai-shek's equivalent of the Gestapo, and a larger number of members of terrorist youth groups sent in by the Syngman Rhee government. Some wore neat American uniforms, others were posing as prisoners. A number of officer prisoners recently in Kuomintang armies were soon recruited.

The immediate task of these servants of American policy was to secure leadership positions in the various prisoner compounds and their continuing task was to locate prisoners who wished repatriation and to do whatever was necessary to dissuade them. Control of the food supplies was a powerful means, and that, threats, beatings, slashings and the killing of the most stubborn, led to a gratifying number who muttered "Taiwan, Taiwan, Taiwan" when asked the key question.

Admiral Charles Turner Joy, chief negotiator at Panmunjom, wrote in his diary, citing army interpreters, that those who expressed a wish to return home at a preliminary screening were "either beaten black and blue or killed... the majority of the PWs were too terrified to frankly express their real choice. All they could say in answer to the question was 'Taiwan' repeated over and over again."[138]

Of course Joy's public view was very different but, as he also wrote in his diary, he emphatically told Ridgway that the prisoners, especially the Chinese, should be re-screened.

The U.S. Ambassador, John Muccio, thought that the Taiwanese representatives were "members of Chiang Kai-shek's Gestapo." He passed on easily verified reports that Chinese prisoners were being forced to sign petitions in blood and undergo tattooing to prove they were anti-Communists and wanted to go to Taiwan.

Two State Department officers, A. Sabin Chase and Philip Mansard, sent to ascertain why such large numbers of prisoners were refusing repatriation reported forthrightly that the main reason was "the violent tactics of the PW trusties before and during the screening process." They found that "a police state type of rule" had been created over the main Chinese compounds, that the prisoners were the victims of "an information blockade" and that physical terror included organized threats, beatings and murders, before and even during the polling process. They did not find significant lack of support for Beijing or the People's Liberation Army among the Chinese prisoners.[139]

A British officer on duty in Korea charged that Americans in the camps treated the prisoners "as cattle, thought little of withholding their mail for four months or more, and regularly addressed the prisoners they dealt with as "you slant-eyed yellow bastards."

The South Korean army provided most of the guards and their brutality and venality persuaded the International Red Cross to recommend in May of 1952 that they be withdrawn.

Former Chinese Nationalist officers organized anti-Communist organizations in the camps and were made trusties by American administrators. According to a State Department official, they intimidated fellow prisoners by "beatings, torture and threats of punishment."

American troops and prisoners clashed on February 18, 1952—one U.S. soldier and at least 69 prisoners were killed. See following section.

In May, outraged by killings and abuse, prisoners seized Major General Francis T. Dodd, commandant, during a discussion of complaints and took him to Compound 75, releasing him only after General Charles F. Colson, who had succeeded him, admitted "instances of bloodshed" and inhumane treatment of prisoners and agreed to ameliorating reforms—which General Mark Clark, who succeeded Ridgway in May of 1952, countermanded as soon as Dodd was freed.

Dodd read a statement at a press conference but reporters were not allowed to ask questions. He said his captors told him they would kill him if troops tried to break into the compounds but that he was treated with the "utmost respect and courtesy." He was quartered in a separate tent and provided with medical treatment and flowers. His meeting with them, he said, "was conducted according to the best parliamentary procedure."

Freed, Dodd talked his way out of staying for a ceremonial farewell. "Apparently I was to be decorated with flowers and escorted to the gate between formed lines of PWs."[140]

He and Colson were reduced in rank to colonel. The promises to the prisoners were derided as "unadulterated blackmail" and ignored. General Clark insisted that the Koje incidents resulted from "the deliberate and planned machinations of unprincipled Communist leaders intent on embarrassing the UN command and influencing truce talks." Troops with tanks reinforced the garrison.

U.S. policy then had two basic elements: Some 70,000 to 80,000 prisoners were to refuse to home and a greatly expanded bombing of the north was to bring about reluctant Communist agreements.

But the Koje revelations resulted in publication of at least fragments of the embarrassing truth. I. F. Stone was again helpful. The U.S. responded with elaborations of its falsifications. Writers of its public statements, it was later revealed, were instructed not to mention the Taiwan role in the screening or the brutalities in the compounds.

A group of correspondents was allowed to tour Koje but not allowed to talk to spokesmen for the prisoners. A prisoner shouted in English a plea for a chance to talk and several others sought to get written statements to them but these were seized by the guards. A guard tried to drown prisoner jeers and shouts by singing "Sweet Aleline" at the top of his voice.

But a correspondent for the *Toronto Star* got in with a British delegation and reported that "physical threats, often carried out" were the reason why so many voted against repatriation. He wrote that Chinese prisoners were told by Kuomintang personnel they could ask to go to Taiwan or "stay here and rot."

General Clark in effect blessed the camp brutalities. In instructions to the guards he said that "prisoners who throw or attempt to throw rocks at guards should be shot while in the act... I will be much more critical of your using less force than necessary than too much."[141]

Clark may or may not have known of violence in the compounds more serious than rock throwing. Prisoners prominently involved in the seizure of Dodd were for weeks subjected to torture and beatings, some of them fatal.

Bloody clashes continued. One was the subject of this report in *Life* on December 2, 1952: "In the worst prisoner of war riots since the Koje Island outbreak of last February, 3,600 North Korean Communists mutinied in the Pongan Island compounds last week. Linking arms, singing Communist songs, they ignored orders to disperse and marched straight into machine-gun and small arms fire. Some continued singing even as they lay wounded. Before the fanatical advance faltered and finally broke, 81 were killed, 118 were wounded."

The British had misgivings, but Winston Churchill said that they had to be "good comrades" both in the "field of action" and "at the council table." Nevertheless Britain and other allies hoped for some compromise on repatriation. Chester Ronning and Lester Pearson of Canada, Krishna Menon of India, and declarations by British and U.S.

Quakers at various times pressed for softenings, specifically proposing involvement of neutral nations in re-screenings.

The Soviet line on the issue was modified further after the death of Stalin on March 5, 1953, and Zhou Enlai retreated on it later that month, making resumption of negotiations and a truce possible.

Zhou also approved General Mark Clark's February proposal (initially urged by the International Red Cross) that wounded and ill prisoners be immediately exchanged, and what was called Little Switch began April 20. Correspondents on the U.S. side were seated in a stand where they could just watch, but were allowed to interview released prisoners several days later. Correspondents on the Communist side mingled with the prisoners in the northern exchange area and took many photos of skeletonized amputees from the south accompanied by burly guards.[142]

The principal change resulting from the softened exchanges was formation of a Neutral Nations Repatriation Commission to handle disposition of prisoners unwilling to be sent home. But the effect of the compromises was essentially to save Communist face. The principle that prisoners could refuse repatriation was of course embodied in the functions of the neutral commission and the U.S. successfully defeated moves to oust the thugs it had championed as compound leaders. The abuse of prisoners went on as before. A candid report by a State Department official said that "pro-KMT trusties" were "again putting the heat on" and that there had been "an upsurge in beatings and killings by self-styled anti-Communists."[143]

But in its final report the Commission did state the all too evident truth: "…any prisoner who desired repatriation had to do so clandestinely and in fear of his life."

Thus many Chinese who didn't want to go to Taiwan found themselves there. Of the Chinese prisoners 6,670 were repatriated to China, 14,235 were sent to Taiwan.

Released Korean women prisoners told tales of horror which were collected by Winnington and Burchett, *Plain Perfidy*, and thus summarized in John Toland's *In Mortal Combat: Korea, 1950-1953:* "… Some Americans were equally brutal. One girl, Kim Kyung-suk, told how they had forced a group of women prisoners into a large room. Here they were stripped. Then nude male North Korean prisoners were shoved in. 'We heard you Communists like to dance,' an American shouted. 'Go on! Dance!' They pointed bayonets and revolvers at the prisoners, who began to dance, while drunken, cigar-smoking, guffawing American officers stubbed out cigars on the girls' breasts and committed indecencies.

"At the Inchon camp two mothers with babies were repeatedly dragged off at bayonet point. The children had their mouths gagged while their mothers were taken into the American guards' quarters and raped."[144]

Big Switch, the final exchange, took place in August and September. On September 6, the last day, an ambulance pulled up and inside was Pak Sang Hyon, PW leader and principal organizer of the kidnapping of General Dodd. After Dodd's release he had been interrogated repeatedly, kept in solitary confinement, half-starved and beaten many times.

For three winter months he was kept outdoors in a six-by-three-foot cage. No walls, just strands of barbed wire. One blanket, no shoes. "I lived like an animal. I collected every scrap of refuse. Every bit of dried grass or grain stalk was a treasure to me. I used everything I could find for padding in my clothes. I burrowed into the dirt like a rabbit and wrapped my feet up with bits of grass, straw, paper and old rags."

For weeks prisoners returning earlier had carried banners demanding his release. He said he did not believe he was being repatriated until the ambulance door opened and he saw KPA uniforms. A minute later a Korean general was hugging him.[145]

The South Korean handling of prisoners is described in a U.S. Army study as "a tendency to mistreat or kill prisoners at the slightest provocation." On several occasions Captain Kim Chong-won, called Tiger Kim, had several groups of about 50 northern prisoners beheaded. The reaction of the U.S. Army when the Red Cross made inquiries was to worry that the correspondents would find out about it.

Accurate accounts of the prisoner of war issue are most scarce in the U.S. media. A book length reversal of the realities is Hal Vetter's *Mutiny on Koje Island*. General Clark's account in his *From the Danube to the Yalu*, evidently written with the help of Hearst correspondent Howard Handleman, is a shorter version of the untruths. But the falsification of it in its most influential form is that in the *Encyclopedia Britannica*, which attributed U.S. insistence on voluntary repatriation solely to "humanitarian considerations" while the Communists— apparently they alone—argued that the prisoners had been terrorized."[146]

CIA Director Allen Dulles declared that the resolution of the prisoner of war issue was "one of the greatest psychological victories so far achieved by the free world against communism." The general misinformation and disinterest then were such that this was virtually unchallenged.

The Red Cross Report on the February 18 Killings

The trusted spokesman saw some of the troops kick the dead. The remains were placed on a truck, without check-up and without medical check of each corpse.

—RED CROSS REPORT

An International Red Cross delegation was inspecting camps in Koje in February of 1952 and, though not an eyewitness to the killings of the 18th, interviewed both inmates and camp officials immediately afterwards. Its report was written in its usual bland language and conclusions were expressed cautiously, but it told in detail what happened, revealing realities that the U.S. was suppressing.

The report appeared only in French in the April issue of the International Red Cross review published in Geneva. Normally it would have been published also in the English edition, the omission indicating a high-level intervention. Correspondents covering the Korean war did not receive copies of the report and the British Red Cross Society by evasions denied it to the London *New Statesman and Nation*. A short account of that frustration by a *New Statesman* columnist alerted the *Compass* and I. F. Stone.

Stone soon located a copy of the report at the United Nations and on May 27, 1952, the *Daily Compass* published it in full in translation. Stone, in a precede, commented that "This document has a double value. Its publication may help to focus public attention on the way in which news coverage of the Korean war continues to be restricted by the American military, even in regard to matters which bear no relationship whatsoever to security."

This is the gist of what happened: South Koreans serving in the North Korean army were screened and virtually all declared they did not wish to be sent north following an armistice. They were reclassified as "interned civilians."

But soon some of the prisoners changed their minds and said they really wanted to be returned to the north. The authorities then directed that a second screening take place. The prisoners adamantly refused to take part, saying they had been coerced in the first screening and did not want a repetition.

American troops in the area for R and R (rest and recuperation) reinforced the regular security force and staged a surprise re-screening at four in the morning of February 18th. Several PWs coming out of their tents to find out what was happening were shot. Then many prisoners, fearing the worst, came out and were killed or wounded by rifle fire and posted machine guns. Sixty-nine prisoners were killed and 142 wounded seriously enough to be hospitalized. One American was killed and several wounded.[147]

The American press release in Tokyo distorted what happened by the omission of two letters—"re." It said the PWs were being screened when they were actually being re-screened. A "re-screening" would have alerted the better correspondents to trouble and raised questions about the supposedly voluntary repatriation process.

The Red Cross delegation selectively inspected conditions at camps in which 152,832 prisoners were held. It summed up its findings on lodging, toilets, nutrition, medical care and discipline. Learning of "some very grave incidents" taking place on February 18 it gathered information about them and included it in the report. Key excerpts follow:

> "On February 8, the Red Cross delegates conferred with the camp security chief about the reclassification of the internees. The latter did not want to hear anything about it. Then they went back to Section 62 to confer with the internees. A demonstration (speeches, songs, banners) organized by the internees, with the agreement of the camp authorities, on the occasion of the anniversary of the Korean People's Army (North), was in progress. Great excitement reigned among some 6,000 who took part (practically all of the internees of Section 62)..."

> "The trusted spokesman (of the prisoners) told the Red Cross delegates that the internees would not allow themselves to be questioned anew, alleging that pressure had been brought to bear on them during their first interrogation."...

> "They became aware of an unaccustomed movement of armed men in the proximity of the section: some soldiers of an American regiment, resting at Koje, embarked in a number of military trucks; the guards had been quadrupled before the barbed wire and some machine-guns posted...two ambulances were placed in front of the entrance to the camp..."

> "On the 18th of February, about 4 a.m., troops representing about one regiment, armed and without warning entered the section.

> "Nearly all the internees were kept under guard in a tent. The troops surrounded the other tents, including that of the

trusted spokesman. Thus the latter did not have a chance to get in touch with the camp authorities.

"The internees were forced to stay in their tents under the threat of bayonets. When, not knowing what had happened, one or the other tried to leave his tent, he was greeted with shots. Seized with fear, thinking they were all about to be killed, the internees went out to defend themselves and to see what was going on. The troops attacked them, using their arms."

The chief of the third battalion of internees "was killed by a gunshot, when he approached the troops at the head of a crowd of internees."…

"The trusted spokesman saw some of the troops kick the dead. The remains were placed on a truck, without checkup and without medical check of each corpse. Certain of the internees were thus, in the belief of the trusted spokesman, treated as dead while they still lived. The trusted spokesman and the internees employed at the dispensary were unable to count the number of corpses."…

The trusted spokesman said that "to his knowledge 189 internees were hospitalized after the incident: 128 others, although wounded, did not wish to leave the camp and remained lodged in four tents; 56 internees had been killed and others probably died in the hospital."… The delegates inspected a number of tents, among them four where the wounded and sick were located. "They went also to the chief medical officer at the infirmary and received from him a list of medical supplies which he needed urgently."

On February 20 the delegates received the following statement by the commandant, Colonel (Maurice) Fitzgerald:

"Following the instructions from higher HQ that POWs and CIs should express individually and privately whether or not they desired to be re-screened, POWs from Compound 62 refused to comply with this procedure. Accordingly the matter was thoroughly discussed and it was finally decided that the use of troops be assigned to separate the inmates into small camps.

"A plan was developed and approved and put into effect to accomplish this purpose. The compound was secured and the inmates separated into small groups. Everything was going smoothly until the Communist agitators, of whom there are a considerable number in this compound, incited one of the POW battalions to attack UN troops.

"All the inmates were heavily armed with iron bars and clubs. Homemade grenades were thrown at the troops. In order to protect themselves, it was necessary for the troops to use strong measures to subdue the attack. Throughout this demonstration, Communist flags and banners were displayed and every indication was given that the attack was planned for the purpose of overrunning the UN troops..."

Fitzgerald eventually halted the re-screening effort and withdrew the additional troops. When he announced that re-screening would be resumed, the delegates warned him against use of force. The delegates had been told by the trusted spokesman and others that a number of urgent appeals had been made to Fitzgerald before and during the bloody clash. Fizgerald denied hearing any appeals.

I. F. Stone commented that "Even if the PWs' own story of a pre-dawn raid which led to a virtual massacre is discounted as one-sided, there is enough here to indicate that force and pressure were playing their part in the "screening" and "re-screening" of prisoners."

The American effort to maximize the number of prisoners rejecting repatriation continued, leading to further abusing of prisoners, violence and bloodshed. Fitzgerald was replaced as commandant by Major General Francis T. Dodd, who would be seized by prisoners and replaced and demoted in a matter of months.

The Prisoner Guinea Pigs

FROM THE GENEVA CONVENTION:

The Detaining Power shall be bound to take all sanitary measures necessary to ensure the cleanliness and healthfulness of camps and to prevent epidemics.

—ARTICLE 19

In particular, no prisoner of war may be subjected to physical mutilation or to medical or scientific experiments of any kind not in the specific interest of the prisoner.

—ARTICLE 13

Some hundreds—possibly thousands—of the ill or wounded Chinese and Korean prisoners were subjected to medical and surgical experimentation or operated on primarily to give young beginner surgeons practice.[148]

Circumstances were propitious. A sufficient number of prisoner patients was always available and a long lasting epidemic supplied more than enough with the major diseases being studied—bacillary dysentery and other forms of dysentery. The American doctors, if they had qualms, could always remind themselves that the purpose was to add to medical knowledge, making possible saving of more lives, and that the victims were inferior beings, gooks to many, near animals to others.

The principal organizational innovation in Korean war medicine was MASH—medical and surgical units located immediately to the rear of the front line so that the seriously wounded could get quick attention. Like the TV series that publicized them, they combined commitment to hard work with irreverence for rules and hierarchy. Very little criticism has been brought against them.

The malpractices were concentrated in two large hospitals in the rear, the U.S. 14th Field Hospital at Pusan POW camp and the U.S. 64th Field Hospital at Koje, both in areas of major epidemics. Present also at Koje and engaged in related laboratory work was the Fleet Epidemic Disease Control Unit—General Crawford Sam's so-called Bubonic Plague Ship, Landing Craft No. 1091—the ship accused of involvement in bacteriological warfare.

The evidence of malpractice falls into three categories: Somewhat candid articles in American medical journals, the later recollections of North Korean Army doctors who had been prisoners, and interviewed and photographed Chinese and Korean prisoners repatriated at Little Switch or Big Switch. Much of all this has been brought together by Alan Winnington and Wilfred Buchett in their book *Plain Perfidy*. China's Hsinhua agency independently made similar charges

First, the medical journals: According to the January 1952 issue of *The American Journal of Tropical Medicine and Hygiene*, an extraordinary epidemic at Koje resulted in 19,320 hospitalizations and an enormous nine percent fatality rate (1,729 deaths). Serious measures to cope with what was called "150 epidemics in one" were delayed and four months passed before it was reported to Washington. Treatments varied: "...some 1,600 cases of proven or suspected bacillary dysentery were followed on 18 different treatment or dosage schedules...." The article observed that "The Korean outbreak demonstrated again that an epidemic situation provides an opportunity to accumulate valuable scientific data very rapidly."

The treatment of 1,408 cases of bacillary dysentery at Koje was described in two articles in the March and April 1953 issues of *The American Medical Association*. A control group, more or less doomed, was given no treatment other than bed rest, fluid replacement, sedatives and nutritional supplements. The others got five types of treatment—five different drugs in various dossages. Of 644 cases of acute amoebic dysentery, 66 patients were the control group, denied real treatment.

The November 1951 issue of *Surgery, Gynecology and Obstetrics* reported that 87 out of 630 UN frost-bitten cases were amputated. Of

644 cases of acute amoebic dysentery, 66 patients were the control group, denied real treatment.

Second, the northern doctors: Four prisoner doctors were assigned to surgical work as assistants. Three were transferred after protesting what they viewed as unnecessary amputations and subsequently repatriated and interviewed by Burchett and Winnington. The fourth was arrested and not heard of again.

Dr. Kim Sok Yu was a prisoner patient at the No. 4 Compound of the 14th Field Hospital. According to him, over 4,000 prisoners died there between October 1950 and August 1951, most of them of dysentery. In the beginning, he recalled, "we were living in tents, two patients sharing an army stretcher and one blanket. It was bitterly cold. For the first twenty days after my arrival, there was no medical attention at all. Patients were merely ordered to remain on their stretchers.

"Later the dysentery patients began to get treatment that can only be described as experimental—patients in the same stages of disease receiving widely different treatments. One group would be ordered to take 8 sulfadiazine tablets, another group 16 or 24, 32 or up to 48 tablets daily. The maximum liquid they got with the pills was two cups of cold water daily and patients became seriously ill... Many patients were suffering from hunger edema...There could be no doubt that it was experimentation to test the effects of very high sulfa intake and many patients died of sulfa poisoning."

Dr. Kim also reported that "Schistosomiasis cases were not treated at all, but were examined under the direction of an American, Dr. Berry, who was interested only in determining the distributions and localization of this disease."

Dr. Pak Chu Bong, in Compound No. 1 at Pusan, was barred from the surgical section after he protested unnecessary amputations. He said limbs stiff merely because of lack of exercise or because they had been released from plaster casts were amputated. He said also that "From June 1951 until December 1952 there were a great many operations carried out. A continuous pool of 300 patients was kept at the hospital and the pool was replenished strictly in accordance with daily death rates. Some 350 patients died monthly, we computed."

Dr. Rhee Tok Ki, former chief of the KPA 10th Division Hospital, also was removed from surgery for protesting what he perceived as malpractices and sent to Compound 6, which was largely for TB cases. "This 'hospital' had no floors in the tents. Twenty patients were packed on stretchers into each tent as close as they could be fitted. Air circulation was very poor. There was no regular medical treatment and if patients needed medicine, the POW assistants were supposed to inform the American doctors who would hand it out if they felt well-disposed, Then it mainly consisted of aspirins, stomach powders, diarrhea and cough medicines.

> "Patients went where they wanted for toilet needs. Later they built their own toilet. There was no purified water. If we POW medical assistants asked too often for drugs, or if the American doctor was in a bad mood, or didn't like the patient, we would be taken off and beaten up for 'agitation'...TB patients especially need rest, but they were hounded day and night as a sort of specially refined torture to get them to renounce repatriation. Twice daily and nightly all patients were forced to strip naked to prove they had no concealed weapons or 'propaganda.'"

From January 1951 to August 20, 1952, some 2,700 patients died—mostly from prolonged starvation and lack of medical treatment.

The Little Switch, Big Switch revelations: The American ambulances and trucks bringing wounded and ill prisoners to the exchange site at Panmunjom were an appalling sight—many were emaciated and so many lacked one or more limbs. The American correspondents heard their angry words at press conferences but knew better than to report them. Clicking rapidly, Winnington and Burchett took graphic photos of the amputees and included them in their book *Plain Perfidy.*

Accompanying interviews confirmed and added details to the American shame. For some months what passed for hospitals were thin mats in tents. There was little or no organized sanitation, rarely latrines, no water purification. Teams of young surgeons arrived every few months, served several months and were replaced. They operated in surgeries from which other medical personnel were barred and performed many amputations, on occasion as many as five or six on a single prisoner. Repeated amputations were performed on a single limb. Of 170 chest operations on prisoners suffering from bronchitis or pleurisy between April 1951 and July 1952 only 37 survived.

In the view of Winnington and Burchett, the "most obvious answer to all the questions posed by these epidemics on Koje Island seems to be that they were part of a large-scale American experiment to work out certain aspects of germ warfare, using Korean and Chinese prisoners of war as human laboratory material for the purpose." Bacteriological warfare reportedly began on a small scale in the autumn of the year the epidemics raged in the camp hospitals.[149]

Armistice and Aftermath

The truth was that Eisenhower realized that unlimited war in the nuclear age was unimaginable, and limited war unwinable. That was the most basic of his strategic insights.

—STEPHEN E. AMBROSE

The truce talks at Panmunjom began on July 10, 1951 when some in the American command still thought victory was possible and that led to a succession of American efforts to try to wring a substitute victory out of them. Concessions on the Communist side almost invariably led to new demands.

This became the view of more and more embattled GIs as the negotiations dragged on. In *The New York Times* of November 12, 1951, George Barrett reported the results of a number of front-line bull sessions. He found that the way an increasing number "see the situation right now is that the Communists have made important concessions while the United Nations Command, as they view it, continues to make more and more demands... The United Nations truce team has created the impression that it switches its stand whenever the Communists indicate they might go along with it."

The truce team was United Nations in name only. The negotiators for the UN were American generals and admirals and they got their instructions from General Ridgway in Tokyo, who got them from Washington. A South Korean general, Paik Sun Yup, was present at the meetings but never spoke, though away from negotiations he echoed Syngman Rhee's opposition to them. The British requested representation but were turned down.

Supposedly important negotiating positions had to be cleared with the sixteen nations with troops in Korea, but the U.S. when pressed took short cuts, giving allies only a matter of hours before announcing agreement. *The New York Times* sometimes printed Washington decisions before allied foreign offices received them. The Chinese and North Koreans, also seeking a substitute for victory on the battlefield, repeated lengthy ideological assessments and insisted on raising issues proper to actual treaty negotiations, such as withdrawal of foreign troops from Korea and the holding of Korea-wide elections. Eventually Stalin himself was moved to offer some observations on the proper scope of truce negotiations.

On the advice of Ridgway, American negotiators tended to be uncivil. Early in the talks Ridgway offered this advice to Admiral Joy, chief UN negotiator: "...to Communists the use of courtesy on your part is synonymous with concessions and concessions with a sure sense of weakness. I suggest you govern your utterances accordingly, employing such language and methods as these treacherous Communists cannot fail to understand, and understanding, respect."[1]

General William K. Harrison, later the chief negotiator at Panmunjom, was so rude that the UN Secretary General felt obliged to suggest to him that his tone might be less harsh.

The Americans had relaxing amenities to get back to and ease the boredom of seemingly endless talks. Their base camp in a nearby apple orchard had a volleyball court, a baseball diamond, horseshoe pits, a skeet range, a social club and a tent for showing movies.

After the Communists agreed that the actual battle line, some of it north of the 38th parallel, was to be the truce line, Ridgway insisted that the truce line be advanced some 32 miles into Communist-held territory, arguing that, unlike the Communists, the UN would have to give up air and naval attacks as well as a ground war halt and was entitled to territorial compensation. When that demand, for weeks officially denied, was finally publicized (Wilfred Burchett and Alan Winnington, reporting on the Communist side, broke the story), he had to abandon it.

As observed earlier, the U.S. imposed strict censorship and behind that cover on occasion issued misleading accounts of proceedings. Some correspondents on the UN side therefore went to Burchett and Winnington for the truth as they saw it, even for a look at maps prepared to correct the U.S. versions.

The early weeks of the negotiations, in July and August 1951 especially, were characterized not only by rudeness but by violations of the neutral zone. The Americans were guilty of some, South Korean partisans bent on disrupting the talks were responsible for the most serious ones. The Communist side was guilty of a number of penetrations of the neutral zone by its forces.

A major incident took place on August 22, the Communists charging that the conference site in Kaesong had been bombed and strafed. Ridgway seized on what may have been misinformation about the subsequent confrontation to suspend negotiations. He and General Van Fleet then ordered limited offensives which included the assault on Heartbreak Ridge and other ridges.[2]

On August 31 a B-26 dropped two 500-pound bombs near the changed Communist headquarters and on September 10 an American plane machine-gunned Kaesong. But the pressures for a truce were being felt. On the 11th Ridgway surprised correspondents by admitting that violation and in October admitted another.

Agreement was reached on moving the negotiations to the village of Panmunjom and on October 25 of 1951 they resumed, at first progressing fairly amicably. On November 27 an agreement on the demarcation line was reached, strengthening forecasts that a truce was near. But the American introduction of the prisoner of war issue, as observed, ended progress and the talks dragged on.

Eisenhower, campaigning for the presidency, said what his right-wing backers wanted him to say. Addressing the American Legion, he called for "a great moral crusade" to roll back the Communist tide. Sharing a Milwaukee platform with McCarthy himself, he declared that tolerance of Communism had "poisoned two whole decades of our national life," even penetrating "our government itself." The truce negotiations? He described them as a trap.

But he pledged in a speech in Detroit that he would go to Korea and see what could be done to end the war. That helped to win him election by a wide margin. An irascible Truman belittled the Korea trip. A President whose search for a truce was a confusion of morality, strategy and domestic politics was succeeded by one with a specific strategy that would serve his resolve to end the war.

Early in December of 1952, Eisenhower flew to Korea with a number of leading associates. For three days he tramped around front-line units and talked to both privates and commanders. He knew that both General Clark and Syngman Rhee had planned major win-the-war offensives but did not discuss them even with Clark, who on October 16 had cabled the Pentagon that he deemed it necessary to plan atomic bombing of Manchuria and North China.

"My conclusion as I left Korea," Eisenhower wrote later, "was that we could not stand forever on a static front and continue to accept casualties without any visible results. Small attacks on small hills would not end this war."[3]

This pointed to his developed strategy. A composite of private resolution and a measure of public duplicity, its fundamentals were avoidance of resort to atomic weapons and expansion of the war while threatening the contrary. He initiated it in Hawaii on his way home. "We face an enemy," he said, "whom we cannot hope to impress by words, however eloquent, but only by deeds—executed under circumstances of our own choosing."[4]

Back in New York, he and Secretary of State John Foster Dulles called on MacArthur and listened to his extremist proposals set forth in a memo titled "On Ending the Korean War." Eisenhower responded evasively, pleading a need to study them and consult others. But privately, according to his principal biographer, Stephen Ambrose, "he was appalled at McArthur's willingness—and that of so many others—to advocate the use of atomic weapons by the United States against Asian people only seven years after Hiroshima. To Eisenhower's way of thinking, that was the sure way to make all Asians into enemies of the United States."[5]

Dulles was opposed to a truce. He did so by calling for unrealistic demands. He insisted that the Chinese had to agree to refrain from further aggressive actions in Asia and he proposed that the truce line be moved northward to the waist of the peninsula, increasing Rhee's territory to 80 per cent of Korea. He regarded with equanimity a war with China fought with atomic weapons.

Eisenhower purposefully echoed Dulles's hard line rhetorically and seemingly he and his Secretary of State saw eye to eye. But unlike Dulles he was truly for a truce. He once remarked to Emmet Hughes, an assistant and speech writer, "If Mr. Dulles and all his sophisticated advisers really mean that they cannot talk peace seriously, then I am in the wrong pew..."[6]

If he talked like Dulles, it was because of his conviction that only an escalation of threats would persuade the Communists to agree to a truce. And he knew that his verbal bellicosity served also to placate the Republican old guard and reduce the chances of a right-wing backlash on foreign policy.

Eisenhower long had been convinced of the horror and strategic futility of a nuclear war. In his diary he reflected on a report that in the event of a nuclear war, the United States would suffer a minimum of 65 percent casualties. That was appalling. Even if the United States were victorious, "it would literally be a business of digging ourselves out of ashes, starting all over."[7]

At a press conference Eisenhower asked reporters if they could imagine a war fought with atomic missiles. His own answer was that it would not be a war in any recognizable sense "because war is a contest, and (with missiles) you finally get to the point where you are talking merely about race suicide, nothing else."[8]

Not once but a number of times Eisenhower assured those closest to him of his opposition to nuclear bombing. He said this in 1953 in connection with Korea and in 1954 at the time of the Dienbienphu crisis in Vietnam. When Admiral Radford and others proposed recourse to atom bombs in the Dienbienphu area , he expostulated, "You boys must be crazy. We can't use those awful things against Asians for the second time in ten years."[9]

But Eisenhower was commander-in-chief of the armed forces, commander of an arsenal with an assorted complement of nuclear weapons. He commented matter-of-factly and positively on use of them, made sure the Communists were informed that continued adamance at Panmunjom would result in ending restraints on choices of targets and weapons. He said he thought the bomb might be used tactically in Korea itself and noted that bombings were cheaper than ground assaults. And he had to consider the consequence of a final Communist no.

Biographer Piers Brendon observed that "Ike often stressed there would be no victors in a nuclear war...that peace was therefore essential. He could, it is true, mention with terrifying calmness the prospect of using atomic weapons, seeming to regard them as a mere extension of conventional arms. In general, though, this was a propaganda tactic..."[10]

Similarly Callum A. MacDonald observed that Eisenhower "appears to have regarded the atomic threat primarily as a means of diplomatic pressure and preferred accommodation in Korea to escalation."[11]

In January of 1953, in an action that was little more than a gesture, the new President "unleashed" Chiang Kai-shek, withdrawing the 7th Fleet from the Taiwan straits where it had barred an entirely unlikely Kuomintang invasion of the mainland. The British were upset because he hadn't consulted them.

More substantially, Eisenhower approved intensified bombing efforts and the expansion of the ROK forces. These were added to the list of well publicized threats.

China's leadership was inclined to doubt that the bomb would be dropped, expecting another major amphibious landing instead. But, General Nie Rongzhen in command, it prepared for the bomb as best it could. American views on protective measures found in confiscated pamphlets were translated and distributed to all Chinese commanders. Qian Sanqiang, a leading nuclear scientist, and others were consulted and their ideas distributed. At the front a work force that came to total 500,000 worked days and nights constructing more tunnels, trenches and reinforced concrete bunkers.[12]

Mao's words to Americans: "You can follow the way you choose to go, and we will go our own way. You can use the atom bomb. I will respond with my hand grenade..."

In a major speech, his first as President, to the American Society of Newspaper Editors in April Eisenhower said this about the ongoing arms race: "Every gun that is fired, every warship launched, every rocket fired signifies... a theft from those who hunger and are not fed, those who are cold and not clothed. This world in arms is not spending money alone. It is spending the sweat of its laborers, the genius of its scientists, the hopes of its children...We pay for a single fighter plane with half a million bushels of wheat. We pay for a single destroyer with new homes that could have housed more than eight thousand people..."

The speech, titled "The Chance for Peace," was addressed to pacific overtures from post-Stalin Moscow but suggests why Eisenhower truly sought a truce. In it he specifically proposed an armistice in Korea on terms that did not include Dulles' extremisms. It sought a general peace "that is neither partial nor punitive… The first great step along this way must be the conclusion of an honorable peace in Korea."

The New York Times called the speech "magnificent and deeply moving" and both *Pravda* and *Isvestia* published it in full. Dulles was absent from Washington when the speech was prepared and delivered and on his return did what he could, not all that much, to minimize it as "nothing new." The speech and other evidence favorably impressed even some on the left. I.F. Stone came up with the slogan, "Back Ike for Peace."[13]

On May 20, acting on Eisenhower's instructions, the National Security Council toughened the repertoire of threats, declaring that "if conditions arise requiring more positive activity in Korea," meaning essentially a Communist refusal to accept final truce terms, air and naval operations would be undertaken against China. A blockade of China would entail mining of harbors. Diversionary operations by the Chinese Nationalist forces would be supported. In Korea a coordinated offensive would seek to move the cross peninsula line north to the waist, as urged by Dulles. Expansion of the ROK military role and the strengthening of the U.S. Eighth Army were to be undertaken, with the aim of completion in a year.

Eisenhower made much of continuing the threats. But he had to be aware that for several months the Communist line on a truce had been softening. In March Zhou Enlai had retreated on the prisoner repatriation issue and had not only agreed to the exchange of injured and ill prisoners called Little Switch, but suggested that it might lead to a truce agreement. Eisenhower said he was heartened by Little Switch, which took place in April. He told Dulles that it would be "impossible to call off the armistice now and go to war in Korea." He said the American public would not agree to this.

While he authorized the savage bombing of the Yalu area dams in May—the purposes included destruction of the rice crop—he refrained from toughening the truce terms.

In June Syngman Rhee, with the sympathy and connivance of a substantial number of high-up American officers, made outwardly hysterical but inwardly shrewd efforts to stop the talks and continue the war, ordering the immediate release of some 25,000 North Korean prisoners allegedly resisting repatriation. In several compounds politically aware prisoners had to be driven out by club wielding guards. At the Pu

Pyung camp near Seoul a violent clash took place in which scores of prisoners were killed and hundreds wounded by U.S. Marines who had replaced ROK guards.[14] General Clark acknowledged that "in some instances a few prisoners were killed and others wounded."

Simultaneously Rhee ordered the arrest of scores of members of the National Assembly and others thought to favor a truce. This was the political scene in the south as summed up by Sydney Bailey in his *The Korean Armistice:* "Opponents of the regime were being persecuted, alleged collaborators executed without trial, governmental 'goon squads' were at large, ministers with unsavory reputations had been appointed, corruption was rife, Rhee and his supporters were threatening to subvert the constitution, and the campaign against an armistice was gaining momentum."[15]

The Chinese had planned a spring offensive directed at key U.S. positions but, in consideration of encouraging agreements reached at Panmunjom on June 8 and Rhee's threat to reject a truce and order his forces to fight on to the Yalu, they quickly turned their offensive into one entirely aimed at the ROK divisions. A sudden onslaught starting June 10 drove Rhee's troops back and, according to Beijing, eliminated some 41,000 of them at a cost of 19,000 Chinese casualties. The offensive halted when agreement was reached on the demarcation line.

On June 17, Rhee carried out his release of North Korean prisoners and on June 19 Mao directed that another major offensive be launched. After elaborate preparations the Chinese struck on July 13, devastating within 24 hours the ROK Capital, 6th, 8th and 3d divisions and capturing thousands of trucks, tanks and artillery pieces. Thousands of ROK troops did march north but as prisoners.

Two outposts of the U.S. 1st Marine Division in the Panmunjom area whom the Chinese charged with repeated violations of the neutral zone were almost wiped out in 55 minutes. The Marine Corps listed 14 survivors.

As a pacific gesture on the eve of the truce signing on July 27, the Chinese gave back territorial gains south of the 38th parallel but retained 75 square miles, including Heartbreak Ridge, lost to General Van Fleet's 1951 offensives.

General Maxwell Taylor, who in February had succeeded Van Fleet as commander of the Eighth army, summed up the Chinese offensives as follows:[16]

> "1) The ROK Capital Division fought well but was almost literally torn to pieces in the fight.
> "2) At least two ROK divisions on the eastern flank of the attack did not behave with the steadiness that has recently been expected of them.

"3) Weaknesses in command forced the relief of one ROK division commander in mid-battle.

"4) Some ROK troops on the eastern flank retreated too far and too fast.

"5) The Chinese had their usual success in the first stages of the mass attack in overrunning, surrounding and penetrating Allied units.

"6) The ROKs, though this was their best effort to date, still have a long way to go before they are truly a steady and dependable army—despite many small-unit displays of heroism and gallantry.

"7) The front which had been 155 miles long since November 28, 1951 is now about five miles shorter due to Red erasure of the Kumsong bulge."

Away from the battlefield, Eisenhower brought about the abandonment of Rhee's go it alone gambit. He was able to do so by promising him political support, lavish economic aid and continued stationing of substantial American troops in the south. In retrospect he compromised the future for the sake of the present.

For Secretary of State Dulles, the truce agreement was a profound disappointment. Shortly before the signing, he was asked how he would feel if a peace agreement were reached. He replied: "We'd be worried. I don't think we can get much out of a Korean settlement until we have shown—before all Asia—our clear superiority by giving the Chinese one hell of a licking." That hell of a beating was threatened but not attempted and that led to the compromise at Panmunjom.[17]

Eisenhower, Dulles and others insisted that threats to expand the war and resort to nuclear weapons compelled the Communists to yield. Eisenhower asserted this in his memoirs and in conversations. Actually, the Chinese softening at Panmunjom had begun before the threats. In October of 1952 Zhou Enlai in Moscow for the Nineteenth Party Congress got Stalin's agreement that the time had come to end the war in Korea.

The wider truth is that the evident stalemate on the ground in Korea was replicated by a strategic stalemate beyond the peninsula. Fleets of Soviet bombers—totaling some 200—were based north of the Yalu in Manchuria. They held the Eighth Army in thrall by their obvious threat to watery access to the peninsula. Which is why evacuation of the peninsula was widely seen as a necessary preamble to a wider war with China. The central privileged sanctuary of Japan was also obviously vulnerable. The American warships shelling North Korea did so in waters potentially dominated by Soviet submarines. By his hand grenade Mao meant a deployed army. The point counterpoint had to give pause.

On June 8, Beijing and Pyongyang essentially accepted what the U.S. described as the final UN terms regarding repatriation and by the 17th a revised demarcation line had been established. Callum Mac-Donald's comment is to the point: "This breakthrough is often hailed as a triumph of atomic brinkmanship, obscuring the fact that Zhou played his own version of the game and that the UN allies, caught in the middle, had exerted great pressure for a compromise. China was not simply forced to accept terms dictated by Washington. The Americans made concessions.... Dulles' atomic bluster concealed the fact that both sides had retreated to avoid a wider war. Both sides compromised to end a struggle whose costs were out of all proportion to its benefits."[18]

Reaching an armistice had to overcome the residuary illusions of a substitute for victory, as well as lesser misapprehensions and self-serving pride and careerism. The agreement was finally signed on July 27, 1953, two years and 575 plenary and subsidiary meetings after negotiations began, in a T-shaped Peace Pagoda built in five days by northern soldiers. The truce line, determined by heavy fighting and many casualties, was not all that different from the 38th parallel.

General Clark said in his 1954 memoirs, *From the Danube to the Yalu* that "In carrying out the instructions of my government, I gained the unenviable distinction of being the first United States Army commander in history to sign an armistice agreement without victory." The signing "capped my career, but it was a cap without a feather." He repeated his belief that vigorous measures including atom bombing could have won the war.

Peng Dehuai signed for the Chinese Volunteers. Reporters from Beijing asked him to what he attributed his successes in leading Chinese troops. He answered in a word, "Marxism." Peng was a major victim of China's Cultural Revolution. A charge against him was that his answer to the reporters should have been "Mao Zedong Thought."[19]

As word of the signing spread, the American command forbade fraternization. Most units obeyed, but some didn't. More of the British troops joined their adversaries in parties and souvenir exchanges among the bomb craters.

The signing of the truce was not celebrated by cheering crowds in Times Square and press opinion was divided. Eisenhower believed it was his outstanding achievement and said so repeatedly in his diary. According to Ambrose, "From the end of July 1953 onward, whenever he listed the achievements he was proudest of, he always began with peace in Korea."[20]

But he was not congratulated by all in the Republican leadership, in and out of Congress. Some prominent Senators complained that he had not fought for victory and suggested that he had agreed to truce terms that if accepted by Truman might have led to his impeachment. A friendlier comment was that the U.S. had been extricated from a terrible war by a general who was not a militarist and by a Republican who was not a reactionary.

The U.S. suffered an average of 4,666 casualties every month's delay in the truce negotiations—the price for its insistence over Communist objectives that the fighting go on while the two sides talked. Total American casualties in the war rose to 142,091, including 33,629 killed.

In his "The Chance of Peace" speech Eisenhower looked ahead to a time when vast sums no longer had to be spent on arms but were available to finance projects helping people. The signing of the truce gave him a similar thought. The Eighth Army, then under the command of General Maxwell Taylor, could be turned into a giant construction crew, set to work building schools, hospitals, bridges, roads and much else in reconstructing the battered south. He put it all down in a detailed memorandum titled "Assistance to Korea" sent to top subordinates. It would be "something unique in history... the opportunity of an army in a foreign land to contribute directly and effectively to the repairing of the damages of war; to rebuild and revive a nation..." The response of Taylor and other recipients was silence. A second Eisenhower memorandum on the subject lead only to continued silence. Eisenhower failed to press the matter.[21]

If Eisenhower did not then know, he soon would that the Chinese Volunteers did transform themselves into a reconstruction crew that worked until 1958. Its contributions included vital work on an impressive subway in Pyongyang and other major constructions elsewhere.

The truce was followed in April 1954 by a peace conference in Geneva held to deal with Korea and Vietnam issues. The unshaken hand perfectly symbolized American intransigence. Arriving early for the Vietnam discussions, Zhou Enlai held out his hand to John Foster Dulles, who refused to take it and turned away.

The U.S., with some rhetorical help from Rhee and his foreign minister, Y.T. Pyun, made a failure of the Korean conference. Chester Ronning, acting head of the Canadian delegation, has given persuasive testimony of what happened in his memoir: "I was appalled by the great differences in position being taken by the United States and South Korea on the one hand and by most of the rest of us on the other. I thought I had come to participate in a peace conference... Instead the emphasis was entirely on preventing a settlement from being realized.

I was particularly disturbed by statements—especially from the South Koreans and supported by the Americans—giving the impression that the Conference had been called merely to go through the motions."[22]

And Zhou Enlai, whose eloquence in Geneva added to his already impressive reputation, frustrated at the total negativity of the Korea conference, at the end proposed that it be simply adjourned and thought given to a resumption. This is his account of what happened:

"On the final day...as there was no result whatsoever with regard to the Korean question, we put forward the question, what was the use of our coming? We said that at least we should adjourn, we should at least set a date for another meeting. At that time the foreign ministers of certain countries were persuaded... And at that time there was an authoritative representative who was seated at the conference and who waved his hand in opposition and the result was that it was not passed. You probably know who he was: the deputy of Mr. John Foster Dulles, Mr. (Walter Bedell) Smith.. He didn't say anything, he couldn't find any words. He just waved his hand."[23]

Eisenhower's own thoughts on China policy differed from those of Dulles and the Republican leadership generally. He thought, according to biographer Stephen Ambrose, "that with the end of hostilities, the United States ought to reexamine its China policy. Keeping China out of the UN, and refusing to recognize the existence of the Communist government, made no sense to him. But the art of leadership includes the art of the possible, and Eisenhower believed that the American public was not ready to think about a new relationship with China." But he used his clout to defeat a Senate bill barring financial contributions to the UN if Beijing were made a member.[24]

The war perpetuated the division of an utterly devastated Korea and brought death, dislocation and suffering to millions of its people. As Robert R. Simmons has observed, "A potentially swift and relatively bloodless reunification was converted into a carnage."

The civilian death count is estimated at four million, proportionately a greater number than Soviet and Japanese civilian losses. Waging virtually total war, the United States turned cities and towns in the north and much of the south into stretches of rubble. In the north it targeted not only villages but food crops, the latter a war crime by Nuremberg definition.

Faces staring into uncovered mass graves, the long lines of bundle carrying refugees fleeing along the roads and railroad tracks, the scorched bodies in napalmed villages—some of the particulars of a very long count.

A U.S. post-truce survey concluded that the rebuilding of northern industry was "a matter of new construction" rather than rehabilitation.

Korea is the least remembered of the post-World War II American interventions. It ought to be remembered as the most genocidal of them. At the start of the war in 1950, Walter Lippmann wrote: "What we...have to prove to the world is that we can help a country without destroying it." The U.S. didn't even come close.

North Korea did realize an objective, gaining possession of the Onjin peninsula and the city of Kaesong, while losing territory in the east.

The last of the Chinese troops went home in 1958 after over five years of reconstruction work in the north. American troops stayed to serve a succession of Seoul regimes as a permanent garrison. President Eisenhower's effort to get them engaged in construction was a total failure.

Among the American failures in Korea was the failure to learn much from it. In initiating the U.S. intervention in the Korean civil war, Truman ordered support for the French effort to hold onto Indochina. That led to ever increasing military involvement. Again the U.S. intervened with a land army and air power in a revolutionary civil war. Hanoi got the Pyongyang treatment. Again brutality was the counter-revolutionary imperative. But again the West Point uniforms were unable to cope.

The war cost China much blood. Its troops, some two million combat soldiers and logistical noncombatants, suffered 390,000 casualties by Chinese count, including 148,400 killed. They consumed about 5.6 million tons of war materials. The young People's Republic spent 6.2 billion yuan it could hardly afford on the intervention, forgoing much expenditure on economic development and social remedies.

Mao's initial expectations that the tactics that had won China's civil war could succeed in driving the Americans off the peninsula proved unreal. Yet Chinese gains were significant. In 1900 a small army made up of contingents from eight Western countries had easily subdued China. Recently some 700,000 Japanese troops had conquered most of it. But in Korea the armed forces of the greatest Western power and its allies had been fought to a draw—called a great victory and celebrated in China. China's military and international prestige was enhanced.

A succession of Chinese military conferences examined the lessons of the Korean war. Primary credit for successes went to correct military politics, to the human factor. Yet the Chinese command increasingly appreciated the importance of military technology even if the rhetoric downplayed it. China developed its own nuclear weapons.

In November of 1953, just a few months after the signing of the truce, Kim Il Sung and an entourage of high officials came to Beijing to conclude agreements on military, economic and cultural cooperation. He warmly praised China for its "magnificent contributions to the Korean War, which will remain as immortal as Korea's beautiful mountains and rivers." At home he was restrained in his expressions of gratitude to the Chinese for nationalist reasons.

Among Mao's victims in the Cultural Revolution was Peng Dehuai, commander of the Volunteers and later Minister of Defense, a blunt, honorable soldier who had served his country well. He was among the first rehabilitated after the death of Mao.

Appendices

On Villages and the People's Republic: The Frog Gets a New Head

The following account of an American Korean encounter in the countryside early in the fall of 1945 was given me by a well-known Korean writer and scholar who was a local official under the Japanese. I protected his identity so zealously that I now do not know it. He was one of the many Kims.

At the time of the surrender in August 1945 I was in a certain rural district not far from Seoul. About 500 Japanese soldiers were in the vicinity, also some Japanese police and about a hundred Japanese farmers and officials. It was a time of confusion, rumors and robbery.

A few Communists just released from prison came to the district. They were in bad health and had no connection with the people. They could do nothing. But the need for some sort of organization was obvious. The old administrative machinery was breaking down: many officials had left their posts, large numbers of the hated police had fled from the police boxes and the notorious collaborators were afraid to show themselves.

I took the initiative and called all the people of my village to a meeting in the village hall. The elders dominated the meeting, but that was to be expected in view of the ingrained feudal traditions. First we talked about the food problem, which was urgent, and decided on measures to handle it. Then we elected a Self-Government Committee. Perhaps our meeting was not very democratic but it was our first step toward self-rule after forty years under the Japanese. The committee right away organized a night watch of young men armed with sticks. Robbery was checked and the people were hopeful.

What happened in our district happened all over Korea during those first weeks of Liberation. Under one name or another, in one way or another, committees were organized in all the towns and villages. Everywhere there were many gatherings and much talk. Then the farmers began to organize and the workers, the youth and the women. It was a time of change and hope.

The Japanese did nothing at first. The old regime was like a frog whose head, Japan, had been cut off. Its limbs, the collaborators, were paralyzed. The Korean people could do what they liked.

But after a few weeks the Japanese made one last effort. They reorganized the wartime Anti-Air raid Corps and handed out arms to the police in the cities. Anti-Japanese posters were torn down and incidents occurred. These, however, were only the weak convulsions of a headless frog whose nerves have been twitched. Daily the organizations of the people grew stronger.

On September 6th a thousand delegates of the new popular organizations met in Seoul and established the People's Republic. Yo Un-yong's underground group and the patriots just out of prison, some of them Communists, of course—played a leading role. More and more of the local committees affiliated themselves with the People's Republic and a Korean government daily became more of a reality.

Two days later the Americans landed—and soon the frog had a new head. First the Americans kept the Japanese in power—who could have believed it? And then when they finally turned the Japanese out and created the American Military Government, they turned to the frog's quivering limbs, the collaborators. In the countryside the police flocked back to the empty police boxes and the officials returned to their dusty desks. The police were given new armbands and permitted to suppress the people's committees in the name of the U.S. Army. Those who resisted were jailed.

It took some time before the Americans could dispatch enough troops through the provinces to suppress all the popular organizations. In North Cholla province the committees ruled for over two months. Of course General Hodge ordered the frog to be "democratic." But what did this frog know about democracy!

An American named Ross came to our district to arrest me. When I was taken in to see him, I found him surrounded by several Japanese and one leading Korean collaborator. All the Japanese had left previously and now they were back—with the Americans. The Japanese had told Ross that I was behind all the robbery in the district and that the armbands of the new youth organization had been seen on the robbers. Fortunately I could speak English. Others in the same situation at this time could do nothing to disprove such charges and were jailed.

I quoted the Bible to Ross and told him that he was being deceived. I defended our youth. Only they could make Korea independent, I told him. Then I said to him, "Look who is with you. Look what you are doing. Are you pro-Japanese?"

I convinced Ross and he apologized and fined the Japanese police chief. But so many of us couldn't speak English.

The Americans blame everything on the Communists. This is nonsense. Of those there were only a few score, just out of prison. At first they could do nothing. They had no organization. But the more the people were oppressed by the frog with the new head the more they became aware of the faithful, of those who had been in prison. The greater the obstacles placed in the way of the new youth and farmers organizations the more readily did people ask the Communists to help them. It was only natural.

In those days it was hard to understand why the Americans opposed the organization of the people, then painfully taking their first steps along a new road. Had not the American people once organized as we did? For the first year I thought that it was because the Americans were ignorant of the situation, because somehow they had been surrounded by those so polite English-speaking collaborators. Now I know better.

Declaration of the Korean People's Republic

SEPTEMBER 14, 1945

We declare herewith that the date September 6, 1945, together with August 15, 1945, should be regarded as epochal in the annals of the Emancipation of the Korean people. On that September 6, 1945, a Korean People's Council was held, the members of which represented every circle and stratum of the nation and comprised more than one thousand advocates of reform, those who have been resolutely striving in and outside our country for our Liberation from Japanese imperialism. At this meeting the name of "The People's Republic of Korea' at last came into the world, and the people's committee was organized to constitute its government and to enforce functions thereof. Under these circumstances, the Korean people have entered upon the colossal task of consummating what our independence imposes on us.

For nearly half a century the way to our free development and growth in every possible way has been obstructed by Japanese imperialism, by its feudalistic exploitations and oppressions.

Notwithstanding these disadvantages we Koreans have ever maintained our revolutionary resistance for the sake of our Liberation. To our unyielding resistance and the international adjustment of postwar problems through principles and ideals of democracy, our deliverance from the Japanese yoke is much indebted.

This means, however, the continuation of our laborious movements for our Liberation so far. Complete freedom and independence which are yet to be won can be gained only through strenuous efforts. Surmounting every obstacle, adversity, and hardship, in accordance with the basic demand of our revolutionary members and our fellow citizens who have elected us, we are determined to demolish Japanese imperialism, its residuary influences, antidemocratic factions, reactionary elements, and any undesirable foreign influences in our state, and to establish our complete autonomy and independence, thereby anticipating the realization of our authentically democratic state.

Hereafter it should be our aim to secure swift improvement in the living standard of the Korean people as a whole and their political freedom, and to establish world peace through our cooperation with the U.S.A., U.S.S.R., England, China and all the other peace loving democratic countries.

We announce, with the intention manifested above, our platform and our administrative policies as follows:

PLATFORM

1. We are resolved to establish an autonomous and independent state, both politically and economically.

2. We are resolved to demolish imperialism and residuary feudalistic influences in our state and be faithful to the principles and ideals of democracy which must materialize the basic political, economical, and social needs of our nation.

3. We are resolved to secure a rapid elevation in the living standard of the laborers, the peasants, and the masses.

4. We are resolved to establish world peace through our cooperation as one of the democratic countries of the world.

Twenty-seven administrative policies are then listed.

This text of the Declaration is taken from *Kyung Cho Chung, Korea Tomorrow*, New York: Macmillan, 1956, pp. 304-306. Several minor corrective changes have been made.

Statement by Kim Ku and Kim Kyu-sik on Trip to Pyongyang

MAY 6, 1948

Our trip to North Korea has fulfilled, through action, the great expectation of a large number of our fellow countrymen, who are longing for the unification of our fatherland, and the people of the whole world, who have been doubtful about the union of the Korean people. The conference of political parties and social organizations of South and North Korea has proved once again the fact that by action the Koreans, as other able peoples of the world do, can unite together above and over the differences of isms and parties for the purpose of overcoming the crisis of their fatherland and perpetuating the existence of the people. This conference agreed to oppose the unilateral elections and separate government in South Korea and to demand the withdrawal of the two troops in order to rehabilitate a sovereign democratic and united Korea. The authorities of North Korea said clearly that they would not set up a separate government there.

This is a historical new development of our independent movement and gives us the great light of hope. The Joint Communiqué of the conference laid the foundation of the union of our people by promising that after the evacuation of the two troops a National Political Conference should set up a provisional government for a United Korea, and that through a general election the Constitution should be drafted and the official united government should be established. It clearly indicates the direction for the rehabilitation of a sovereign, democratic and united regime in our fatherland. Furthermore, it proves that Koreans are capable of having a peaceful national life, if there is no interference from outside.

We declare with confidence that as the Joint Communiqué indicates, there would be no strife among our people. One cannot be satisfied with the first spoonful of food. But with the developing results of the first conference, the final success is certain to come.

We regret that international harmony and other problems which we discussed have not been solved. We believe that the powers can demonstrate international harmony by practicing it, showing which of them can do most for Korean independence and that the other problems will be solved by frequent leadership contacts and by our united efforts. We have shown by our experience that Koreans can unite and talk over problems. For example, 1) there was a dispute about electric power between the authorities of South and North Korea. The North told the press it would cut off the electricity in the near future. And 2) the Yun Paik irrigation problem was tangled. The conference solved these problems. The North Korean authorities agreed gladly not to cut off the light and water. They also promised to let us take Mr. Cho Man Sik down to South Korea, not at this time but in the near future.

In conclusion we express our thanks to the occupation forces and government authorities of South and North Korea, the press, and others who enabled us to make this trip so pleasantly.

Mao's Telegram to Stalin October 2, 1950

(1) We have decided to send a portion of our troops, under the name of Volunteers, to Korea, assisting the Korean comrades to fight the troops of the United States and its running dog Syngman Rhee. We regarded the mission as necessary. If Korea were completely occupied by the Americans and the Korean revolutionary force were fundamentally destroyed, the American invaders would be more rampant, and such a situation would be very unfavorable to the whole East.

(2) We realize that since we have decided to send Chinese troops to Korea to fight the Americans, we must first be able to solve the problem, that is, we are prepared to wipe out the invaders from the United States and from other countries and drive them out; second, since Chinese troops will fight American troops in Korea (although we will use the name of Chinese Volunteers), we must be prepared for an American declaration of war on China. We must be prepared for the possible bombardments by American air forces of many Chinese cities and industrial bases, and for attacks by American naval forces on China's coastal areas.

(3) Of the two questions, the first one is whether the Chinese troops would be able to wipe out American troops in Korea, thus effectively resolving the Korean problem. If our troops could annihilate American troops in Korea, especially the Eighth Army (a competent veteran U.S. army), the whole situation would become favorable to the revolutionary front and China, even though the second question (that the United States declares war on China) would still remain a serious question. In other words, the Korean problem will end in fact with the defeat of the American troops (although the war might not end in name, because the United States would not recognize the victory of Korea for a long period). If so, even though the United States declared war on China, the confrontation would not be a large-scale one, nor would it last very long. We consider that the most unfavorable situation would be that the Chinese forces fail to destroy American troops in large numbers in Korea, thus resulting in a stalemate and that, at the same time, the United States openly declares war on China, which would be detrimental to China's economic reconstruction already under way and would cause dissatisfaction among the national bourgeoisie and some other sectors of the people (who are absolutely afraid of war.)

(4) Under the current situation, we have decided, starting on October 15, to move the twelve divisions, which have been earlier transferred to southern Manchuria, into suitable areas in North Korea (not necessarily close to the 38th parallel); these troops will only fight the enemy that venture to attack areas north of the 38th parallel; our troops will maintain a defensive warfare, while fighting with small groups of enemies and learning about the situation in every respect. Meanwhile, our troops will be awaiting the arrival of Soviet weapons and to be equipped with those weapons. Only then will our troops, in cooperation with the Korean comrades, launch a counteroffensive to destroy the invading American forces.

(5) According to our information, every U.S. army (two infantry divisions and one mechanized division) is armed with 1500 pieces of artillery of various calibers ranging from 70 mm to 240 mm, including tank guns and antiaircraft guns, while each of our armies (three divisions) is equipped with only 36 pieces of such artillery, The enemy would control the air while our air force, which has just started its training, will not be able to enter the war with some 300 planes until February 1951. Therefore, at present we are not assured that our troops are able to wipe out an entire U.S. army once and for all. But since we have decided to go into the war against the Americans, we should be prepared so that, when the U.S. high command musters up one complete army to fight us in one campaign, we should be able to concentrate our forces four times larger than the enemy (that is, to use four of our armies to fight against one enemy army) and to use a firing power one and a half to two times stronger than that of the enemy (that is, to use 2200 to 3000 pieces of artillery of 70 mm caliber and upward to deal with the enemy's 1500 pieces of artillery of the same caliber), so that we can guarantee a complete and thorough destruction of one enemy army.

(6) In addition to the above-mentioned twelve divisions, we are transferring another twenty-four divisions, as the second and third echelons to assist Korea, from the south of the Yangzi River and the Shaanxi-Ganshu areas to the Long-hai, Tianjin-Pukou, and Beijing-Southern Manchuria railways; we expect to gradually apply these divisions next spring and summer in accordance with the situation of the time.

From *Uncertain Partners: Stalin, Mao, and the Korean War* by Sergei N. Goncharov, John W. Lewis, and Xue Litai, Document 63

North Korea Diary 1997

by Hugh Deane

OCTOBER 22

This is our first full day in Pyongyang.

Arriving from Beijing by a Koryo plane yesterday afternoon, we are immediately taken to bow before a bronze statue of Kim Il Sung. We are handed a bouquet of flowers to add to those at the base of the statue.

We are an American delegation of just three, all with some friendliness toward the north in our past—Dr. Charles M. Grossman from Portland, Oregon, internist, active in the Physicians for Social Responsibility and in a newly formed committee, Americans for a New Relationship with Korea. The others were Howard Glazer, a progressive architect with China experience, also from Portland, and the author, an editor and writer from New York City engaged in writing a book about the Korean war. Grossman and I had served four years on the national board of the US-China Peoples Friendship Association. All three of us had traveled in China together a year earlier.

In the morning we are taken to see monuments—Kim Il Sung's birthplace, a thatched roof farm house, which expanding Pyongyang has enveloped; a triumphal arch honoring the Workers Party (Communist) on its 50th anniversary; a soaring round tower memorializing *juche*, an elusive concept for foreigners which Kim Il Sung has described as a theory "that man is the master of everything and decides everything..."

In the afternoon a request of mine is realized, a visit to the huge war museum. To see all 80 detailed exhibits might take at least a week, so we see only selected ones having to do with the origins of the 1950-1953 war and some of the important battles. Neither on the walls nor in the English-language booklets I bought in the museum shop was there even a mention of the major Chinese role in the war, which indeed, at the cost of enormous casualties, saved the Kim Il Sung regime. I inquired of course and was told that exhibits having to do with the Chinese intervention were being reworked. I learned also that on October 25th, the anniversary of the date Beijing announced its intervention, a Chinese delegation took war artifacts to the museum and requested that they be added to the exhibits. Answers to questions informed us that two monuments honoring the Chinese who fought in the war were erected in Pyongyang years ago.

The account of the start of the war in the museum corrected some obvious American propaganda but did not go beyond Kim Il Sung's statement of June 26, 1950 that the southern army had engaged in a general assault along the 38th parallel. Southern troops may have violated the parallel near the Onjin peninsula in the west in 1950 as they certainly did in 1949, but no peninsula-wide offensive took place.

Revelations in recent years, including Soviet and Chinese documentation, indicate that Kim Il Sung had determined to try to unify the peninsula by force and eventually gained the acquiescence of Stalin and Mao. He waited for the return of the many thousands of Koreans who had served in the People's Liberation Army in the civil war, waited also for or what he could call a provocation and then sent battle-tested divisions south. Kim and Syngman Rhee in Seoul were mirror images of each other in one key respect, both convinced that only military force could achieve unification. Kim ignited the war, but it was a civil war, Koreans invading Korea, a struggle between a revolutionary north and a decidedly rightist south, until the massive American invasion.

At the end of the tour of the museum we found two generals waiting to talk to us. Lieutenant General Kang Tae Mu is a southerner who in 1949 commanded one of two southern companies stationed along the parallel which defected to the north. He told us that he had come to dislike the Syngman Rhee regime and to resent what he saw as American control of the army and that had led him to listen sympathetically to the Pyongyang radio. Many others shared his feelings and so two entire companies went north. Kim Il Sung embraced him as a patriot and he advanced rapidly in the new northern army, becoming a general at age 29.

Major General Kim Tae Hua was there to inform us about the war atrocities. We knew about them but soon found that the general's words had bite. His father, a farmer, had been killed as he worked in a field by a strafing plane, American he was certain. Six other members of his family were killed during the brief southern occupation of the north in the fall of 1950. He said that 200 years from now the atrocities performed by the South Koreans and Americans would live in the hearts of the people.

October 23

Two days a week foreigners are allowed to join in respectful visits to Kim Il Sung's mausoleum, which is his office reconstructed. Today is one of them and we join many Koreans, entire units and individuals. A moving walkway, the length of a football field, takes us to an escalator and a corridor to a large hall occupied solely by a statue of Kim

Il Sung. We line up in front of it and are asked by a guide to pay homage. We bow with the guides. Several long flights of stairs take us to the bier, enclosed in a glass rectangle. We bow four times, once on each side of it. Then we retrace our steps to sunlight.

Kim Il Sung and his son and successor, Kim Jong Il, are rarely out of sight. Statues at the entrance to public buildings, photos of each in public rooms, billboards, quotations cut in slabs of stone. We see in our hotel and elsewhere giant pictures featuring flowers and are told that they depict new varieties of orchid and begonia developed in Indonesia and Japan and named for Kim Il Sung or Kim Il Jong. We are shown a long film in which the two Kims are invariably together at ceremonies and inspections.

OCTOBER 24-28

On each of these days, busy with sightseeing, we learn more about the sad realities beyond what we have come to see as the Pyongyang oasis. We view a long documentary about the floods and talk to both Koreans and UN personnel and other foreigners. One of our two guides had a notebook full of specific data collected on an earlier assignment.

The catastrophe began with the loss of the socialist market—trade with the former Soviet Union, Eastern Europe and pre-capitalist China. Industry was hard hit; many plants shut down. Then came three years of natural disasters, floods in 1995 and 1996, drought and a giant tidal wave this year. In 1995 the Yalu River, along the northern border, flooded south as torrential rains fell, causing mountain avalanches and rock slides as well as inundated villages. The Korean People's Army evacuated many people in peril, dropping down in helicopters where necessary. The 1996 flood came when the earlier flood had not entirely receded and the damage was even more extensive. Close to a million acres of paddy and dry field were covered with mud or otherwise taken out of cultivation. A million tons of stored grain were washed away. Railroads, roads, bridges, dams and irrigation systems suffered, coal mines were flooded, some to such an extent that they have been abandoned. More industries were lost, some soon torn down for scrap. Then this year the usual rainy season was rainless. Nearly all the maize crop, normally a million tons, was lost. The rice crop was reduced, both because of the drought and because there was no fertilizer to apply to it. Such are the circumstances that brought hunger and starvation to a great many.

A visiting delegation of American doctors, some of them ethnically Korea, found that shortage of medicines is about as serious as the publicized food shortage. Hospitals in Pyongyang they visited lacked sufficient medicines and adequate equipment. But outside Pyongyang the situation is far worse. The doctors encountered hospitals without medicine—without even aspirin, iodine or alcohol. Patients were being operated on without anesthesia. Much of the equipment is old and unusable, x-ray machines lacked film. Dr. Grossman, back in Portland, joined in an effort to organize a shipment of medicines and equipment.

Some foreigners are pessimistic about the future of the Democratic People's Republic of Korea, perhaps influenced by ideology. They suppose that for decades it will be a backward third world country, with only vestiges of industry. One offered this shorthand advice, "Make cheap shoes." Others are more hopeful. A Texan distributing sacks of grain donated by Amigos Internaciones told me that the north can count on one asset—its people.

Organizations from various countries, some associated with the United Nations World Food Program, have launched or plan specific projects, both humanitarian aid and the kinds of assistance needed to address the basic hurts of the economy. One instance is the balanced help being received from the American Friends Service Committee, which began work here in 1980. It has raised $600,000 internationally to provide the Sambong Cooperative with seed, fertilizer and vinyl sheeting as well as medicines, food and clothing, including mittens for the 250 children.

OCTOBER 24 (GOING BACK A FEW DAYS)

We are driven northwest in our two Mercedes (North Korea bought a fleet of them some years ago) to view the area drowned by a typhoon-generated tidal wave that struck nearly 50 miles of the coast, penetrating inland to a depth of about three miles. The wave came ashore in daylight and no lives were lost, but farm houses, even entire villages were destroyed or damaged. We see ships of 20 to 30 feet that the wave had borne far inland. And we see a coal mine that had escaped earlier floods which the wave had flooded. A serious effect of the inundation is that the land soaked cannot be cultivated for three years or so. It will take that long for rain to wash away the deposits of salt. In towns we drive through we see factories with broken windows, abandoned.

We end the day with a visit to the largest of the Children's Palaces. Like the similar ones in China, it offers after-school activities to thousands of children of all grades. We make the rounds of classes teaching choral singing, the playing of various musical instruments, sketching, performing solo at gatherings. Pyongyang has two palaces. Throughout the country are smaller ones, we were told.

OCTOBER 25

Today we drive north and somewhat east into the mountains that are North Korea's geographical treasures, the forested mountains which were the scene of skirmishes and battles in the long struggle to win independence from Japan.

The countryside is neat. The rice has been harvested and bundles of straw left in the closely clipped fields; many will be threshed again, a gleaning. The large green cabbage patches are being harvested. Cabbages are the principal winter vegetable and the basic ingredient of the national dish, *kim chi*, made a hundred different ways of fermented cabbage, radish and peppery spices. Some of the villages look new; rows of one-story houses with whitewashed walls, tile roofs and blue painted doors and window frames. Some may replace villages destroyed in the war when the U.S. Air Force bombed the northern dams, sending a torrent of water through fields and villages all the way to Pyongyang.

Our destination is Mount Myohyang, below it a forested valley with a rushing stream. Kim Il Sung was moved to write a long poem on the scene in autumn and chant it from the balcony of the International Friendship Exhibition on October 15, 1979:

> On the balcony I see the most
> glorious scene in the world...
> The Exhibition stands here,
> its green eaves upturned, to exalt
> The dignity of the nation,
> and Piro Peak looks higher still.

The exhibition consists of halls in which are displayed gifts of foreigners to Kim Il Sung and Kim Jong Il. The gifts were declared the property of the people and collected here. Jimmy Carter and wife gave Kim Il Sung handsome glassware and Billy Graham, evangelist, twice in Pyongyang, gave Kim Il Sung gifts twice. Our eyes strayed from the expensive gifts in glass cases inside to the glorious forest and stream outside.

OCTOBER 26

A Sunday, we go to one of the two Protestant churches. It is simply and elegantly designed and the service is well attended. When it ended, a visiting Japanese pastor came to the podium and apologized at length for Japanese misbehavior in Korea and elsewhere in Asia. The Korean pastor translated. Three other Japanese Christians came forward and bowed deeply, their knees on the floor.

Billy Graham, whose wife grew up in North Korea, preached on two occasions at the other Protestant church. Pyongyang also has a Catholic church. The number of Christians in North Korea is about 11,000. Outside of Pyongyang they worship in house churches, as in China.

OCTOBER 27

A well-designed broad highway takes us south to Kaesong, capital of the Koryo dynasty (918-1392), close to the 38th parallel. Again the countryside is harvested rice paddies and much cabbage. Large plots of ginseng, which has to be sheltered as it grows, come on the scene as we near Kaesong. All along young pines tell us of a reforestation effort.

Kaesong, bombed to smithereens like most Korean cities and towns, both north and south, is an almost new city of high rises. A few ancient buildings that survived the bombings can be seen fleetingly between them.

From Kaesong we drive a short distance east to Panmunjom, site of the long truce talks. The large building in which the truce agreement was signed, designed and constructed by a unit of the Korean People's Army, is occupied only by bare tables. General Mark Clark said in his memoirs that he signed reluctantly; Washington ordered him to. Peng Dehuai signed for China. When reporters from Beijing asked to what he attributed his successes as commander of the Chinese forces, he answered in a word, "Marxism." During China's Cultural Revolution, in which he was persecuted, he was criticized for not answering "Mao Zedong Thought."

Americans from the 37,000 occupation force were stationed at the DMZ, the demilitarized zone, up to a year or so ago. They have been replaced by South Korean soldiers from contingents that are integrated into American units. The south has constructed a cement wall across the peninsula and, denying that it has done so, grown grass on it. We saw sections of it through telescopes. We also saw large southern posters appealing to northerners to cross over. Anyone doing so is promised a good life, including foreign travel.

On July 8 of 1994 Kim Il Sung at his desk signed a paper setting forth policies aimed at achieving unification. Two hours later, still at his desk, he slumped over, dead. The media here makes much of Kim's concern with unification in his last hours. A quotation from him on the subject is chiseled into granite at the DMZ.

Without consulting any Koreans, Washington and Moscow divided Korea along the 38th parallel in 1945. The stalemated war did not seriously change the division and it continues to divide families and antagonistic political and military entities. Feelings of shame are shared south and north. The United States is centrally involved. Its garrison is justified as forestalling a northern offensive, but the underlying effect, certainly calculated, is to deny unification.

OCTOBER 28

An inspection of the heavy industry exhibition in Pyongyang is both enlightening and sad. The North Korean engineers sometimes improved foreign machinery as they adapted it to their needs. A number of inventions impressed us: a coal mining machine capable of breaking up many tons an hour, a robot to mine lead and zinc, a robot producer of machine tool parts, an off-white building block, larger than a brick and very sturdy, that won the attention and study of Howard Glazer, architect. The sadness is that the disastrous years have destroyed many of the factories capable of putting the displayed machinery to use.

Driving about, we get an admiring sense of Pyongyang. Surely one of the world's most attractive capitals, it was enabled to become so in large part by American bombs. By northern count, the Air Force dropped 428,000 bombs, high explosive and napalm, converting the city into a stretch of rubble and building fragments. So the city planners and designers after the truce in 1953 had a level field to work with, and the result is broad tree-lined streets, straight and curved, many parks, some along the banks of the two rivers, squares setting off imaginatively designed public buildings, among them museums, theaters, arenas and a home for the circus.

A forest of mostly high rise apartment houses seem overly similar though balconies give some horizontal lines. Unlike New York, Pyongyang has no homeless, a guide cannot resist telling us. The apartments have three or four rooms. Rents and water are free. Residents pay for electricity and, I suppose, for the steam heat piped into buildings by the power plants. Petrol has to be imported and is scarce. Few cars are on the streets but the sparse traffic is directed at intersections by policewomen in neat, light blue uniforms. Electrified trams take people to and from work.

North Korea's serious plight is not visible in Pyongyang. The regime seems to be giving priority attention to keeping its appearance normal. A criticism is that far less effort is being paid to other cities and towns, as those visiting or passing through cannot help but immediately notice.

OCTOBER 29

In North Korea the usual hammer and sickle have a traditional writing brush between them, a consequence of Kim Il Sung's conviction that intellectuals can be good revolutionaries and that humankind must be well educated to advance socially. We visit the huge Korean-style Grand People's Study House which as many 7,000 come to daily. It houses a multi-million volume library which includes books that may be taken out and some 600 rooms, including lecture halls, study rooms, special collections, a photo center and a printing plant. A feature is a Q and A room in which several professors or scholars, serving in rotation, are always on hand to answer the questions of perplexed students.

We are shown a music room composed of scores of listening stations. Those coming to it may sign up for an album of Korean or foreign music, take it to a station, clap on ear phones and listen without disturbing others. We are told about collections for study of science and art.

A quotation from Kim Il Sung begins, "Books are silent teachers...." The study house is described as "an important base of intellectualizing the whole of society and a correspondence university of the working people." Professionals and workers may add to their knowledge by taking short courses or attending special lectures.

OCTOBER 30

We are taken through the Korean history museum and folklore museum. They make evident to observers with China knowledge a truth unacknowledged by the museum guide and the texts on the walls—China contributed very much to the shaping of the society. Confucianism and Buddhism were dominant imports; the written language of the elite was Chinese. Early in the millennium four Chinese commanderies or colonies were established in Korea. The largest, with a population of 300,000, was Lolang, near what is now Pyongyang. I discovered that the commanderies and Chinese influence in general get minimal attention and some misleading comment. Korean nationalism, long suppressed by the Japanese, is naturally assertive. It expresses a truth. Some in the Korean elite were Sinocized but for the most part foreign influences were absorbed in a homogeneous culture. A distinct language with an alphabet is part of it.

In the afternoon we moved from history to a notable and emotional aspect of the present. Some 150 of the most heroic of the men and women killed in the revolutionary struggle, in the guerrilla war in the north or caught in the underground, are interred, reinterred in many cases, in the Cemetery of Revolutionary Martyrs on Taesong

Mountain overlooking the city. Rows of identifying stones surmounted by bronze busts descend a slope from a huge flag made of red marble. Among them is Kim Jong Suk, wife of Kim Il Sung and mother of Kim Jong Il. She began revolutionary work at the age of 14.

Prominently there also was Kim Chaek, revolutionary army commander and Kim Il Sung's closest associate. The city of Kanggye, in the far north he knew so well, has been renamed for him. The average age of the 150 martyrs is 25.

OCTOBER 31

We visit a unique institution called a Health Complex. It is something of a misnomer, since it does not treat the ailing or injured or dispense medicine. Rather it brings together in one place varied facilities for promotion of good health and well-being—two barber shops (50 barbers, most of them women), an equivalent of a beauty parlor, massage rooms, exercise rooms and enough bathrooms (public, family and individual) to accommodate 10,000 people daily. Also a restaurant, soft drink counters, a wading pool for youngsters, a normal one for adults. Swimming teachers are on hand. Mosaics and a circle of fountains add to the attractiveness of the well attended complex.

Later we visit a family in an apartment. The conversation was interesting but what I remember most clearly is that only the men in the family, the husband, a son and a nephew, sat with us in the living room. The wife and daughters prepared and served us delicious things to eat.

On this, our last day, we are asked to write a letter to Kim Jong Il. We agree on one we will all sign. It congratulates him on his election as general secretary of the Workers Party, says that we have learned much on our short visit, and will tell our fellow citizens about it, commits us to working for a nuclear weapons-free peninsula and world, and expresses the conviction that increased dialogue and visitation will help to bring about normalization of diplomatic relations and normalization of human relations.

Chronology
Major Historical Dates

108 A.D.
- Kingdom of Choson overcome by armies of China's Han dynasty.
- Lolang and three other Chinese colonies established.

FIRST CENTURY A.D.
- Korean states of Koguryo, Paekche and Silla established.

313
- Lolang falls to Kokuryo and Paekche.

668
- United Silla period initiated by Silla defeat of Kokuryo and Paekche.

935
- Koryo dynasty succeeds United Silla.

THIRTEENTH CENTURY
- Mongol invasions.

1392
- Long-lasting Yi dynasty established.

1443
- Korean alphabet invented.

1592, 1598
- Hideyoshi (Japanese) invasions.

1883
- First American embassy opened.

1894
- Sino-Japanese war.

1904
- Russo-Japanese war.

1910
- Korea formally annexed to Japanese empire.

1919
- March First movement for independence. According to Koreans, at least 6000 are killed, 45,000 injured, and 49,000 arrested in the Japanese suppression. • A declaration of Korean independence was proclaimed in Seoul and in villages and cities. Thirty-three religious leaders signed it.

1942 DECEMBER 1:
- The Cairo Declaration, signed by the U.S., Great Britain and China, promises a free and independent Korea "in due course."

1945 AUGUST 8:
- Soviet Union declares war on Japan, subscribes to Potsdam Declaration promising Korean independence.

AUGUST 15:
- Roosevelt and Stalin divide Korea arbitrarily at the 38th parallel with Soviet forces occupying the north and U.S. the south. Official liberation day for Korea.

AUGUST-SEPTEMBER:
- People's Committees formed in many places, north and south, leading to establishment of the Korean People's Republic by a broad left-dominated coalition on September 6.

SEPTEMBER 8:
- U.S. troops arrive and shortly the American command, headed by General John R. Hodge, begins the crackdown on the People's Republic and left organizations. • In the north the committees are retained and eventually controlled by the Workers Party (Communist).

LATE SEPTEMBER:
- Kim Il Sung returns to Korea after a stay in Soviet Union.

OCTOBER:
- Syngman Rhee returns to Korea after long exile, is warmly welcomed by the American command, and begins his rhetorical assault on the Soviet presence north of the 38th parallel.

DECEMBER 12:
- U.S. officially bans people's committees.

DECEMBER 27:
- U.S., United Kingdom and Soviet foreign ministers reach Moscow Decision—Korea temporarily to be subject to a four-power trusteeship, provisional government to be formed. South Korean right, with U.S. support, opposed the decision.

1946 MARCH 20-MAY 8:
- U.S.-Soviet Joint Commission meets in Seoul, deadlocked chiefly because of U.S. intransigence

OCTOBER-NOVEMBER:
- Widespread Autumn Harvest uprisings in the south are ruthlessly suppressed.

1947 MAY-OCTOBER:
- Second and concluding vain meeting of the Joint Commission.

JULY 19:
- Yo Unhyong, the principal left-oriented leader, assassinated in Seoul.

AUGUST-SEPTEMBER:
- Assaults on above-ground South Korean left intensified until its destruction largely achieved.

SEPTEMBER 17:
- U.S. takes Korea issue to the United Nations as initial step toward creation of a separate southern regime.

NOVEMBER:
- General Assembly creates UN Temporary Commission on Korea.

1948 APRIL:
- Left uprising on Cheju Island begins and continues into 1949.

APRIL 2:
- Truman approves NSC-48, basic foreign policy document which broadly approves rollback as opposed to mere containment of Communism.

APRIL 19-23:
- Broad political conference representing 56 South and North Korean parties held in Pyongyang opposes separate elections in the south.

MAY 10:
- Elections in the south, boycotted by the left, are a sweeping victory for Rhee and rightists and validated by UN.

JUNE 29-JULY 5:
- Second Pyongyang Conference supports setting up of government in the north and holding of elections.

JULY 20:
- Syngman Rhee elected president of south by Assembly.

AUGUST 15:
- Separatist Republic of Korea established in Seoul, MacArthur present at the ceremony, promises Rhee that he will defend the regime.

SEPTEMBER 9:
- Democratic People's Republic proclaimed in north, Kim Il Sung is premier.

OCTOBER:
- Brief rebellion in Yosu area leads to broad guerrilla conflict in the south that continues, weakened, into 1950.

DECEMBER 25:
- Soviet troops withdrawn from North Korea, advisers remain.

1949 MARCH:
- Kim Il Sung visits Moscow seeking Soviet approval of a North Korean drive south. Much later Stalin agreed.

MAY 4:
- South Korea initiates engagement with northern forces in area of the Onjin Peninsula; two companies defect to the north.

JUNE 30:
- U.S. withdraws troops from South Korea, leaves 500 advisers.

JULY-AUGUST:
- More clashes along 38th parallel accompany southern threats to invade north.

1950 JANUARY 12:
- Acheson, in speech to the National Press Club, seemingly places Korea and Formosa outside U.S. defense perimeter.

MAY 29:
- Assembly elections are serious setback for Rhee.

JUNE 17:
- Dulles arrives in Seoul, there until June 21. Is photographed peering north at the 38th parallel.

JUNE 25:
- General North Korean assault along 38th parallel. Truman orders intervention in the Korean civil war, sends the 7th Fleet into the Taiwan straits and increases U.S. involvement in French Indochina and the Philippines.
- The U.S. carries out its intervention in the name of the United Nations.

JUNE 28:
- Seoul falls to north.

JULY 1:
- First U.S. combat troops arrive in Korea.

JULY-AUGUST:
- Korean People's Army takes 90 percent of south but is withstood by U.S. forces in the Pusan area.

JULY 31:
> • MacArthur flies to Taipei to consult with Chiang Kai-shek.

AUGUST 17:
> • MacArthur sends message to Veterans of Foreign Wars convention critical of Washington policies. • Truman orders it withdrawn but too late to prevent its publication.

AUGUST 20:
> • Zhou Enlai in cable to UN: "The Chinese people cannot but be concerned about the solution of the Korean question."

AUGUST 25:
> • MacArthur declares that Taiwan is part of an island chain from which U.S. "can dominate with air power every Asiatic port from Vladivostok to Singapore."

SEPTEMBER 12:
> • George Marshall succeeds Louis Johnson as Secretary of Defense.

SEPTEMBER 15:
> • Amphibious landing at Inchon, planned and commanded by MacArthur, inflicts major defeat on north and results in recapture of Seoul and reinstatement of Rhee.

SEPTEMBER 30:
> • Zhou Enlai declares "The Chinese people… will not supinely tolerate seeing their neighbors being savagely invaded by the imperialists."

OCTOBER 3:
> • Zhou Enlai informs Indian envoy K.M. Pannikar that if U.S. troops enter North Korea, China will intervene. • The principal American response is that Beijing is bluffing.

OCTOBER 7:
> • UN Assembly supports military unification of Korea. First American troops cross 38th parallel.

OCTOBER 14-16:
> • Units of PLA's Fourth Field Army, called Volunteers, enter Korea.

OCTOBER 15:
> • Truman and MacArthur confer on Wake Island. MacArthur assures the President that China will not intervene.

OCTOBER 19:
> • Pyongyang falls to U.S. Eighth Army.

OCTOBER 26—NOVEMBER 7:
> • Chinese Volunteers batter elements of three Republic of Korea divisions, then halt attacks. On the 7th all Communist units break off action and take shelter in the hills.

NOVEMBER 24:
> • MacArthur launches "home by Christmas" offensive. • Chinese special delegation arrives at UN, briefly stirring peace hopes.

NOVEMBER 27:
> • Chinese and North Korean forces execute massive counterattack, bringing about a swift, chaotic U.S.-ROK retreat. • On the 28th MacArthur declares that "We face an entirely new war."

NOVEMBER 30:
- Truman suggests nuclear bomb may be used, alarming allies and bringing Clement Attlee on a hurried visit to Washington.

DECEMBER 15:
- U.S.-ROK retreat crosses 38th parallel.

DECEMBER 23:
- General Walton Walker killed in road accident, succeeded as commander of the Eighth Army by General Matthew B. Ridgway.

DECEMBER 31:
- Chinese with North Koreans launch third offensive.

1951 JANUARY 4:
- Seoul again taken in Chinese-North Korean offensive.

LATE JANUARY:
- Drive of Sino-Korean forces reaches southernmost point and is followed shortly by a limited U.S. counteroffensive.

FEBRUARY 1:
- UN resolution, pressed by Washington, condemns China as aggressor.

FEBRUARY 13:
- MacArthur issues statement criticizing Administration policies.

MARCH 14:
- Seoul recaptured by American forces.

MARCH 24:
- MacArthur calls on Communist commanders to confer in the field with him, his purpose to undermine a UN peace move.

APRIL 5:
- Another critical MacArthur letter read to House of Representatives by minority leader Joseph W. Martin.

APRIL 11:
- MacArthur dismissed by Truman as UN commander, succeeded by General Ridgway. General James Van Fleet takes command of Eighth Army.

APRIL-MAY:
- Two major Chinese offensives halted in fighting which costs them heavy casualties.

JUNE 23:
- Soviet representative Adam Malik at UN urges cease-fire discussions.

JULY 10:
- Truce negotiations start at Kaesong.

AUGUST 23:
- Talks suspended. • Communist delegates charge serious violations of the neutral zone at Kaesong.

SEPTEMBER:
- U.S. and allies sign peace treaty with Japan.

OCTOBER 25:
- Truce talks resume at a changed site, village of Panmunjom.

SEPTEMBER-OCTOBER:
- Battle of Heartbreak Ridge, heavy casualties.

NOVEMBER 12:
- Ridgway orders end of major offensive action.

NOVEMBER 27:
> • Agreement reached on demarcation line at Panmunjom, briefly arousing truce hopes.

1952 JANUARY 2:
> • U.S. proposes that war prisoners be given repatriation choice—the intent being to be able to show that a large number of PWs refuse to return to their homeland. • The Communists reject the proposal and the issue stalemates truce negotiations for a year and a half.

FEBRUARY—JUNE:
> • Violent clashes take place in Koje compounds, the repatriation issue being an underlying cause.

FEBRUARY 19:
> • Agreement reached at Panmunjom that a political conference would be held 90 days after truce agreement.

APRIL 19:
> • U.S. delegates inform Communists that only 70,000 of 132,000 prisoners are willing to return home.

MAY 7:
> • PWs at Koje seize the commander, General Francis T. Dodd, demanding cessation of abusive policies and practices.

MAY 12:
> • General Mark W. Clark succeeds Ridgway as UN commander.

JUNE 23:
> • Suiho power plant and four major dams bombed by U.S., inflicting heavy damage.

AUGUST 29:
> • Heaviest bombing of the war carried out against Pyongyang.

OCTOBER 8:
> • Truce negotiations indefinitely recessed following Communist rejection of U.S. proposal on PW question.

DECEMBER 2-5:
> • President-Elect Eisenhower tours Korean front, fulfilling an election promise.

1953 MARCH 5:
> • Death of Stalin accelerates movement toward a truce.

APRIL 20:
> • Little Switch of PWs, exchange of sick and wounded, suggested by International Red Cross, proposed by General Clark in February and agreed to by Communists in March.

APRIL 26:
> • Truce talks resume at Panmunjom.

MAY 13:
> • General Clark authorized to activate two more ROK divisions, bringing total to 20.

MAY 13-16:
> • U.S. bombing of northern dams causes heavy flooding of countryside.

MAY 20:
- The U.S. National Security Council decides that "if conditions arise requiring more positive action in Korea," air and naval operations will be extended to China and ground operations in Korea will be expanded. But implementation is delayed.

JUNE 8:
- The PW repatriation issue is resolved as Communists yield.

JUNE 17:
- Rhee orders release of 25,000 Korean War prisoners as part of his effort to prevent a truce.

JUNE-JULY:
- Strong Chinese offensives reveal the continued weakness of the ROK forces and the illusions behind Rhee's threats to continue the war unilaterally.

JULY 27:
- Armistice signed. It has yet to be followed by a peace treaty.

AUGUST 5—SEPTEMBER 6:
- Operation Big Switch, exchange of war prisoners.

1954 APRIL 26—JUNE 15:
- Fruitless Geneva Conference on Korea.

1955 DECEMBER:
- Pak Hon Yong, leader of the southern Communists and minister of foreign affairs in Pyongyang during the war, is executed. Scapegoated for the failure of the drive south in 1950, he was accused of treason and espionage.
- Others are eliminated as Kim Il Sung becomes unchallenged leader.

1958:
- Last Chinese troops, engaged in reconstruction, leave Korea.

Bibliography—Principal Sources

Stephen E. Ambrose,
> *Eisenhower Volume II The President*, New York: Simon & Schuster, 1984.

Roy E. Appleman,
> *South to the Naktong, North to the Yalu*. Washington, DC: Government Printing Office, 1961.

Roy E. Appleman,
> *Escaping the Trap: The U.S. Army X Corps in Northeast Korea*. Texas A and M University Press, 1950.

Frank H. Armstrong, editor,
> *The 1st Cavalry Division and Their 8th Engineers in Korea*. South Burlington, Vermont: Bull Run of Vermont, 1996.

James Aronson,
> *The Press and the Cold War*. New York: Monthly Review Press, 1970.

Sydney D. Bailey,
> *The Korean Armistice*. London: Macmillan, 1992.

Keyes Beech,
> *Tokyo and Points East*. Garden City, New York: Doubleday, 1954.

Clay Blair,
> *The Forgotten War: America in Korea 1950-1953*. New York: Times Books, 1987.

Piers Brendon,
> *Ike: His Life and Times*. New York: Harper, 1986.

Wilfred Burchett,
> *Again Korea*. New York: International Publishers, 1968.

Wilfred Burchett and Alan Winnington,
> *Koje Unscreened*, Peking, Published by the Authors, April, 1953.

Malcolm Cagle and Frank A. Manson,
> *The Sea War and Korea*. Annapolis U.S. Navy Institute, 1957.

John C. Caldwell,
> *The Korea Story*. Chicago: Henry Regnery Co., 1952.

Chen Jian,
> *China's Road to the Korean War*, New York: Columbia University Press, 1996.

Charles Allen Clark,
> *Religions of Old Korea*. New York: Fleming H. Revell Co., 1932.

Hilary Conroy,
> *The Japanese Seizure of Korea, 1868-1910*. Philadelphia: University of Pennsylvania Press, 1960.

James Cotton & Ian Neary, editors,
> *The Korean War in History*. Atlantic Highlands, New Jersey: Humanities Press International, 1989.

Bruce Cumings, editor,
> *Child of Conflict: The Korean-American Relationship, 1943-1953*. Seattle: University of Washington Press, 1953.

Bruce Cumings,
> *The Origins of the Korean War, Volume I, Liberation and the Emergence of Separate Regimes, 1945-1947, Vol II: The Roaring of the Cataract, 1947-1950*. Princeton, N.J.: Princeton University Press, 1983 and 1990.

Bruce Cumings,
> *War and Television.* London and New York: Verso, 1992.

Bruce Cumings,
> *Korea's Place in the Sun.* New York: W.W. Norton, 1997.

William F. Dean, with William L. Worden,
> *General Dean's Story.* New York: Viking, 1954.

Hugh Deane,
> *Good Deeds & Gunboats: Two Centuries of American-Chinese Encounters.* San Francisco: China Books and Periodicals, 1990.

Jurgen Domes,
> *Peng Te-huai: The Man and the Image,* Stanford: Stanford University Press, 1985.

Robert J. Dworchak and others,
> *Battle for Korea: The Associated Press History of the Korean Conflict,* Pennsylvania: Combined Books, 1993.

Raymond A. Esthus,
> *Theodore Roosevelt and Japan.* Seattle and London: University of Washington Press, 1966.

Rosemary Foot,
> *A Substitute for Victory.* Ithaca and London: Cornell University Press, 1990. *The Wrong War,* Cornell University Press, 1985.

Mark Gayn,
> *Japan Diary.* New York: William Sloane Associates, 1948.

Andrew Geer,
> *The New Breed: The Story of the U.S. Marines in Korea.* New York: Harper, 1952.

Sergei N. Goncharov, John W. Lewis, and Xue Litai,
> *Uncertain Partners: Stalin, Mao and the Korean War,* Stanford: Stanford University Press, 1993.

A. Wigfall Green,
> *The Epic of Korea.* Washington, D.C.: Public Affairs Press, 1950.

John Gunther,
> *The Riddle of MacArthur.* New York: Harper, 1950.

Joseph C. Goulden,
> *Korea—The Untold Story of the War.* New York: New York Times Books, 1982.

Andrew J. Grajdanzev,
> *Modern Korea.* New York: Institute of Pacific Relations and John Day, 1944.

Jon Halliday and Bruce Cumings,
> *Korea: The Unknown War.* New York: Pantheon Books, 1988.

Han Sungjoo,
> *The Failure of Democracy in South Korea.* Berkeley: University of California Press, 1974.

Max Hastings,
> *The Korean War.* New York and London: Simon and Schuster, 1987.

Takashi Hatada,
> *A History of Korea.* Santa Barbara, California: American Bibliographical Center—Clio Press, 1969.

Gregory Henderson,
> *The Politics of the Vortex.* Cambridge: Harvard University Press, 1968.

Marguerite Higgins,
> *War in Korea.* Garden City, New York: Doubleday, 1951.

Robert Jackson,
> *Air War Over Korea.* New York: Scribner's, 1973.

D. Clayton James with Anne Sharp Wells,
> *Refighting the Last War.* New York, Toronto: The Free Press, Macmillan, 1993.

C.I. Eugene Kim and Han-kyo Kim,
> *Korea and the Politics of Imperialism, 1876-1910.* Berkeley: University of California Press, 1967.

Joyce and Gabriel Kolko,
> *The Limits of Power: The World and United States Foreign Policy, 1945-1954.* New York: Harper, 1972.

Richard Lauterbach,
> *Danger From the East.* New York: Harper, 1947.

Dr. Channing Liem,
> *The Korean War: An Unanswered Question.* Albany, New York: The Committee for a New Korean Policy, 1989.

William Manchester,
> *American Caesar: Douglas MacArthur, 1880-1964.* Boston, Toronto: Little, Brown, 1978.

Matray, James I., Editor,
> *Historical Dictionary of the Korean War.* Westport, Connecticut: Greenwood Press, 1991.

Callum A. MacDonald,
> *Korea: The War Before Vietnam.* New York: The Free Press, Macmillan, 1986.

David McCullough,
> *Truman.* New York: Simon and Schuster, 1992.

Gaven McCormack, Mark Selden, editors,
> *Korea North and South: The Deepening Crisis.* New York: Monthly Review Press, 1978.

Evelyn McCune,
> *The Arts of Korea: An Illustrated History.* Rutland, Vermont and Tokyo: Charles E. Tuttle, 1962.

George M. McCune,
> *Korea Today.* Cambridge: Harvard University Press, 1950.

James McGovern,
> *To the Yalu. From the Chinese Invasion of Korea to MacArthur's Dismissal.* New York: William Morrow, 1972.

E. Grant Meade,
> *American Military Government in Korea.* New York: King's Crown Press, Columbia University, 1951.

John Merrill,
> *Korea: The Peninsular Origins of the War,* Newark: University of Delaware Press, c. 1989.

Nie Rongzhen,
> *Inside the Red Star: Memoirs of Marshal Nie Rongzhen,* Beijing: New World Press, 1988.

Glenn D. Paige,
> *The Korean Decision.* New York: The Free Press, Macmillan, 1968.

Paik Sun Yup,
   From Pusan to Panmunjom. Washington, New York: Brassey's (US), Inc., 1992.
Matthew B. Ridgway,
   The Korean War. Garden City, New York: Doubleday, 1967.
Chester Ronning,
   A Memoir of China in Revolution: From the Boxer Rebellion to the People's Republic. New York: Pantheon Books, 1974.
Robert Scalapino & Chong-Sik Lee,
   Communism in Korea. Berkeley: University of California Press, 1974.
   2 volumes.
Harrison E. Salisbury,
   The New Emperors: China in the Era of Mao and Deng. Boston: Little Brown, 1992.
Michael Schaller,
   The American Occupation of Japan: Origins of the Cold War in Asia. New York and Oxford: Oxford University Press, 1985.
Michael Schaller,
   Douglas MacArthur, The Far Eastern General. Oxford University Press, 1989.
Shu Guang Zhang,
   Mao's Military Romanticism: China and the Korean War, 1950-1953. Lawrence, Kansas: University Press of Kansas, 1995.
Robert R. Simmons,
   The Strained Alliance: Peking, Moscow, Pyongyang and the Politics of the Korean Civil War. New York and London: The Free Press, Macmillan, 1975.
Russell Spurr,
   Enter the Dragon: China's Undeclared War Against the U.S. in Korea, 1950-51. New York: Henry Holt, 1988.
Shelby L. Stanton,
   America's Tenth Legion: X Corps in Korea, 1950. Novato, CA: Presidio Press, 1989.
I.F. Stone,
   The Hidden History of the Korean War. New York: Monthly Review Press, 1952, paperback 1970.
Anna Louise Strong,
   Inside North Korea: An Eyewitness Report. Pamphlet published by the author at Montrose, California, 1950.
Donald G. Tewksbury, compiler,
   Source Materials on Korean Politics and Ideologies. New York: Institute of Pacific Relations, 1950.
Reginald Thompson,
   Cry Korea. London: Macdonald & Co., 1951.
Rudy Tomedi,
   No Bugles, No Drums, An Oral History of the Korean War. New York: John Wiley & Sons, 1993.
John Toland,
   In Mortal Combat: Korea, 1950-1953. New York: William Morrow, 1991.
Shigeto Tsuru,
   Japan's Capitalism: Creative Defeat and Beyond, University of Cambridge Press, 1993.

Clarence Norwood Weems, editor,
   Hulbert's History of Korea. New York: Hilary House, 1962.
Whiting, Allen S,
   China Crosses the Yalu: The Decision to Enter the Korean War. New York: Macmillan, 1960.
William W. Whitson with Chen-hsia Huang,
   The Chinese High Command: A History of Communist Military Politics. New York: Praeger, 1973.
Peter Williams and David Wallace,
   Unit 731, The Japanese Army's Secret of Secrets. London, Glasgow: Grafton Books, 1990. The American version, published by The Free Press, Macmillan , lacks Chapter 17, "Korean War".
Alan Winnington and Wilfred Burchett,
   Plain Perfidy. Peking, Published by the Authors, April, 1954.

Notes

HISTORY THAT SHAPES THE PRESENT

1. John K. Fairbank, Edwin O. Reischauer, Albert M. Craig, *East Asia: Tradition and Transformation*, p. 279. Cumings, *Korea's Place in the Sun*, pp. 25–26.

2. In the words of Sir George Sansom, quoted by Evelyn McCune (page 31), Korea was a "terrain in which cultural elements from various sources were combined before they were transmitted..."

3. The visitors were Dr. Charles Grossman, Howard Glazer and the author. We were in North Korea October 22—November 1, 1997.

4. Tom Kaasa observes in his historical review of the Korean language that "during the historical period of the evolution of the Korean language there were established basic language forms of sufficient strength and vitality to withstand centuries of domination and influence by foreign nations and to retain intact the fundamental outline of its linguistic identity" (*Korean Review*, June 1948.)

5. *Korea Old and New: A History*, p. 32.

6. *New York Times*, September 14, 1997. In addition to the Kyoto Ear Mound, others, usually smaller, exist elsewhere in Japan. Toyotomi Hideyoshi is regarded as a national hero by Japanese, as a brutish villain by Koreans.

7. *Korea Old and New*, p. 215.

8. Chong-Sik Lee, *The Politics of Korean Nationalism*, pp. 24-25.

9. Donald G. Tewksbury, *Source Materials on Korean Politics Korea and Ideologies*, pp 12-14.

10. Chong-Sik Lee, *The Politics of Korean Nationalism*, p. 31.

11. Kim and Kim, *Korea and the Politics of Imperialism.* p. 77.

12. Bruce Cumings, *The Origins of the Korean War*, Vol. I. p. 368.

13. The text of the Declaration of Independence is in Tewksbury, *Sources*, pp. 48-50.

14. The text of Hasegawa's proclamation is in Tewksbury, *Sources*, p. 33.

15. Harries and Harries, *Soldiers of the Sun*, pp. 127 and 364.

16. Nym Wales (Helen Foster Snow), "Rebel Korea" in *Pacific Affairs*, March, 1942.

17. *The Rule of the Taewongun, 1864-1875*, by Ching Young Choe, pp. 110-125. Also *Hulbert's History of Korea*, Volume II pp.207-208. For many years the *General Sherman's* anchor chain hung on one of Pyongyang's gates and now, with a cannon, is in a museum.

18. Kim Il Sung's *Reminiscences*, Vol. 1, p. 10.

19. Lyndon G. Van Deusen, *William Henry Seward*, p. 522.

20. *Korea Old and New*, pp. 195 and 197. Cumings, *Korea's Place in the Sun*, pp. 96-98.

21. Principal articles in the treaty are in Tewksbury, *Source Materials,* pp. 3-4. The key clause is in a number of contemporary treaties with Korea.

22. Cumings, *Korea's Place in the Sun,* p. 132. The information came from Angus Hamilton, *Korea,* Scribner's, 1904.

23. Frank G. Williston in *Korean Review,* June 1948, pp. 7-9.

24. The text of Taft's memorandum sent Roosevelt on July 29, 1905 is in Tewksbury, *Source Materials*, pp. 20-21. Tyler Dennett's account of "President Roosevelt's Secret Pact with Japan" appeared in *Current History,* October 1924, pp. 15-21.

THE TRUE START OF THE KOREAN WAR

1. Cited in Cumings, Vol. II, p. 617.

2. Cumings, Vol. I, p. 126.

3. Cumings, Vol. II, pp. 186-187.

4. Mark Gayn, *Japan Diary,* p. 428.

5. Cited in Robert Smith, *MacArthur in Korea,* New York, Simon and Schuster, 1982, p. 43.

6. Cumings, Vol. I, Preface, p.xxi.

7. My original papers are in the archives of the University of Chicago, copies at the State University of New York at Binghamton. My China papers are at the University of Missouri, Kansas City.

8. Abuses of students and teachers in various schools and school closings are detailed in an unpublished paper titled "List of Persecutions in the Fields of Culture and Arts in South Korea," Deane papers, University of Chicago archives. Sample entries:

"In April and May, 1946, more than seventy schools and 100,000 and more students participated in the all-out strike and they demanded democratization of school, purging of Japanese imperial-ist beasts, democratic teachers returning to school, no more police interference in school..."

"Police arrested and detained the middle school boys and girls who joined May Day commemorating great meeting held under the co-auspices of Democratic National Front and Korean Federation of Trade Unions, and up to May 9... (24 students expelled, 47 suspend-ed, 167 sentenced to home confinement.)

9. A typical beginning of a Richards article, this one published in the *Baltimore News-Post* of October 8, 1947 follows: SEOUL, Oct. 8 ...You have to come to a place like this to see the substance of Communism... It is a slimy sight. Russia is putting on the dirtiest kind of fight to capture all Korea as an essential part of her Asiatic domination.

10. Gayn, *Japan Diary*, p. 384.

11. Cumings, Vol. II, pp. 224-225.

12. Hugh Deane, *Notes on Korea,* March 20, 1948. unpublished, University of Chicago archives, Deane papers.

13. Marguerite Higgins, *War in Korea,* p. 162.

14. Han Suyin, *Love Is a Many Splendored Thing,* pp. 347-348.

15. Halliday, Cumings, *Korea: The Unknown War,* p. 92. Cameron wrote: "I had

seen Belsen, but this was worse. This terrible mob of men—convicted of nothing, untried, South Koreans in South Korea, suspected of being 'unreliable.' There were hundreds of them; they were skeletal, puppets of string, faces translucent gray, manacled to each other with chains, cringing in the classic Oriental attitude of subjection, the squatting fetal position, in piles of garbage. Around this medievally gruesome marketplace were gathered a few knots of American soldiers photographing the scene with casual industry... I took my indignation to the (UN) Commission, who said very civilly: 'Most disturbing, yes; but remember these are Asian people, with different standards of behavior... all very difficult.' It was supine and indefensible compromise. I boiled, and I do not boil easily. We recorded the scene meticulously, in words and photographs. Within the year it nearly cost me my job, and my magazine its existence."

16. Han Suyin, *Love Is a Many Splendored Thing*, p. 343.

17. Haliday, Cumings, *Unknown War*, pp. 161-162.

18. Cited in Toland, *In Mortal Combat*, p. 503.

19. Winnington and Burchett, *Plain Perfidy*, Chapter II, "The Ball-Point Pen Murders."

20. Reginald Thompson, *Cry Korea*, pp. 39 and 84.

21. Gayn, *Japan Diary*, p. 478.

22. Cumings, *Origins*, Vol. II, pp. 690-697. Thompson, p. 252. I have added some racist instances to those set forth by Cumings.

23. Bradley F. Smith, *The Shadow Warriors*, p. 130, other indexed references.

24. Cumings, *Origins*, Vol. I, pp. 246-247.

25. A. Wigfall Green, *The Epic of Korea*, pp. 58, 100-101. Green observed that "entrapment, illegal in the United States, was declared legal in apprehending Koreans."

26. Meade, p. 134.

27. Gayn, p 398

28. Meade, p. 165. Meade's views in the main were conformist, but he began a summary this way: "By suppressing the People's Republic and identifying themselves with a minority group, the Americans distressed and antagonized the people; by providing a highly centralized government, they classified themselves with Japanese." p. 235.

29. Gayn, *Japan Diary*, pp. 387-389. Gayn added 12 of the police reports dated September 26 to October 20. Substantial excerpts from the October 20 report follow: "A democratic leader killed in Kaesong... Fifty-four leftists arrested. Jail full, and now using school as arrests continue. District station at Yonan captured by rebels; 64 rifles stolen. Rebels seize police station at Pakchon...but station retaken by U.S. troops... Three hundred and fifteen prisoners being moved from Kaesong to Seoul. Choy Chan Ki attacked a police station, and then committed suicide..."

30. Cumings, Vol. I, p. 381.

31. Extracts from the biography are among my papers at the University of Chicago. Toward the end they declare that Yi "is awaiting the order of the million compatriots as a loyal subordinate of them. If the nation desires him as a soldier or if the country needs him as a servant, he will be most satisfied to serve them faithfully. If they do not desire his abilities, he will resign himself to his fate and go back to the primitive life in the deep forest as a hunter."

32. Hugh Deane, *China Notes*, May 23, 1948, unpublished. Also "Extracts from the Quarterly Report of Korean National Youth, Inc. For Period Ending March Thirty-first 1948." Also Deane, "South Korea's New Premier," *The China Weekly Review*, Shanghai, October 2, 1948.

33. Burchett and Winnington, *Koje Unscreened*, p. 104.

34. My principal source for the section on labor is naturally my contributions to Allied Labor News, New York, 1947-48, and the notes I kept. See also Cumings, Vol. II, p. 204.

35. Cited in Hugh Deane, "Rhee Regime Wrecked Unions," *New York Daily Compass*, July 17, 1950.

36. Cited in Robert Smith, *MacArthur in Korea*, New York: Simon and Schuster, 1982. Baldwin, American Civil Liberties Union, had pressed the Occupation to introduce a declaration of civil liberties and take other democratic initiatives. Mark Gayn, as observed earlier, was the independent-minded correspondent of the *Chicago Sun-Times*.

37. Hugh Deane, "Economic Deterioration in South Korea," *China Weekly Review*, October 30, 1948. Also Kolko, *Limits of Power*, p. 287. Kolko commented generally: "Within the overriding framework of containing the Left and the Soviets there remained a number of economic options. The measures that the AMG introduced early in the occupation reflected the dogmatism of conservative men, essentially ignorant of economic affairs, in imposing their concepts of a laissez fair capitalist state on an underdeveloped agrarian economy. Their policies created indescribable chaos in the South Korean economy, vastly magnifying already serious political problems." (pp. 286-287)

38. My unpublished notes on a trip to Chonju, August 13-17, 1947, Deane Papers. Also Cumings, Vol. II, p. 242.

39. The preliminary report of the WFTU delegation to Korea is published in *Facts and Documents Concerning the Far East*, prepared by the Committee for a Democratic Far Eastern Policy, 1948.

40. Cumings on Moscow Decision, Vol. I, p. 226.

41. "U.S. Saved Rhee from Korean Defeat," Hugh Deane, *New York Daily Compass*, July 4, 1950.

42. Johnston's slant in the *Times* of July 20, 1947: "Mr. Lyuh's murder provoked much speculation among Korean political circles today. While there is still no indication which of My/Lyuh's political enemies was responsible for the assassination, it is a matter of record that Mr. Lyuh's efforts to escape Communist domination have met with strong disapproval from the extremist elements among his associates."

43. *The Voice of China*, August 15, 1947. Green, *The Epic of Korea*, p. 74.

44. Baldwin's statement to the press appeared in *The New York Times* of June 23, 1947. He said he "was reporting the consensus of opinion of those qualified to judge. "

45. Hugh Deane, "South Koreans Rebelled Against Rhee Government," *New York Daily Compass*, July 18, 1950.

46. John Merrill, Korea, p. 64.

47. "Information Concerning Organization and Activities of People's Guerrilla Forces on Cheju-Do," Office of the Assistant Chief of Staff, G-2, APO 235, June 8, 1948. Recruits at this camp were given Japanese army uniforms, rubber

shoes and mess kits and told that the guerrillas called each other comrade instead of by individual names. They were given lectures on communism and government.

48. Cumings, Vol. II, p. 256.

49. Merrill, p. 126.

50. Seoul, Associated Press, March 25, 1950.

51. See Carl and Shelley Mydans, *The Violent Peace*, Section IX, "Police Action in Korea."

52. Merrill, p. 114.

53. Merrill, pp. 120-121.

54. Hugh Deane, *Notes on Korea*, March 20, 1948. University of Chicago papers. Also Cumings, Vol. II, p. 282.

55. *Encyclopedia Britannica, The Korean War*, 1973.

56. Cumings, Vol. II, pp. 282-283.

57. Walter Sullivan quote cited as an epigraph by Cumings, Vol. II, p. 268.

58. First Part of the Report of the United Nations Temporary Commission on Korea, Vol. I, p. 17.

59. First Part of the Report, p. 34. Text in *Source Materials on Korean Politics and Ideologies*, Donald G. Tewksbury, compiler, p. 95.

60. Text of the conference declaration against southern elections follows, p. 97.

61. Hugh Deane, *New York Daily Compass*, July 13, 1950.

62. John Merrill, "Internal Warfare in Korea," in *Child of Conflict: The Korean-American Relationship 1943-1953.*

63. Deane, *Korean Notes*, June 9, 1948. Also Cumings, Vol. II, p. 221

64. The text of MacArthur's grandiloquence is in Tewksbury, *Sources*, pp. 117-118.

65. Hugh Deane, "Syngman Rhee's Victory at the South Gate," first published in the *China Weekly Review*, July 24, 1948. I learned of Choi's execution from Dr. Channing Liem, *The Korean War: An Unanswered Question*, p. 34.

THE 1950 WAR IN THE MAKING

1. Cumings, Vol. I, p. 388. The demonization of North Korea and the Soviet role there was abetted by CIA fabrications. The September 26, 1950 issue of *The Reporter*, reputedly a liberal magazine, featured an article by an ex-Soviet officer on: "How Russia Built the North Korean Army." The article was a CIA concoction. The officer, a Colonel Kalinov, did not exist. But the article was widely quoted in serious publications.

2. See "North Korea. Development and Self-Reliance: A Critical Appraisal" by Aidan Foster-Carter in Gavan McCormack and Mark Selden, editors, *Korea North and South: The Deepening Crisis*, p. 125.

3. *In North Korea* was published by Soviet Russia Today. An expanded version titled *Inside North Korea* was published in California by Anna Louise Strong herself. This followed Moscow's absurd charge that she was a spy, which made *Soviet Russia Today* her enemy. See also Cumings, II, pp. 351 and 835-836.

4. Cumings II, pp. 157-182. Hugh Deane on "Japan: U.S. Pacific War Base," a series in the *New York Daily Compass* (January 28-February 1, 1951) and a similar pamphlet published by the Committee for a Democratic Far Eastern Policy

5. Joseph C. Goulden, *Korea—The Untold Story of the War*, pp. 465-475. Goulden's account is based on candid interviews with a top CIA agent, Hans Toft. His remarks on the creative Japanese film industry are entirely in error. Both the CIA and General Willoughby ran nets of agents in North Korea, as of course did South Korean intelligence. According to Tofte, the CIA focused on developing evasion-escape means for downed fliers, who were at risk if northern peasants got to them first.

6. Deane, "Japan—U.S. Pacific WarBase." In his book *The Age of Hirohito* Daikichi Irokawa points to a long-term consequence of the American policy reversal in Japan—the continuing refusal of the Japanese leadership to really acknowledge and regret aggression and war crimes. "The occupation authorities allowed conservative nationalists, purged for their wartime activities, to return to public office and discontinued the investigation of the conservatives' responsibility for the war." p. xv.

7. Goncharov, *Uncertain Years: Chinese-American Relations, 1947-1950*, p. 111. Cumings, *Korea's Place in the Sun*, p. 277, states that a Defense Department paper favoring rollback was hopeful that as a result Manchuria "would lose its captive status."

8. Chen Jian, *China's Road to the Korean War*, pp. 85-91, 155- 156. Alexandre Y. Mansourov, "Stalin, Mao, Kim and China's Decision to Enter the Korean War," Cold War International History Project Bulletin. Evgueni Bajanov, "Assessing the Politics of the Korean War, 1949-51," Cold War International Project Bulletin.

9. Goncharov, *Uncertain Partners*, p. 130. Dieter Heinzig comment, Cold War International Project Bulletin, p. 240.

10. Chen Jian, *China's Road to the Korean War*, pp. 142-143.

11. Haliday and Cumings, *Unknown War*, pp. 50-54. Also Cumings, Vol. II, pp. 568-580.

12 Henderson reported this conversation in a memorandum dated August 26, 1948, classified restricted. It was captured by the North Koreans in Seoul and is in the Pyongyang war museum. The text is Appendix F in Dr. Channing Liem's *The Korean War: An Unanswered Question*.

13. Gupta, *China Quarterly*, no. 52 (1972). Various comments followed in No. 54.

14. Cumings, *Korea's Place in the Sun*, pp. 257-258.

15. *Korea's Place in the Sun*, pp. 263-264.

ARMIES AT WAR, 1950-1953

1. David Halberstam, *The Fifties*, p. 71.

2. Dean, *General Dean's Story*, p. 29.

3. Han Suyin, *Love Is a Many Splendored Thing*, p. 342 and p. 349.

4. Cited in Cumings, Vol. II, p. 693.

5. "A Preliminary Study of the Impact of Communism on Korea," U.S. Air Force, Air University. Based on about 100 interviews, none with ardent northern partisans, conducted by a team of social scientists, led by Wilbur Schramm, with ties to the CIA. Cited by Bruce Cumings, Vol. II, Chapter 20. Cumings has written what is far and away the best account of the northern performance in the south and I am much indebted to it.

6. New China News Agency dispatch from Pyongyang, July 10.

7. Thompson, *Cry Korea*, p. 92.

8. See "Japan's Involvement in the Korean War" in *The Korean War in History*, pp. 129-130. Forty-six Japanese vessels, mine sweepers mostly, manned by 1,200 former Japanese navy personnel, were on combat duty in the harbors of Wonsan, Kunsan, Inchon, Haeju and Chinanpo between October 2 and December 12, 1950. Two vessels were sunk by the North Koreans.When Pyongyang reported Japanese activity in the war, the U.S. effectively used the charge to point to the lunacy of Communist propaganda. The U.S. also secretly brought several thousand Japanese technicians to Korea to help operate power plants and other key industries and to operate dredges and lighters in harbors. Intensive studies of the military situation in Korea led the PLA's General Staff to the conclusion that the U.S. was most likely to turn to amphibious operations. They listed five possible port locations and picked Inchon as the one the Americans would probably choose. They warned the North Koreans, who were then too confident of swift victory to pay much attention. In any case, without air or sea power, they could have done very little. See Cumings, Vol. II, p. 726 and Chen Jian, p. 147.

9. Higgins, *War in Korea*, p. 170.

10. Joseph W. Alsop with Adam Platt, *I've Seen the Best of It*, p. 322.

11. Cited in Robert Jackson, *Victory at High Tide: The Inchon-Seoul Campaign*, p. 229.

12. Thompson, *Cry Korea*, p. 94.

13. Henderson, *Korea: Politics of the Vortex*, p. 167. Kim Tae-pon, head of the South Korean National Police, admitted the earlier 1200 figure in an interview with a correspondent.

14. Cited in Robert Smith, *MacArthur in Korea*, p. 228.

15. Telepress, November 9, 1950. "The Marines Capture Seoul"

OPERATION RAT KILLER

16. Cumings, *Origins*, p. 688.

17. Paik, *From Pusan to Panmunjom*, p. 183. On Operation Rat Killer, pp. 179-193.

18. Historical Dictionary, p. 356.

ROLLBACK: MACARTHUR'S DRIVE TO THE YALU

19. Acheson at cabinet meeting. Cumings, *Origins*, Vol. II, p.715

20. Cumings, *War and Television*, pp. 217 and 218-223.

21. On Kim Tae Hua see *North Korea Diary*, appendix, October 22 entry.

22. Stone, *Hidden History*, pp. 264-265.

23. *New York Compass*, February 2, 1951.

24. MacArthur to Truman on Wake: "Had they interfered in the first or second months it would have been decisive. We are no longer fearful of their intervention." McCullough, *Truman*, p. 804.

25. David Halberstam, *The Fifties*, p.77.

THE CHINESE CROSS THE YALU

26. Goncharov, *Uncertain Partners*, p. 181.

27. *U.S. Policy in the Korean Crisis*, Department of State Publication No. 3922. July 1950, p. 18.

28. The Progressive Party concluded that "we should oppose any intervention in the civil war in Korea by the United States or any other power as essential to the speedy settlement of the conflict..." The party's two statements were written by John J. Abt. The second includes Congressman Vito Marcantonio's remarks on Truman's action with regard to Taiwan.

Cumings, *Origins*, p. 638, describes the comments of the *Monthly Review,* George Seldes's *In Fact,* and Scott Nearing's *World Events.* In the *New York Compass,* I. F. Stone had more or less orthodox views for a number of weeks but then began writing the columns which later went into his *Hidden History.* I wrote a series of 10 comprehensive articles on Korea published in *The Compass* soon after the outbreak of war but also for a time accepted the establishment view on how it began. The Committee for a Democratic Far Eastern Policy, headed by Maud Russell, issued a comprehensive statement on June 27. American left-oriented statements, pamphlets and leaflets are listed in the first appendix.

29. Chen Jian, *China's Road to the Korean War,* p. 143. Zhou, in his years in Chongqing, had encounters with Koreans in exile in China and offered this comment at a dinner in the fall of 1940: "The Sino-Korean relations will be of great importance in the future. At the time of the first Sino-Japanese war, China failed in Korea and this was the signal for the collapse of the Qing dynasty."

30. Mao's first choice had been Lin Biao. But Lin, in an early stage of his conspiracy to eliminate Mao and seize power, pretended to be ill. An examination of him by a group of physicians, ordered by Mao, revealed no serious ailments though his drug addiction was revealed. Yen Jiaqi and Gao Gao, *Turbulent Decade: History of the Cultural Revolution,* p. 229.

31. Complete text with notes in Goncharov, *Uncertain Partners,* pp. 275-276. Partial text differently translated in Chen Jian, *China's Road to the Korean War,* pp. 175-177. No copy of this telegram has been found in Moscow but what has been found in the Russian archives is a very different telegram from Mao to Stalin also dated October 2. This one focuses on the negative aspects of a Chinese intervention perceived in the Chinese leadership and reports that a decision had not been reached. This telegram reflected the early reality of the disinclination to enter the war and may also have been a form of pressure on Stalin to pledge real support in the way of air cover and military supplies. Beijing had threatened to intervene if U.S. troops crossed the 38th parallel and on October 2 Mao did not know if they had done so. The first Mao telegram, whether sent or not, set forth Mao's true convictions, doing so in his own handwriting. In the event, Mao finally gained the support of the enlarged Politburo in the October 4-5 discussions. The early October meetings in Beijing are summarized in Shu Guang Zhang, *China's Military Romanticism,* pp. 77-82. A discussion of the two telegrams by Shen Zhihua is in the Bulletin of the Cold War International History Project, pp. 237-242.

32. *Selected Works of Mao Tsetung,* Volume V, p. 41. Goncharov, *Uncertain Partners,* pp 278-279. A different translation: Chen Jian, *China's Road to the Korean War,* pp. 186-187.

33. Remarks on January 19, 1951. *Selected Works of Mao Tsetung,* Volume V, p. 44.

34. Goncharov, p. 195. Stalin was said to have been on the point of tears. Shu Guang Zhang, *Mao's Military Romanticism,* p. 84.

35. According to Goncharov, p. 200, the Soviet Union sent 13 air divisions (fighters as well as bombers) to the Northeast (Manchuria) and China coastal

areas. Ten Soviet tank regiments were stationed in four cities in the Northeast. Shu Guang Zhang, *Mao's Military Romanticism,* p. 84, gives the most details. Also Cumings, *China's Place in the Sun,* p. 291.

36. Donald Knox, *The Korean War,* pp. 434-438. Also Cumings, Vol. II, p. 741.

37. Nie Rongzhen, *Inside the Red Star,* p. 648. Nie wrote that in working to organize supplies of parched flour for the troops Zhou joined in making some himself.

38. Appleman, *Escaping the Trap,* pp. 37-38.

39. On October 25th, the date of the first Chinese action in Korea, the Associated Press was told by "informed sources" that "most American troops may be out of Korea by Christmas" and that MacArthur expects "the first elements of the 8th Army to begin moving back to Japan by Thanksgiving."

40. Frank H. Armstrong, editor, *The 1st Cavalry Division and Their 8th Engineers in China,* p. 111.

41. Hastings, *The Fifties* p. 109.

42. MacDonald, *Korea: The Last War Before Vietnam,* p. 216.

43. Spurr, *Enter the Dragon,* p. 284. Cumings commented: "It would be foolish to discount the importance of the Chinese intervention in destroying the American rollback into North Korea. But the Korean contribution to the outcome both in strategy and in fighting power, has been ignored in the literature. The primary, day-to-day evidence makes the indictment of McArthur's generalship all the more devastating. He not only dismissed the palpable Chinese threat but got badly outmaneuvered by Korean generals, *Origins,* Vol. II, p. 744.

The *Encylopedia Britannica* eventually mentioned the North Koreans by implication when it said that by the end of 1952 three-fourths of the 800,000 enemy ground troops were Chinese. Its doubtless widely read account of the war is palpably falsified.

44. Thompson, *Cry Korea,* p. 259.

45. Paik Sun Yup, *From Pusan to Panmunjom,* pp. 106-108.

46. Spurr, *Enter the Dragon,* pp. 220 and 224. Other lines include:

> *See the pretty girl on the hill?*
> *She won't lay but her sister will*
> *I'm movin' on...down to Pusan*
> *I'm comin' on fast…*

47. Tomedi, *No Bugles, No Drums,* p. 77.

48. Peng Dehuai, *Memoirs of a Chinese Marshall,* p. 478.

49. Frank H. Armstrong, editor, *The 1st Cavalry Division and Their 8th Engineers in China,* p. 128.

50. Whiting, *China Crosses the Yalu* includes key excerpts, pp. 132-133. One excerpt recalls the gauntlet in which the U.S. 2nd Division was mauled: "To achieve quick decision we should generally attack, not an enemy force holding a position, but one on the move. We should have concentrated, beforehand under cover, a big force along the route through which the enemy is sure to pass, suddenly descend on him while he is moving, encircle and attack him before he knows what is happening, and conclude the fighting with all speed."

51. Sun Zi, *The Art of War,* Beijing: People's China Publishing House, 1944.

52. Peng gave similar speeches to command audiences on October 9 and 14. See Shu Guang Zhang, *Mao's Military Romanticism,* pp. 89-92. Peng's entire

October 14 speech is in Goncharov, *Uncertain Partners*, pp. 284-289. He said, "It is surely our task to defend territory, but it is more important for us to annihilate the enemy's effective strength...All of us should make specific adjustments to the situation as it develops on the battlefield." On positional warfare, "we should adopt defense in depth. Each squad should be divided into three or four teams. So as to ensure mutual support through crossfire, these teams should be deployed in plum blossom-shaped pillboxes 20-30 meters apart. By constructing such defense works, we can reduce casualties from the enemy's bombing and shelling."

CHINA AND THE UNDOING OF MACARTHUR

53. Evans Fordyce Carlson, *The Chinese Army*, 1940, and *Twin Stars of China*, 1940. Also *Evans F. Carlson on China at War, 1937-1941*, Hugh Deane, editor, 1993. James McGovern, *To the Yalu*, was one of the very few Korea authors with something to say about Carlson: "Colonel Evans Carlson of the U.S. Marine Corps was the first foreign military observer to gain access to areas of north China held by the Communists In 1937 and 1938, Carlson traveled on foot with them for more than two thousand miles. He was impressed by the toughness, mobility and uncomplaining endurance of these Chinese soldiers. Carlson once observed a march of fifty-eight miles in thirty-two hours in mountainous country.

54. McGovern, *To the Yalu*, p. 312.

55. David Caute, *The Great Fear: The Anti-Communist Purge Under Truman and Eisenhower*, p. 415.

56. Cumings on "The Panic in Washington," *Origins*, Vol. II, pp. 745-747.

57. Cumings, *Origins*, Vol. II, p. 750.

58. Kolko, *The Limits of Power*, p. 605.

59. Thompson, *Cry Korea*, p. 252.

60. Stone, *Hidden History*, pp. 228-229.

61. Peter Lowe, "The Frustrations of Alliance: Britain, The United States, and the Korean War, 1950-51" in *The Korean War in History*.

62. Ridgway, *The Korean War*, pp. 93-94. This book is the source of two quotations from him that shortly follow.

63. Peng Dehuai, *Memoirs*, p. 478. Peng was demonized during the Cultural Revolution but one accusation rings true. "Peng often complained about the poor logistics service. Returning from Korea in April 1951, he complained that the cloth of the army uniforms sent from China to Korea was poor in quality and that the soldiers suffered from diarrhea after eating the fried rice given them. Taking advantage of this, he banged on the table and scolded Premier Zhou. 'Are the volunteers at the front not human beings?'" Zhou needed little scolding. He publicly exhorted Chinese families to bake flour for the volunteers.

64. The changes pushed by Ridgway early in 1951 included the beginning of integration of Blacks, then called Negroes, into all-white units. The results were gratifying—fears of racist hostility proved largely unfounded and combat performance improved. On Ridgway's recommendation, percentages of Negroes were added to all army units in the Far East. Robert Smith, *MacArthur in Korea*, p. 228.

65. Ridgway, *The Korean War*, pp. 143-145.

66. The greater part of the text is in D. Clayton James, *The MacArthur Years*, Vol. III, pp. 586-587.

67. Stone, *Hidden History*, pp. 201-202.

68. Cited in David Halberstam, *The Fifties*, p. 113.

THE WAR FOR FROZEN CHOSIN

69. Tomedi, *No Bugles No Drums*, p. 68.

70. Appleman, *Escaping the Trap*, p. 355.

71. Cumings, *Origins*, Vol. II, pp. 730-732, 743-744.

72. Stanton, Shelby L., *America's Tenth Legion*, Chapter 10.

73. Appleman, *Escapimg the Trap*, p. 103. McGovern, *To the Yalu*, pp. 125-126. Cumings, *Origins*, II, p. 742.

74. Cumings, *Origins*, p. 742.

75. Appleman, *Escaping the Trap*, pp. 367-368.

THE FAILED CHINESE OFFENSIVES

76. Peng Dehuai, *Memoirs*

77. Jeffrey Grey, *The Commonwealth Armies in the Korean War*, p. 82.

78. Paik, *From Pusan to Panmunjom*, p. 148.

79. Shu Guang Zhang, *Mao's Military Romanticism*, pp. 154-156.

80. Goncharov, *Uncertain Partners*, pp. 200-201.

81. Paik, *From Pusan to Panmunjom*, p. 238.

82. Zhang, *Mao's Military Romanticism*, p. 257. He was long bitter about abandonment of "the carefully prepared but never implemented offensive."

THE BLOODY YEARS OF STALEMATE

83. Frank H. Armstrong, editor, *The 1st Cavalry Division and Their 8th Engineers in Korea*, p. 189.

84. Burchett, *Again Korea*, pp. 59-60.

85. Ridgway, *The Korean War*, pp. 186-187.

86. Quoted in Dworchak, *Battle for Korea*, pp. 236-237.

87. Walter G. Hermes, *Truce Tent and Fighting Front*, p. 97.

88. Ridgway, *The Korean War*, pp. 150-151. Ridgway was persuaded that the American people would not support "an endless war in the bottomless pit of the Asian mainland."

89. James, *Refighting the Last War*, p. 245.

90. Rod Paschall, *Witness to War in Korea*, pp. 101-102.

91. Ridgway's comment is in *The Korean War*, p. 22. In a postwar interview Ridgway was asked why North Korean troops fought so well and valiantly, while their southern counterparts generally didn't. He answered that he had long pondered the question and could only conjecture that the northern troops had been given drugs, though he had never found evidence that they did. Ridgway could not imagine that the revolutionary character of the war was a factor.

General Dean of the 24th Division, commander at the battle of Taejon, told MacArthur: "I am convinced that the North Korean Army, the North Korean soldier and his status and training and quality of equipment have been underestimated."

92. Quoted in Robert J. Dworchak, *Battle for Korea,* p. 158.

93. Ridgway, Cited by Paik, p. 97. A somewhat different translation in Cumings, *Origins,* Vol. II, p. 741.

94. Ridgway, *The Korean War,* p. 22. Zhang, *Mao's Military Romanticism,* pp. 106-107.

95. Walter G. Hermes, *Truce Tent and Fighting Front,* p. 511.

96. Tomedi, *No Bugles, No Drums,* p. 151.

97. Hugh Deane, "A War That Argues for Peace," *New York Daily Compass,* December 20, 1951.

98. Cited in Stone, *Hidden History,* p. 256.

AIR WAR

99. Callum A. MacDonald, *Korea: The War Before Vietnam,* p. 228.

100. Robert Jackson, *Air War Over Korea,* p. 61.

101. O'Donnell, no more targets Stone, *Hidden History,* p. 312.

102. Cited by Stone, Hidden History, p. 313.

103. *Truman and Attlee.* Cumings, *Origins,* Vol. II, pp. 748-749.

104. Cumings, *Origins,* Vol. II, pp. 750-752.

105. Ridgway on Pyongyang bombing. Cumings, *Origins,* Vol. II, p. 753-755.

106. Dean, *General Dean's Story,* pp. 274-275. Dean, in command of the 24th Division, had been captured near Taejon in July of 1950.

107. Burchett, *Again Korea,* p. 30.

108. Dean, p. 278.

109. Dean, pp. 272-273.

110. Callum A. MacDonald, *Korea: The War Before Vietnam,* pp. 241-242; Cumings, *Korea's Place,* pp. 296-297.

111. MacDonald, *Korea: The War Before Vietnam,* p. 152.

112. Stone, *Hidden History,* p. 258.

113. Dworchak, *Battle for Korea,* pp. 130-131. Also Clay Blair, *The Forgotten War,* p. 515 and Cumings, *Origins,* Vol. II, P. 707.

114. MacDonald, *Korea: The War Before Vietnam,* p. 229. Jackson, *Air War Over Korea,* pp. 9, 10.

115. MacDonald, p. 247.

BIOLOGICAL WARFARE

116. Stephen Endicott, "Germ Warfare and Plausible Denial," in *Modern China,* January 1979.

117. John W. Powell of San Francisco did much of the critical early exploration of the germ warfare issue and brought the shadowed truth to light. He has published his findings in four articles: "Japan's Germ Warfare: The U.S. Cover-up of a War Crime," *Bulletin of Concerned Asian Scholars,* October-December, 1980—the comprehensive article cited above. The others are "A Hidden Chapter in History," *The Bulletin of Atomic Scientists,* October 1981; "The Human Guinea Pigs," *San Francisco Chronicle,* November 3, 1985; "The Gap Between the Natural and Social Sciences Sometimes Leaves the Public Poorly Informed," *Bulletin of Concerned Asian Scholars,* July-September, 1986.

118. Haries and Haries, *Soldiers of the Sun,* pp. 360-361. I have taken a number of other particulars from this account.

119. Williams and Wallace, *Unit 731,* p. 339.

120. See Chapter 20, "The Powell-Schuman Case: Truth Was the Defense" in Hugh Deane, *Good Deeds and Gunboats: Two Centuries of American-Chinese Encounters,* 1990.

121. The book *Unit 731* was first published in Britain by Hodder and Stoughton Ltd in 1989. In 1990 a paperback edition was published by Grafton Books; a copy, bought in Scotland, is used here. Only the British editions, in Chapter 17, state and look at critically the evidence having to do with the question of American guilt in the Korean war. The American publisher, Macmillan, insisted on the omission of Chapter 17, The Korean War.

122. *Unit 731,* p. 381.

123. *Unit 731,* pp. 395.

124. *Unit 731,* pp. 353-354.

125. *Unit 731,* pp. 374-376. See Stephen Endicott's biography of his father, *Rebel Out of China.* Obituary by Hugh Deane in *US-China Review,* Vol. XVIII, No. 2, Spring 1994.

126. Zhang, *Mao's Military Romanticism,* pp. 182-183.

127. Powell, "Japan's Germ Warfare," *Bulletin of Concerned Asian Scholars,* pp. 11-14.

PRISONERS IN CHINESE CAMPS

128. Cumings. *Origins,* pp. 702-703.

129. Deane, *Good Deeds and Gunboats,* Chapter 22.

130. Pascall, *Witness to War,* p. 173.

131. Tomadi, *No Bugles, No Drums,* pp. 229-230.

132. Stone, *Hidden History,* Chapters 25 and 26.

133. Dean, *General Dean's Story,* pp. 191-192. Dean had this exchange with a guard who knew very little English. the guard drew a map of Korea in the dirt and said, "Chosen (Korea) home, okay? Dean agreed. "Chosen not America home. okay?" Again Dean agreed. "America in Chosen home, why?" Dean thought there is a good but complicated answer.

134. **Tales of Americans in Soviet Jails,** in the July 19, 1996 issue of *The New York Times.*

135. Winnington and Burchett, *Plain Perfidy,* p. 20. Hastings, *The Korean War,* p. 287.

136. Cited in *Plain Perfidy,* pp. 21-22. Elsewhere *Time* reported: "For every man or tired U.S, soldier who walked or hobbled or was stretcher borne along the quick road home last week there were stories to tell… " The price of a ticket along the quick road home was simply a story—"atrocity or sensation. "From Joy's diary, *Negotiating While Fighting,* quoted in Foot, *A Substitute for Victory,* p. 116. Also *Unknown War,* p. 178.

KOREAN AND CHINESE PRISONERS

137. Hastings, *The Korean War,* p. 287.

138. From Joy's diary, *Negotiating While Fighting,* quoted in Foot, *A Substitute for Victory,* p. 116. Also *Unknown War,* p. 178.

139. Foot, *A Substitute for Victory,* pp. 116-117, Clark cited in Foot, *A Substitute for Victory,* pp. 120-121.

140. Hugh Deane in *The Compass,* May 13, 1952.

141. Clark cited in Foot, *A Substitute for Victory,* pp. 120-121.

142. Winnington and Burchett, *Plain Perfidy,* pp. 14-16, photos of crippled and amputated Chinese and Korean prisoners...In the days before the switch, according to Agence France Presse, the number of American air sorties increased by a third—the aim was "to deal a heavy blow to Chinese lines of communication." The main target was bridges along the main north-south road, the aim being to delay the arrival of PWs coming to be exchanged. the *Plain Perfidy,* pp. 86-88. Summarized in Toland, *In Mortal Combat,* p. 587.

143. Foot, *A Substitute for Victory,* pp. 191-192.

144. Winnington and Burchett, *Plain Perfidy,* pp. 86-88. Summarized in Toland, p. 587.

145. *Plain Perfidy,* pp. 92-93.

146. *Encyclopedia Britannica,* 1973, Vol. 13, p. 474. Clark, in a foreword to *From the Danube to the Yalu,* thanked Handleman "for his valuable help in writing this book."

The Red Cross Report and the February 18 Killings

147. The additional troops reinforcing the security personnel were the 3rd Battalion, 27th Infantry.

The Prisoner Guinea Pigs

148. *Plain Perfidy,* by Winnington and Burchett, especially Chapter X, assembles the key evidence of medical malpractices. A summary account that adds particulars and reports the Chinese charges is in Williams and Wallace, *Unit 731,* pp. 385-387. It cites an Associated Press dispatch dated May 18, 1951 that reported that some 3,000 tests on oral and rectal cultures obtained from prisoner patients were made daily at Koje.

149. *Plain Perfidy,* p. 108.

Armistice and Aftermath

1. Ridgway, *The Korean War,* p. 198

2. Burchett, *Again Korea,* pp. 38-44.

3. Stephen E. Ambrose, *Eisenhower The President,* Vol. III p. 31.

4. Foot, *A Substitute for Victory,* p. 159. Ambrose, *Eisenhower,* Vol. III, p. 34.

5. MacDonald, *Korea: The War Before Vietnam,* p. 179. Zhang, *Mao's Military Romanticism,* pp. 237-238.

6. Ambrose, *Eisenhower The President,* pp. 94-95. Leonard Mosley, *Dulles: A Biography of Eleanor, Allen and John Foster Dulles,* pp. 334-335.

7. Ambrose. *Eisenhower The President,* p. 295.

8. Ambrose, *Eisenhower The President,* p. 313

9. Ambrose, *Eisenhower The President,* p. 194.

10. Piers Brendon, *Ike: His Life and Times,* p. 256.

11. MacDonald, *Korea: The Last War Before Vietnam,* p. 179.

12. Zhang, *Mao's Military Romanticism,* pp. 233-234, 237-238.

13. Brendon, *Ike: His Life and Times,* p. 256.

14. Winnington and Burchett, *Plain Perfidy,* pp. 48-50. "The story at Pu Pyung camp near Seoul was even more terrible and was witnessed by dozens of western journalists..." Clark's admission was in his *From the Danube to the Yalu,* p. 280.

15. Bailey, *The Korean Armistice,* p. 937.

16. Winnington and Burchett, *Plain Perfidy,* p. 64. The source was an Associated Press dispatch.

17. Dulles to Emmet Hughes, April 1953. MacDonald, *Korea: The Last War Before Vietnam,* p. 178.

18. MacDonald, *Korea: The Last War Before Vietnam,* p. 190.

19. I am indebted to my friend Israel Epstein, Beijing, for this anecdote.

20. Ambrose, *Eisenhower The President,* pp. 107-108.

21. Ambrose, *Eisenhower The President,* also pp. 107-108.

22. Ronning, *A Memoir of China in Revolution,* Chapter 14.

23. Interview, Committee of Concerned Asian Scholars Conference in China, July 19, 1971. Cited in *Quotations from Premier Chou En-lai.* Crowell, pp. 64-65.

24. Ambrose, *Eisenhower The President,* p. 99.

Index